The Seven Ranges

The Seven Ranges

Ground Zero for the Staging of America

WILL HOYT

Front Porch Republic *Books*

THE SEVEN RANGES
Ground Zero for the Staging of America

Copyright © 2021 Will Hoyt. All rights reserved. Except for brief quotations in critical publications or reviews, no part of this book may be reproduced in any manner without prior written permission from the publisher. Write: Permissions, Wipf and Stock Publishers, 199 W. 8th Ave., Suite 3, Eugene, OR 97401.

Front Porch Republic Books
An Imprint of Wipf and Stock Publishers
199 W. 8th Ave., Suite 3
Eugene, OR 97401

www.wipfandstock.com

PAPERBACK ISBN: 978-1-7252-8735-8
HARDCOVER ISBN: 978-1-7252-8736-5
EBOOK ISBN: 978-1-7252-8737-2

03/08/21

Portions of chapters 1, 8, and 9 appeared in December 2015 and January 2016 editions of New Oxford Review, and portions of chapters 2, 3, 6, and 7 appeared in June 2012, March 2014, and January 2017 editions of Front Porch Republic. The author is grateful to these publications for permission to reprint that material here, in slightly altered form.

for Dru

America is all one prairie, swept by a universal tornado. Although it has always thought of itself in an eminent sense as the land of freedom, even where it was covered with slaves, there is no country in which people live under more overpowering compulsions.

—**George Santayana,** *Character and Opinion in the United States*

Here opened another, entirely new education, which promised to be by far the most hazardous of all. The knife edge along which he must crawl, like Sir Lancelot in the twelfth century, divided two kingdoms of force. . . .. The historian's business was to follow the track of the energy; to find where it came from and where it went to; its complex source and shifting channels; its values, equivalents, conversions.

—**Henry Adams,** *The Education of Henry Adams*

Contents

Acknowledgements | ix
Introduction | xi

1 Chop Wood Carry Water | 1

2 Geographer's Line | 29

3 Rock and Roll | 52

4 Son of the Morning Star | 71

5 Allegheny Courthouse | 100

6 Draglines | 125

7 Organized Crime | 151

8 Disturbed Area | 174

9 Forty Acres and a Mule | 190

Endnotes | 207
Bibliography | 225
Index | 231

Acknowledgements

Special thanks to Ed Asbury (Superintendent of Wheeling-Pitt Steel Company Furnace #5 at Mingo Junction), Sandy Day (Librarian of Local History at Steubenville Public Library), Bill Griffen (Manager at Harrison Mining in East Cadiz), Bill Porter (Director of Sales at Ingram Barge Company), Marty Sammon (Referee for World Boxing Association), James Slater (Professor of Chemistry at Franciscan University), and Ocie Clark crew members Jack Lynch, John Kirvin, Stephen Haber, Dave Davis, Frank Workman, Bradley Pogue, Jim Hemby, Etta Smith, and Dennis Galloway, each of whom gave graciously of their time.

Thanks also to Joe Almeida, Dominic Aquila, Jeremy Beer, Hal Clifford, John Crosby, Bill Kauffman, Jim Kunstler, Dick Lyon, John Lukacs, Dan Nichols, Jason Peters, Mark Ryland, and David Scott who served in varying capacities as outfitters, law enforcement officers, and guides.

Works of historical, sociological, and philosophical scholarship to which I am indebted can be surmised by studying angles I employed while writing this book, but I also leaned heavily on other, lesser known works that deserve special mention: Evan S. Connell's *Son of the Morning Star* (published by former neighbor North Point Books), Alexander Fenton's *A Farming Township: Auchindrain Argyll*, Tim Flannery's *The Eternal Frontier: An Ecological History of North America and its Peoples*, and George Mosul's *Under the Buckeye Trees* and *Through the Rear View Mirror* (remembrances of Steubenville in the 1920s and 1940s). John Suiter's *Poets on the Peaks: Gary Snyder, Philip Whalen and Jack Kerouac in the North Cascades* was a touchstone, and I also made practical use of the annotated Lewis and Clark Bicentennial edition of the US Army Corps of Engineers' *Ohio River Navigation Charts* (Foster KY to Montgomery Locks and Dam).

Acknowledgements

Last but not least I owe a debt of incalculably large magnitude to my son Luke, otherwise known as Fr. Luke Hoyt, O.P., who lent me unflagging support by helping to conceptualize the book's shape over the course of dinner table conversations, reading every draft, and providing orienteering and trail-finding expertise during times when I got lost on "the mountain" and needed bearings.

Mistakes, where they exist, are the fault of the author and no one else.

Introduction

This book, written between 2010 and 2015, explains cultural and political polarization. The book describes what such polarization is, where it comes from, how it happens, what it costs, and why the phenomenon is especially likely to appear in the United States. Additionally, the book explains how polarization dynamics can be disabled. But the book wasn't begun with these talking points in view. Rather, it was simply a log I kept while journeying up the Ohio River from Marietta to the Ohio/Pennsylvania State Line on a towboat owned by Ingram Barge Company.

My purpose, in taking the trip, was to visualize freshly and to some degree chart the eastern Ohio region I had emigrated to nine years earlier, for instead of becoming less mysterious after I'd settled here, the area had become increasingly new and passing strange. Indeed, I dare say that it had become as mysterious to me as the North American continent must have been to the first European mariners who made landfall in Maine. We had different names for the object of our attention. Their name for land captivating them was "Norumbega"—a kingdom of legendary wealth and perhaps eternal youth.[1] Mine was "The Seven Ranges"—Congress's term for federal land west of the Alleghenies that got imprinted in 1785 with a rectilinear grid to make it ready for sale. But in other respects our situations were similar. Like them, I was (at least nominally) a Christian. And though we stood, historically speaking, on different sides of the Enlightenment and the French Revolution, let alone the Reformation, we were both of us Catholic. Were Cabot and Allefonsce and the other European explorers like Champlain who followed them as sobered by what they eventually saw on a line vessel's bridge? I suspect not, but on the other hand perhaps many of them were, for though they were not yet Moderns they can't, ultimately, have been any better prepared than I was to contextualize the evening aspect to our New World.

It wasn't so much that, thanks to the sheer splendor of givens, I wound up cataloguing biological, economic, and cultural damage on a scale I had previously not imagined. (The West Virginia panhandle boasts the longest record of continuous inhabitance in North America, let alone bracingly lush ecosystems, and the United States territory that became The Seven Ranges was specifically planned by Thomas Jefferson to function as a constellation of self-governing "ward republics.") Nor was it that, thanks to the brilliance of resourceful native sons, Ohio hill country began to manifest as a staging area for the dissemination of gaming and mining technology that was destined to wreak world-class havoc. Rather, it was that I saw some of the logic behind eastern Ohio's ravaged aspect—the sense of it, if you will, and perhaps even the inevitability of it. Moreover, the region itself appeared to draw in and trap a beholder to the very same degree that it afforded vision, for upon studying Pittsburgh and points immediately west, doors opened on their own accord as in a fun-house, and some of those doors led to Melville-like "try-work" places that, if you value secure kinds of North, are better left buried in the recesses of deepest time. Which meant that while conducting research I had to close as many doors as I eventually walked through.

Though it may appear otherwise (one of my chief theses, in this book, is that post-1776 Ohioan culture cannot be understood without reference to the end of the Medieval era and the beginning of the Renaissance, in the late 1300s) I made it a rule on my journey to defer at each and every turn to a sense of economy, and thanks to supplementary reliance on studied naiveté (a most under-rated skill), respect for my commission's limited aspect (stay local), and homemade diagnostic tools (incarnation meters), I believe I was relatively successful in my attempt to chart the land I had moved to. The map is not definitive. It is just a sketch of how things looked to one observer at one particular moment, and its mode—if one can call it that—bears more resemblance to street-based investigative reporting than to historical scholarship. Nevertheless, the chart I made over the course of that voyage has proved surprisingly reliable, and it can furthermore be said that the drama of its making has no small amount of entertainment value. After all, the place I had emigrated *from* was California, a zone where history matters as little as surf and redwoods loom large, and who could not enjoy a plotline that involves a Californian backpacker unwittingly placing himself at the country's center rather than at its edge and then colliding, head-on, with colossally inertial facts like the Rust Belt and the all-determining Civil War?

The surprise was that the book turned out to have practical value in addition to the diversionary sort, given the accelerating polarization now on view in the country at large and my coincidental discovery that polarization is a reliable marker for forces that could have been powerful enough to cause the damage I was cataloguing. My goal, while writing, was simply to come up with a satisfactory explanation for why land around me looked the way it did, but as I searched across Harrison County for clues, I began to see the shape of a convincing, if unexpected, answer, and the crystallization of that answer turned out to be heralded at each and every point by one thing—the removal of an integrative center and the consequent arrival of a polarity-driven storm.

Sixty-six years ago, Berkeley-based sociologist Robert Nisbet suggested that the simultaneous appearance of the modern centralized state, on the one hand, and the atomized individual, on the other, was not a coincidence. Then, in 1977, Kentucky farmer Wendell Berry observed that while appearing to oppose one another, advocates of Puritanism, on the one hand, and sexual licentiousness, on the other, were in fact "locked in a conflict that is really their collaboration in the destruction of body and soul both." And in 1992, fifteen years after Berry's insight, Yale literary critic Harold Bloom remarked that American religion was best defined by "antithetical intensity" that gets generated when "extreme supernaturalism," as on view in Appalachian snake handlers, comes close to "abundant materialism" resulting from Gilded Age wealth. These were three different thinkers pursuing three different questions about America, yet they all intuited that answers to their respective lines of inquiry could best be found through the examination of what might tentatively be called false-opposite sets.[2] Whence the appearance of these sets, and to what extent have we become entrapped by them? When I started my study of eastern Ohio these were still open questions, but after concluding my investigation I have begun to see that I may in fact have answered both of them.

Therefore, I have decided to organize and publish these river notes so that they can function for others as the steadying report they currently are for me, and, too, so that they can serve as an occasion for reinvigorated declarations of American citizenship.

Endnotes

1. Samuel Eliot Morison, *The European Discovery of America: The Northern Voyages A.D. 500–1600*, (New York: Oxford University Press, 1971), 464–470.

2. Robert Nisbet, *The Quest for Community: A Study in the Ethics of Community and Freedom* (Wilmington: ISI, 2014), 128, 133, 145, and 225; Wendell Berry, *The Unsettling of America: Culture and Agriculture* (Berkeley: Counterpoint, 2015), 108–110; Harold Bloom, *The American Religion* (New York: Chu Hartley, 2006), 188.

1

Chop Wood Carry Water

Willow Island Pool, 1500 hours, Mile 146. There are no bends on this reach-like section of river, and headwind is strong. The temperature is wintry and skies are grey. Water sliding by the port-side deck (just inches down owing to forward momentum) is oily and brown, and foam on the pillow of churned water astern is closer to yellow than to white. On shore, two hundred feet away, you can still see the high-water mark of last month's flood thanks to a line of plastic rubbish in trees that overhang Sheets Ripple. There are long views to the east and north, on the far side of a navigational beacon marking an industrial intake, and beyond that there is a glimpse of distant hills.

I clap my mitten-clad hands together in an effort to keep warm, then stomp my feet.

No good.

Moving toward the bow I pass an open galley door and just miss colliding with Dave, who has been scraping paint. We sway some, while regaining balance, then brace ourselves to sway again, this time because the vessel has slowed. I look up. Spectra lines are tight, and there are no other vessels in the sailing line. Water has started to break over the bows of the leading rakes, though. Maybe the pilot is protecting steerage.

The boat I am standing on is the Ocie Clark, which belongs to Ingram Barge Company, whose corporate offices are in Nashville, TN. Ingram operates about 90 line-boats on the Mississippi, Ohio, Cumberland, and Tennessee Rivers, and the Ocie Clark, whose twin 4800 horsepower engines enable it to push twenty loaded barges at a time but not the thirty-five often pushed on the mile-wide lower Mississippi, usually works the Ohio. Its homeport is

Paducah, KY. The vessel is 40-feet wide by 154-feet long, and its steersman sits in a wheelhouse on top of three decks fitted out with bunkrooms, showers, crew lounge and galley, dining area, maintenance lockers, water and fuel tanks, and an engine room. The boat weighs 403 tons, draws 9 feet, and burns 4000 gallons of fuel per day on a typical "hard" tow, working 24/7. I got on board late last night by climbing down a long metal ladder after the boat (lights blazing) entered Willow Island Lock, but the crew—one forward and one back watch consisting of three men each plus a cook, an engineer, and an "eighth man"—is two weeks into a four-week shift that began when my hosts relieved last month's crew at a fueling stop in Owensboro, KY. Two days ago they were running empties to Huntington, WV, and now, having just put in at South Point a few miles south, the current crew is northbound again, this time pushing three football fields of coal to a power plant on the Mon. It's called a 15-barge tow, this amount of freight. It measures three barges wide by five barges long, and when you add tonnage and the length of the vessel to which the tow is fastened via hydraulic winches and wire rigging, the load being moved by Ocie Clark engines weighs 23,000 tons and measures a quarter of a mile long.

    Standing now on the lee side of tow knees, I try to calculate inertial forces but soon I give up. I focus instead on eyes, shackles, and links stored there, close by the capstan, and then—as before—on the long view. Looking first across the tow to the jack staff with its flag snapping crisply in the wind far away at the bow, then across the long stretch of water leading toward a wall of steeply sloped hills beyond, I am struck by how the river at this point looks like a highway leading up and in. There is the sense of an interior—of a place so laden with fastnesses and strange scents and sharp tastes that it exerts a kind of pull. Can it be possible that the high country on view here is of a piece with the mountain terrain I sought in my youth? Of course not. That was a land of bright green tarns with talus slides and feeder creeks that were thick with rock flour milled by glaciers high, high above. It had dippers and rock wrens, marmots, scat from grizzlies. It had trails built out of riprap with gooseberry bush on the turns. It had dense fog combed by stands of fir and then sun so bright you needed fur-lined goggles with dark coke-bottle lenses just to see with. Here, at the headwaters of the Ohio, the lure is different. This country beckons owing to its iron, its sassafras and ginseng, its bluestone, ash, and pignut hickory. Elevations being lower, you think in terms of springhouses, tilth, and straw hats rather than snowmelt, granitic scree, and zinc oxide. Turning away, though, there is a flash. Somewhere off the port bow I see a preternaturally green forest with clear, fast-running streams on terrain so rugged that access is limited to mule tracks and footbridges. And at the very corner of my eye, just for a second, I see a bird, circling. The bird is large, it's got a wing-span like a condor's, and it appears to be adversarial. I hesitate, eyes locked (weirdly) on a small beach that will soon sport waves thanks to the Ocie Clark's wake, but by the time I turn back to figure out what I saw, the greenness and the bird are gone.

❧

I used to live in Berkeley. Not so much the Berkeley of the Free Speech Movement and the 1964 appearance by Mario Savio at Sproul Plaza during a student strike ("There is a time when the operation of the machine becomes so odious, makes you so sick at heart, that you can't take part, you've got to put your bodies upon the gears and upon the wheels"), or the Berkeley that Hendrix played on Memorial Day in 1970, a year after the fatal shooting of a student protester at People's Park and a year and a half after the release of Susie Q and the rise of local band Creedence Clearwater Revival, or even the Berkeley that George Santayana addressed in 1911, when, in the town's first incendiary speech act, the Spanish philosopher turned his back on Harvard (his employer), delivered a sly critique of this country's "genteel tradition," and then left for Rome, never to return. No. When I say I used to live in Berkeley I mean, rather, the Berkeley of Bernard Maybeck and Bay Tradition architecture, which crossed the natural-wood, "craftsman" look with an emphasis on industrial materials, Prairie School horizontality, and Beaux Artes classicism. I mean the Berkeley of poet William Everson, a.k.a. Br. Antoninus, who ran a letter press in the basement of St. Albert's priory after doing time at internment camp #56 for pacifists in Oregon, and then wrote in his spare time about ravens "sloping above the lonely fields" and cawing on "the farthest fences of the world"; the Berkeley where the owner of every other Queen Anne "brown shingle" rented out a cottage in the back to a card-carrying bohemian like Allen Ginsburg, who lived at 1624 Milvia while preparing for the 1955 Gallery 6 poetry reading, or his buddy Gary Snyder who faced the Far East, slept on a straw mat, and read by the light of a kerosene lamp while living at 2919 Hillegass; the Berkeley of Pauline Kael, who lost it at the movies almost every single week while writing for the New Yorker in the Seventies; the Berkeley of film-maker Les Blank and his friends over at Arhoolie Records, keepers of the flame before the altar of "raw" folk expression, be it zydeco, scratchy Lemon Jefferson blues, or steel drums; the Berkeley of Christopher Alexander, whose "pattern language" in the key of southern France guided the construction of Apple Computer as well as livable houses in pedestrian-friendly neighborhoods; most of all, perhaps, the Berkeley whose leading lights thought in terms of "meanders" and "rhizomatic structure" and "bee swarms" when it came time to explain social reality, and so helped to hatch the idea of "city-nature" (call it the West Coast version of Jane Jacobs' New Urbanism) and various "re-wilding" projects like uncovering creeks hidden under city streets, or building lettuce farms in factory districts.

Which is to say, I write as a romantic.

Of course, in America, all of us are romantics. We think our life stories begin the day we are born, we prize nature over tradition, we imagine that history has to do with ruins. Originality, for us, is an achievement rather than a starting point, and we are forever reminding our children that they can break the shackles of convention, pull themselves up by their bootstraps, and be whoever they want to be. We have, at least putatively, an enormous respect for manual labor—indeed, if our presidents don't show at least some sort of prowess with a broadaxe, gun, or horse we tend to vote them out of office, for we look on the unschooled aspect to cowboys, dockhands, and steelworkers as a badge rather than a handicap. And we positively idolize "straight shooters"—which is to say, anyone who expresses impatience with artifice and exalts, in its stead, something called "frankness." If there is one cardinal rule to which Americans all adhere, it is that we (and our products) must be "natural." Hence it would be foolish to imagine that anyone in this country could ever *not* be infected with romanticism.

In Berkeley, though, the strain is particularly virulent, and there are three reasons for this virulence.

First, the city has a strong Emersonian heritage thanks to the Bostonian roots of the university's founders. (Street names, in Berkeley, sound like names in Cambridge ought to sound: Channing, Bancroft, Dwight.) Second, the city is set in a stunningly beautiful area. It is built on the west side of dry, chaparral-themed coastal hills where streams function as moist creases that permit redwoods, ferns, and flowering currant to prosper, and it looks out over a bay formed by the confluence of the San Joaquin and Sacramento Rivers, each of which bears huge loads of wetland-building, migratory bird-supporting mountain nutrient. Owing to the proximity of deep ocean currents just offshore, fog forms nearly every morning, and when that fog comes in off the ocean it is like a fresh breath drawn by the city upon waking. If you climb into the Berkeley hills shortly after sunrise the sky is blue but the city itself is invisible. All you see are spires and clock towers sticking up out of fog, and then, around midday, as the sun gets hot and the city starts to exhale, offshore breezes arrive to carry away the carbon dioxide. There is industry in the bay, and up near Martinez there are even oil refineries, but thanks to the morning fog and afternoon breezes, air in the East Bay is usually fresh, and this fact, in turn, makes the place an ideal site for the cultivation of romantic "vision." But, as I say, there is also another reason romanticism is strong in Berkeley. It's that, thanks to the city's edge-of-continent location, the American civilization v. nature dynamic ("westward the course of empire takes its way") gets tripped up, exposed for the sham it is, and then swept aside in order to make room for a more formidable, less easily deconstructed romanticism, which is the idealization of pre-modern ideas of nature.

As with any other pyramid scheme, the idea of civilization triumphantly displacing nature is credible solely to the extent that true costs are hidden or at least deferred—as is the case when fresh, unspoiled land is available just a stone's throw west. The early residents of Berkeley, however, saw nothing but ocean in front of them and a lot of used land behind them. They were not distracted from wondering whether the civilization v. nature dynamic might have more to do with a craven need for fresh land to despoil than any inherent merit to the civilization invoked to legitimize that conquest. Hence it makes sense that they would pioneer efforts to protect wilderness via institutions like John Muir's Sierra Club, and lobby for the creation of National Parks. The surprise is that they would also, one hundred years later, be in the vanguard of the movement to undercut the philosophical premises on which both the Sierra Club and National Parks are based, but in the last analysis even this makes sense, for thanks to being finely tuned to the problematic aspect of civilization displacing wilderness, Berkeley citizens have also been in a good position to recognize that the idea of wilderness serving as a refuge from civilization's destructive energies is just another version of the same problem.

Be that as it may, the folks who now dominate Berkeley's intellectual life push for a definition of nature wide enough to include villages and town life, in addition to rivers and trees. The precedents for defining nature in this way are all pre-modern. They have roots in classical Greece and reach their fullest flower in medieval Europe during the Cistercian renewal. But you wouldn't know this from Berkeley's intelligentsia, and that fact is problematic. Given that the Middle Ages, in particular, are fundamentally alien to our current, post-Christian age, thinkers who uphold some of those former eras' achievements without at the same time saluting the beliefs that made those achievements possible have no choice but to relate to those ages as romantics. And in Berkeley people do so happily, for the idealization of pre-modern ideas of nature blends seamlessly with the city's well established, Maybeck-driven architectural bias in favor of pre-Raphaelite aesthetics, not to speak of the city's rather messianic Marxist bias in favor of pre-industrial craft.

In the case of this particular Berkeley citizen (I moved to the city on purpose, directly after graduating from college) the romanticism showed up twice. It showed up in the choice I made regarding a profession—carpenter—and then, increasingly, in my attention to mountains—both the literal sort that you find in the high Sierra, and, too, the kind you traverse when you read books.

I lived in "the flats," between the hills and the bay, in a section of town known as "Ocean View." Prior to 1848, the land on which my house sat (close by recently uncovered Codornices Creek) belonged to Domingo Peralta, whose father (Don Luis Maria Peralta) had been granted the entire east side of the San Francisco Bay in return for military service at the Presidio. Domingo built a small adobe structure just a few yards north of what is now a produce market and lived there with his wife Maria Edenviges and their children behind a low wall that was covered with honeysuckle vines, a crucifix, and some Jericho roses. They called the place "Rancho Codornices" and had no intention of living anywhere else. After the war between the United States and Mexico, however, the Peralta family was asked to register land according to American title rules rather than Spanish ones, and because the Peraltas were unable to afford associated legal fees, they lost their investment. The new territorial government sold the Peralta property to American cattlemen, who continued to manage the land as Domingo had, i.e. by using it as a kind of staging area for the conversion of sunlight into beef, and there the land sat until finally it was bought in 1911 by a developer named McGregor, who converted it into lots that were just a little bit bigger than the stucco houses he started right away to construct on those lots, in six different period-revival styles.

Up in the hills things were different. After the University of California was chartered in 1868, the slopes above the new school's campus became a magnet for clergymen, architects, Nobel laureates, moneyed professorial types, and the sorts of corporate directors who functioned as (or imagined themselves to be) trustees of the arts and sciences. All of them had means, and given that the vaguely Teutonic arts-and-crafts sensibility popularized by William Morris and John Ruskin was at that time pretty much the rule, given too that the steepness of the East Bay hills lent themselves well to systems of interlocking carriage drives and long, often winding flights of stone steps, and given finally that the quiet of fog-watered redwood groves meshed nicely with the contemplative quiet that was reinforced by pipe tobacco wafting from the many open windows that belonged to resident philosophers—given all that, you had a neighborhood with tremendous allure. Part of it was the rarified atmosphere, the way the region functioned as a kind of magic mountain lifted from the pages of Thomas Mann. But the chief appeal, at least for someone like me, was the built aspect—the way the homes there made use of wood.

Berkeley is paradise if you're a carpenter. One season you may find yourself working in the flats on a straight-down-the-middle-of-the-road craftsman bungalow with stick-style trim, exposed rafters, clapboard siding, and a modestly pitched gable roof that incorporates a porch with overly sized square wood columns. Next season, you find yourself working on Frederick Olmstead's "Rose Walk," where stairs leading to second story apartments twist and turn like stairs leading to a choir loft in Transylvania, or on a Maybeck-designed Buena Vista Way house with strong horizontal lines, a poured concrete chimney, stenciled steel signage, and massive Japanese outriggers. All that before heading back to the flats again, this time to work on a turreted Queen Anne with shingled walls that swell out, here and there, to accommodate generously sized bay windows. There is no other city in America with that kind of variety to its carpentered infrastructure, and I reveled in the opportunity to learn tricks of the trade by maintaining and improving that infrastructure.

Given that a lot of my jobs were in the relatively upscale hills, I of course learned to recognize and admire classical joinery—the art of fitting pieces of wood together without the use of nails. I could tell the difference between a half lap and a mortise-and-tenon joint with a pin, and I took pride in my ability to square a tenon's shoulder and chamfer its end. Most of the time, though, I used a worm-drive power saw, a 24-ounce framing hammer (smooth head), and then (after the technology appeared) a pneumatic nail gun made by Hitachi, and in truth I preferred it that way, for I liked the speed and relative ease with which complex three-dimensional shapes could thereby be erected.

I would start by building "on paper" the addition or cottage I had been hired to construct. This meant checking an architect's drawings against field notes and then, by closing my eyes and visualizing every aspect of construction, creating a series of charts that took into account offset dimensions for hold-down bolts, locations of studs and joists in relation to pipes and wires, the exact length of every board, even the angle settings I'd need to make the cuts. In one sense, this was an exercise involving ideal forms, as when I calculated the "line length" of a valley jack before subtracting for the thickness of the ridge, but in another sense it was an opportunity to get down into some nit and grit while there was still time to change an architect's plan—as when I calculated the sometimes prohibitive challenge of installing a cast-iron closet bend in an unavoidably tight joist space, or getting a vent pipe to a wall as per Uniform Building Code rules. You can burn a lot of calories building on paper! But the process did have an end, and after reaching that end I got to move outside, into a more skilled phase called "demolition."

I'm serious when I call this phase skilled. You don't want a bunch of yahoos taking apart a house. As with an offensive rush in football, you want people who think before attacking and know how to use the weight of whatever they are attacking to their own advantage. Otherwise, the house comes down on you or the neighbor and—back now at your own twenty—you wind up with twice the work you bargained for. Who wants that? Better to wield a sledge like the fine instrument it is and work surgically. Minimize dust, remove debris quickly so you stay nimble on your feet, and then hit hard where (and when) it counts.

And then? Then the good stuff happened.

Once planning and demolition hurdles were crossed, jobs pretty much played themselves, and I was able simply to go along for the ride—batter boards with line strings so taut you could almost pluck them, stunningly clear cross hairs on West German theodolites that depended for accuracy on natural light and finely etched glass, bobcats that turned (literally) on a dime, cages of #4 or #5 steel, pump trucks and rubber boots and reverse-gear warning signals, 4-inch diameter hoses filled with wet concrete heavy and dangerous as elephant trunks, standard-and-better plates and studding, plumb bobs on 20' strings that pointed (exactly) to the center of the earth, and—best of all—rafters. Can there be anything better than climbing into the sky and making something out of thin air? One day there is nothing and then—voilà!—there is a ridge beam and a set of commons sitting squarely on a plate with a rightly oriented bird's mouth and a well-placed plumb cut. I wasn't so keen on applying siding and roof shingles, I must admit. Buildings don't change much, doing those things, and you have to use a lot of tar. But those jobs come into play about the same time that plumbing and electrical work do; therefore, I was often able to delegate waterproofing tasks and focus instead on flux, solder, and Mapp gas, or (one beat later) service drops, breaker panels, and foursquare boxes with rings. Even if I couldn't perform that little evasive maneuver, though, I was still fine, because at bottom I liked all of it, even the maintenance stuff I used to do at St. Albert's between jobs.

How could I not? This was Berkeley. I worked for myself on houses whose lines I admired next to lemon trees. I drove to work with a cup of Peet's coffee in my hand, after purchasing it at the famous corporation's first and at that time only location on Walnut Square. My job was to cut, plane, and install woods that ranged from kiln-dried vertical grain fir to Alaskan yellow cedar so fresh that sap spurted out when you sank a nail into it. Lunch, prepared by my wife, came with a thermos. When it was time to eat

I sat outside, usually in the sun in order to warm up after working in heavy fog. Skies became bright and blue in the afternoon, and hammer sounds became less muffled. You needed shades. There were techno covers of the Supremes on the ra-di-o and sometimes even young mothers tanning, topless, in the yard next door—nothing prurient here, mind you, just thanksgiving that a world with such sights should actually exist, and gladness for the privilege of inhabiting it.

As the years went by, though, it became apparent that my real interest was mountains. I hungered for the walking I had been introduced to as a teenager in the Sangre de Cristo range in northern New Mexico, the kind where you carry a weight and ration your breath according to your steps—the kind where your head is down, your thumb is wedged under a pack strap, and your eyes are focused sometimes on a patch of gold aspens to your right but usually on the cobbled or root-bound track passing under your booted feet. So I started making regular visits to the high Sierra, usually in the fall, theoretically before the snows. Sometimes I brought my wife and children; other times I went alone. I explored Yosemite's Tuolomne meadows, which is a kind of high-altitude table ringed by peaks and bisected by bright stream water running over a pebbled bottom, then (in the relatively unpeopled northern part of the park) the serrations along Paiute Ridge, and after that (sixty miles to the south) the approach to lush Tully's Hole with its wildflowers and pack-train hay. Usually I slept at timberline in a tent that weighed a mere three pounds. When I heated food it was with a twig fire under a bowl of stars, and when I left in the morning things looked as they had when I arrived—unless of course the night had brought a dusting of snow.

But that was only half of it.

At the same time that I began touring the Sierra I also started visiting more regularly the kinds of mountains you encounter when you read books, and thanks to the juxtaposition of good pay, low living expenses (my family was still young), and the serial nature of carpentry jobs, I often set off on these kind of trips for weeks rather than days. They took place in an attic room and then, later, in a hut that I built in our back yard. Both these staging areas were small, but when I left them in the evening to go "home" to my family I felt like I was coming in from a place that A. R. Ammons would have called "out," a place where you are invited to stop and look and listen, a place where you measure your steps and travel in silence across exposed ridges on narrow paths that accommodate just one person at a time—in short, a mountain.

Words "shaggy and combed" on the one hand, trees and rivers on the other—I was amazed at how they were the same place, how when you read

Dante or Nabokov you walked through (and on) a lettered world of vowels and consonants that were every bit as real, or available to the senses, as ferns, sap blisters, and rock faces beside a switchback. Similarly, when I toured the Sierra I marveled at the verbal underpinnings to the world I tasted and saw, how one essentially "read" feldspar and sequoias and columbines the way one read words in a book.

What was it that I was after? What was I hunting when I put down my hammer to walk in lettered ecosystems?

I suppose one word for it would be freedom, but I am wary of that word. It is used by too many people as cover for a power play, or as a means to an end that is hard to distinguish from enslavement, and even when the word isn't used that way, even when people make a genuine effort to define the word in a disinterested fashion, there is *still* cause for wariness, for here the word usually winds up getting pinned to some notion of engaged citizenry, and I am talking about something more basic, something prepolitical. Let us, then, call it residency in a certain climate—specifically, the climate that comes to pass when things are oriented toward their source and they "mean." In a book, characters and objects have revelatory power to the extent that they are oriented toward an authorial intelligence that has their end in view. And in a meadow it is the same: assuming they live at all, plants grow and shine with thereness and selfhood because they are always turning to face the sun. What, then, of the person who reads a book or a meadow? Though we most of the time face ourselves or a project of our own making and so are not available to be illumined or "grown" in these respects, the person who reads in the way I am talking about does in some way participate in the free, which is to say source-oriented, life that he observes all around him. He breathes the air of a rightly ordered world, and, to that limited extent, he becomes rightly ordered himself.

At the time, of course, I didn't think too much about why "the mountain" compelled attention. All I knew was that I liked visiting the place and wanted to spend as much time there as I could. Hence I committed to more than a few years of back-and-forth shuttle operations, until one day it finally dawned on me that if I only changed my overall household economy, chances were good that I could actually live in mountains, full time.

Call the plan "Walden, take two."

Like Thoreau, my idea was to make an uncompromised, no-strings-attached study of books and ecological wholeness the top priority in my life rather than something I did in my spare time, and I proposed to accomplish this feat by a kind of downward mobility that would lessen my need for cash. Given, however, that I was conceiving this plan in the 1990s rather than the 1840s, there were bound to be important differences, and though I liked to think Thoreau himself would have similarly altered his plan should he have instituted it during the first Iraq war rather than during the Mexican war, there was no getting around the fact that my changes amounted to corrections.

The most serious flaw in Thoreau's original Walden project was that he defined wilderness in opposition to civilization and so fell prey to a false dichotomy whose destructive impact was worse than anything he thought he was fleeing. Nowadays we know better; therefore, if a new Walden project is to have any credibility it must be premised on the redefinition of wilderness as land managed for the extraordinary fertility and diversity that constitute genuine "wildness." Which is to say, it must be premised on agri-culture, which comprises civilization. How much better Thoreau's book would have been if he had understood agriculture for the miracle it is. It would have been a journey *toward* families and vibrant town life rather than away from them, and his startlingly clear vision of nature's sheer otherness would most likely have intensified. Alas, Thoreau let that particular opportunity go. It was staring him in the face via John Field, the Irish laborer with a big family who came to Henry David for advice on how he, the laborer, could achieve what Thoreau had achieved, but Thoreau just shook his head and filed John Field's plight with that of those who are unable to walk away from material possessions. Well, the rest of us need not make the same mistake. We are free to incorporate agriculture into a Walden-derived project, and I even began to wonder whether farming might be a better inroad to the mysteries of biological life than backpacking, given that cultivating and planting and harvesting contribute as much to a rightly ordered climate as do animals, vegetables, and minerals.

The other important change that needed to be made to Thoreau's program, if it was to be credible in the 1990s, was to adjust compass settings so that embarking on a Walden project meant steering toward *used* land rather than pristine land. Thanks in no small part to the use of "virgin soil" as an indicator for absolute worth, this nation's land is a lot less fertile than it used to be. We farm in such a way as to use land up, rather than build it, in no small part because, as noted earlier, there has always been "new" land just a few miles west. Now that there is no more "new" land (it was never really new; it just looked that way thanks to being farmed by Native Americans rather than Europeans) we are of course in crisis, but currently we are able to forestall collapse thanks to the input of chemical fertilizer and the use of fungicides and pesticides that control the kinds of bugs that appear when soils are depleted or stressed. How long that evasive tactic will work is anybody's guess, but certainly it can't hurt if people at least start the job of disowning emphases on "unspoiled" landscapes. And given that the people who most need to do this are followers of Thoreau, I tried especially hard while designing our move to think in terms of environmental restoration rather than environmental protection—even going so far as to conceive of our Walden project as restorative by definition.

This nation featured a depopulated countryside in 1995! Sometime around 1970 family farms started disappearing in direct proportion to the rise of agribusiness giants like Cargill and Monsanto, and by the early 1990s it was becoming clear that small, crop-diversified farms and the Midwest towns they once supported would soon exist solely as exhibits in museums if people didn't actively try to reverse the process. Might not a wave of new Walden projects at least partially accomplish that goal? I was convinced that it would, and I thought of myself and people like me as a new sort of pioneer—one who would practice genuine, place-specific agriculture rather than mining soil and "lighting out for the territory." True, I was in the process of pulling up stakes myself. As Frederick Jackson Turner would be quick to note, I was "breaking for the high timber" every bit as thoroughly as the original nineteenth century pioneers did. In my mind, however, there was a difference, for I would be "clearing out for the new purchase" in order to put in place an entirely different ethic, which would correct a wrong turn taken.

This idea of re-settling the continent, like the idea of subverting the nature v. civilization dynamic, had considerable appeal, and I regularly leaned on it to justify our plan. Yet the ultimate selling point for a twenty-first-century Walden project proved not so much to be its remodeled, ecologically correct aspect as its original, still revolutionary promise concerning the extension of a formerly aristocratic privilege to tradesmen. What, after all, was the reason Thoreau became famous? Was it that he indulged a primitivistic impulse and tried to live simply in the woods? On the contrary, it was because he presumed to practice leisured contemplation without an inheritance or some form of institutional largesse and, as well, to write a book about his experience in order to demonstrate to the rest of the world that the maneuver was possible. Even today the glad tidings of his achievement ring out like a bell on a hilltop. "For more than five years," he announces, "I maintained myself . . . solely by the labor of my hands." Then he sharpens things a little: "I found that, by working about six weeks in a year, I could meet all the expenses of living." Implication? "The whole of my winters, as well as most of my summers, I had free and clear for study."

The idea was not exactly new. There is a blueprint for Thoreau's project in St. Thomas More's *Utopia*, where More explains that the inhabitants of his fictional island paradise have a six-hour workday so as to "give each person as much free time from physical drudgery as the needs of the community will allow, so that he can cultivate his mind."[1] Nevertheless, it would be wrong to think of the idea as old, for the simple reason that until America appeared on the world stage, people in developed societies almost uniformly assumed that the human race could and should be divided into two classes—one that thinks and practices the liberal, or "free" arts, and another that sees to basic human needs (food, shelter) and practices, thereby, the "servile" arts. Take classical Greece, the culture that first came up with the terms. Though carpentry and farming were respected and thought of as ennobling in the polis (you can tell this just by reading Homer and imbibing his respect for the way Odysseus "trues a board to a chalk line," and then feels at home, even honored, sleeping alongside swineherds dressed in "rough tunics, oxhide leggings, and goatskin caps"), by the time Plato and Aristotle appear (courtesy of Athenian democracy with its imperialist navy) "hewing wood" and "drawing water" are depicted as activities that *interfere* with the practice of finer arts and ought to be *delegated* to slaves or at least hired hands. Romans confirmed this distinction, and though the divide was to some extent subverted during the early Middle Ages owing to the Benedictine linkage of "ora" to "labora," the split between "liberal" and "servile" arts mainly got a boost at that time owing to the scholastic enthronement of decidedly liberal arts in still valuable curriculums. (The "trivium" consisted of rhetoric, logic, and grammar, the "quadrivium" of arithmetic, music, geometry, and astronomy.) All told, the idea of categorizing work as either "liberal" or "servile" has proven durable over the years, and citizens everywhere have worked hard to maintain the distinction. Hence, it was something of a surprise when Thoreau claimed to have vaulted the wall that enforced the split. He didn't ask for anybody's permission or blessing. He just went out and did it. And after he did it, he made the act sound almost casual. "I preferred," he said, "that society should run amok against me, it being the desperate party."

Thoreau's wager—and it was a distinctly American wager in which our very identity as a people was staked, not just Thoreau's own well-being—was that there was a way to practice the contemplative arts without, at the same time, breaking someone else's back. Did he win? Given that his move to Walden Pond inspired a host of similar moves whose success or lack thereof has yet to be tallied, the jury is of course still out. But if you confine your gaze to Thoreau's own venture on the shore of Walden Pond, there is no question that he failed. I don't mean that he failed because he withdrew from society and so precluded the option of politically engaged contemplation. Even Aristotle recognized the importance of mountaintops as nurseries for contemplative life, and certainly it could be argued that Thoreau's decision to leave Walden Pond and re-enter society proves that importance. When

I say Thoreau failed, then, I mean something different, which is that Thoreau (like More) focused simply on changing the *ratio* of hours spent doing servile work relative to hours spent practicing the so-called liberal arts, not on subverting the dichotomy itself. As a result, he remained trapped by the twin categories and couldn't think beyond them, even if in some of his actions (like sounding the pond) he clearly went beyond them. If you're going to think in terms of fault lines and try to put limits on one mode of being relative to another, might not a more serviceable distinction be "leisured labor, as practiced by clerks, tradesmen and thinkers," versus "distracted, hence slavish labor, as practiced by clerks, tradesmen and thinkers"? I, for my part, wanted to find out. Accordingly, I set a course that would allow me to cultivate received liberal arts in such a way that my experience as a carpenter would have a chance to figure as crucially in the practice of those arts as thinking had in the practice of received, allegedly servile, arts.

Or so the story line went.

As I intimated earlier, the idea of subverting the liberal/servile distinction was a selling point for our move, and in that respect it was neither more nor less truthful than other story lines about agricultural and environmental restoration. Though each of these tales agreed with "the facts" and in that sense avoided falsehood, both were mostly built *after* the decision to move had been made in an effort to ferret out implications, get a handle on significance, and (even more importantly) provide cover for a deeper, less easily justified motivation regarding mountains that I couldn't even name, let alone understand. Hence our story lines concealed as much as they revealed. Was it the same for Thoreau? I suspect that it was exactly the same. In the last analysis, Thoreau didn't build that cabin on Walden Pond in order to wake fellow Americans to their place in history any more than he built it to satisfy a primitivist urge. Rather, he built the cabin in order to cast his lot with bums (Thoreau was an un-credentialed practitioner of a formally useless philosophical art) and pursue an almost religious interest in poverty and the fruits it brings. Which is to say, he set out to build a hermitage—a place where, with quieted mind, you watch and wait. I don't know what Thoreau's code name for this place was, when he was planning his move—for all I know he simply used "Walden"—but I do know mine. I used "chop wood carry water."

Years later, upon returning to Berkeley for a visit after building my house in Ohio, I saw a sign on a message-of-the-day-type billboard above a bookstore that featured the same words with exclamation points, thereby referencing the spirituality of medieval Zen masters like Daito Kokushi, who said, "Ever, ever be on the lookout!" Then, a few years after that, I realized one day that the "chop wood carry water" phrase also functioned as a kind of shorthand for hewers-of-wood and drawers-of-water conceits deriving from Aristotle's definition of servile arts. When I first used the phrase, though, I was unaware of these associations. To me the phrase just meant splitting wood and hauling water in a tin pail. I *liked* doing those things, and given that the mindset they made possible was the same mindset I hoped to achieve once we made our move, I started using it as a file heading for the notes I made while getting my bearings.

Migratory birds apparently navigate via on-board bacteria which have magnetic crystals in their cells that allow the winged creatures to read the pitch of magnetic lines of force relative to the ground.[2] If you put a locator beacon on a Hawaiian tern's leg in the springtime and then let that tern go, it turns out that the tern flies straight as an arrow to the Aleutian Islands. How, though, does a bird *pioneer* a given route? Is it accident? Or is the bird part of something larger than itself that tilts it toward a certain place? This is a big mystery, and the mystery doesn't get any smaller when you plug humans instead of birds into the equation. Lewis and Clark, of course, were led directly by a mother (Sacajawea) and child (Sacajawea's baby). But that was unusual. Most of the time we have to depend on less efficient, more scatter-shot means, and in my family's case (seeing as how there was no GPS) the means consisted of DeLorme atlases, yellow highlighter pens, rental cars, and a kind of interior "mountain" detector which told me whether or not a given piece of ground would serve well as a site for the kind of life I wanted to build. We looked in California, up near the Oregon border, and then ("bi-coastal" people that we were) in Vermont and Maine—all without success. Everywhere we looked, land that could become (as it were) "land" had fallen into the hands of either (a) large, heavily capitalized farms, (b) doctors from a neighboring city who had the money to subsidize and maintain a strong beauty quotient, or (c) people who were content to sell it off, piece by bull-dozed piece, to shopping centers, purveyors of log cabin "get-aways," and car dealerships. That established, we turned inland (or "back") in a far more radical sense than we, Gary Snyder's cultural descendants, had originally dared to go, and that is how I found myself driving south and east one day across Ohio's Allegheny plateau on roads that, if it weren't for remarkably precise atlases, would normally be called "uncharted."

The country was strange to me. No ocean, no ski area, no second homes. Odd-sized fields owing to ruggedness of terrain, little evidence of agribusiness, dirt roads consisting of grass growing between tire tracks. Land parcels shaped, probably, like they had been one hundred years ago. At the same time obvious fertility: lots of hardwood forest in addition to soy-beans and corn. What was this place? Looking at my watch, I decided that I had about an hour to spare, and without a moment's hesitation I turned my car around to explore a road I had not yet followed. Five miles north of the ridge upon which my family and I now live I passed an abandoned farmhouse with a spring that delivered good, cold water. Then, a few hundred yards beyond that, I swung right onto a track that led to a cornfield that would soon be ready for harvest. Turning off the motor, I climbed out of the car, stretched my back, and listened. The silence was huge. It was full, not empty, and at that moment I knew our search was done.

What I didn't know was that the land we had chosen was situated on the edge of a wasteland that had no precedent.

Oh, I "knew" all right. I had learned in libraries and newspapers about the dying "rust belt economy" and the environmental devastation wreaked by that economy when it was in its prime. I had even learned that eastern Ohio had lost not just one but three key industrial props in the early 80s and hence faced a particularly bleak future.

During World War II this region was booming. More steel was produced here, on the upper Ohio, than anywhere else in the world, and it was made in furnaces that were fired by locally mined coal. This meant that in addition to manufacturing armored plate there was a lot of digging going on, both by wildcatters and big players—so much so that Ohio's Hanna Coal Company was commonly referred to, during WWII years, as United States Coal. And given that when you dig for coal you tend to find it over seams of clay, that in turn meant that there was a near-continuous supply of raw material for potteries and clay-block factories, some of which grew big enough to produce nationally and even internationally recognized "product."

Scroll ahead, now, to 1986: eastern Ohio coal output halved, potteries dead, nine out of ten steel mills closed. If newspaper articles were to be believed, a regional identity that not too long ago invited comparisons to the celebrated civilizational giant in Nebuchadnezzer's dream had fallen down right there in the tri-state area's midst, and all that was left was rubble. This giant may have kept his eyes on Rome "as if" (according to the Poet) "on a mirror," but his (the giant's) feet had been made out of clay and iron, and each of those, in turn, was planted on coal. All of that: toppled.

Thanks to the rapid globalization of the steel and clay industries, the increasing scarcity of easily available coal, the mechanization of deep mines that continue to feed power companies, and EPA rules constricting the use of locally produced "soft" (high sulphur content) coal, the tri-state regional economy had imploded, and though Pittsburgh was apparently trying to reinvent itself along post-industrial, silicone chip-lines, it seemed that the future for most of the area's residents and businesses was bleak. Steubenville-Weirton population dropped faster, between 1980 and 2000, than any other urban area in the nation, losing a full 50 percent of its people, and during the late 90s, when the rest of America experienced a real-estate boom, Pittsburgh's real-estate market was flat. Add to that the widely trumpeted fact that people who didn't move out stood a better chance of *dying* than other people did—in 1994, the year before our move, Harvard University released a landmark study on the health risks of airborne particulate matter, which concluded that Steubenville residents had a 26 prcent higher chance of dying early than residents in Portage, Wisconsin—factor that in and a prospective emigrant couldn't help but "know" that he or she was headed someplace grim.[3]

But in another sense I didn't know at all. I just didn't have the mental equipment necessary even to imagine (let alone measure) the kind of destruction that came into view, exhibit by exhibit, once I began living here. Hearing that Harrison County was ravaged was like reading a graph in a textbook, and I processed the fact in exactly the same way that I processed other facts that helped me to contextualize our move. Honey, did you hear? The first federal land office was in Steubenville! The land west of there is coal country! Colerain was the home of Josiah Fox, the naval architect who designed the *USS Constitution*! If some people called Harrison County a wasteland, so much the better, for tourists would then give the region I was moving to a wide berth.

We live on a ridge just north of Cadiz, which is a half-hour drive northwest of Wheeling, West Virginia, and—it's a picturesque place. If you climb the hill behind my house, face north, and then run your eye from west to east, you see a kind of scrunched-up, ragged patchwork quilt made out of woods and fields. Some of the woods have been recently logged; there brambles and soft maple dominate. On other quilt pieces oaks are mature, and the canopy is full of squirrels and bird nests. Fields are either in hay or corn, if they're level, and if they're not they serve as pasture—usually for Angus cattle or horses. There's a Methodist church with a steeple on the next ridge over, to the west. That church has a cemetery attached to it, and in that cemetery, along with a statue of a Union soldier, there are graves dating back to 1800 that feature the same names that appear on mailboxes outside current-day homes. The church also has a big bronze bell, and on Sundays someone manually rings it. Other times we hear chain saws, hay-making equipment, car tires on the state highway, the lowing of cattle and the honking of geese, the clip-clop of horses pulling Amish buggies on the county road snaking along the ridge, or the rumble of diesel locomotives hauling freight on a valley floor that is half a mile to the north.

Travel a few miles to the south and east, however, and you enter a very different landscape. It's green, in the summertime, and there are numerous lakes that on first appearance look like fjords, but contour lines are confused, roads peter out for no discernible reason, and old farmsteads—where they still exist—seem to be poorly situated on land they once presumably commanded.

Upon first moving here I didn't think about these oddities much. Focused as I was on buying property and building a farm, I tended to note only those things that lined up well with those interests. Later, though, I got to wondering why neighboring land looked as it did, and one day the answer hit me. It was like the moment in a sci-fi movie when the hero suddenly sees past the trees to the forest and realizes that the "planet" his spaceship landed on is in fact an organism that is alive. He had never before known that something alive could be that big; hence, he had been fooled. Well, I was similarly fooled. In my case the key insight was that the "land" that I had puzzled over wasn't in fact land at all. It was merely upended earth. Rather than being shaped by rainfall over centuries, it had been thrown and piled, helter-skelter, by shovels in search of a quick buck, and therefore it was in an important sense dead. How could it support life? Life is adaptation, and if a given region's human, biological, and geological history have all been erased, there is in effect no landform there, no identity worth adapting to and enriching, and hence little to no "yield." Like the space traveler in the sci-fi movie I had been fooled, and the reason I had been fooled was that I did not know land could be dead on this scale. I had thought of this area's ravaged aspects as a kind of moat whose existence would serve to protect a secret kingdom from unwittingly destructive tourists. Now, however, my eyes were opened. All those strangely abbreviated ridges over near Hopedale with the covering of poplar and poison ivy? Those were spoil banks. And the winding fjords on view in all three eastern Ohio counties where people sometimes park campers and set out chairs with pockets for fishing poles? Those were puddles resulting from ruts made by a giant shovel following a seam of coal along a contour. This was not just a moat I was looking at. Rather, it was an entire salted *sink*, and I was on its rim, looking out, as amazed as Lewis and Clark must have been when they, in their turn, finally "saw" the Pacific.

If I had first traversed this sink in areas where extensive stripping operations had either just concluded or were still in progress, I would not have been fooled. If I had approached from less traveled regions in the southern part of the county, for example, I would have been struck by a sudden absence of farmsteads, and their replacement by either defunct power stations, rusty tipples, and old signs that say "explosives in use," or (if the mining was completed after reclamation laws went into effect) by immaculately groomed hills and *no trees*. Alternatively, if I had entered the sink via even less frequented roads in the southwestern part of the county, I would have noted hilltops in the process of being decapitated and places where the ground is on fire owing to smoldering coal seams, and hillside seeps that look like sores (open wounds) owing to acidic content stemming from the forced exposure of pyrite, and a form of bacteria called "yellow boy" that leaves a slick, reddish-yellow precipitate on "streambed" rocks. Given sights like that, it is hard not to know that one has entered a lifeless environment. But this doesn't mean those approaches are the best ones, if one's intent is to grasp the truth about this region. On the contrary, they are useful mainly for providing supporting evidence, for the biggest measure of the ills besetting my region is probably the relative normalcy of the devastation—which is to say, the ability of people to continue living in its midst.

Let us, then, head for the river on well-traveled roads.

Now that our eyes have been opened, what do we see?

The first thing we see is "township" after "township" in which land has been stripped for coal so thoroughly that the only undisturbed land is the land under a church, or a lone farmhouse whose owner would not part with mineral rights, or a graveyard, or a state road. County roads, in many instances, have disappeared, but state roads are less easily discontinued; hence, they continue to channel traffic, even when land that used to be abreast of the road has disappeared and all that's left is a "highwall" or cliff-like border to a previously subterranean bench 100 feet below. This is the region where topography is deranged and one sees ponds shaped like Norwegian fjords, sometimes with fishing "camps" attached to them. Call the landscape badlands. Trees descended from the original hardwood forest look gnarly and misbegotten, if they aren't already smothered by poison ivy and grapevines, and once productive bottomlands, where they still exist, tend now to be flooded owing to high silt content in the water draining the mines. Otherwise, it's just benches with a thin covering of grass, oddly shaped troughs with stagnant water in them, and a wandering assortment of debris piles with hybrid poplar growing on top. It's a region so infertile, so thoroughly devoid of reason and rhyme, so flat-out undetermined by geologic forces and weather, that its principal use now is to serve as a terminus for trains hauling municipal waste out of New York City. This region used to export massive amounts of Pittsburgh #8 coal via "unit trains" that were 100 cars long. Now it imports trash via unit trains outfitted with tip/hook cars, and in general those trains are traveling to the very same place where they first picked up the coal.

There are bright spots, of course. There is an area north of Cadiz that serves as a mecca for ATV enthusiasts. And to the east, at least one enterprising fellow has converted his topographical jumble into a "fair hunt" elk preserve where the meat grinder is as prominent as the cover for elk to hide in is sparse. Most of the time, though, residents are less opportunistic. Billboards here advertise lightning rods sold by a man doing business as "Dr. Boom," and so far as I can tell the principal reason for this man's entrepreneurial success is that folks in these parts know they've been hit.

What do you see after you cross the badlands?

After the badlands, but before you start descending to the river, you cross a different kind of desert. Here the placeless-ness is due not so much to re-ordered topography as to re-ordered town life—viz, the dual substitution of chain stores for locally-owned ones, and car-oriented strips for coherent, pedestrian-friendly downtowns.

As in the first, more westerly zone, there are bright spots. Some of the businesses that moved out of downtown Steubenville (once an outlying mall started mining the local economy) actually managed to keep their customers—usually by maintaining large parking lots with clearly marked lines and plastic signage that blends in well with the more cartoonish, instantly-recognizable signage of corporate neighbors. Additionally, several people run thriving, relatively new businesses out of homes along the strip thanks to winning emphases on toupees, tuxedos, and taxidermy. But you really have to look to glimpse this kind of economic life. If you aren't paying close attention, all you see is an 800,000 square foot Walmart distribution center on the site of a former mine, and then a long winding "strip" lined with Rite-Aid dispensaries, Burger King establishments, and Jiffy Lube depots—at which point you descend to the river proper with its hollowed-out town on the river's generous west bank.

Whenever a visitor drops down out of the hills onto the brownfields on the upper Ohio's valley floor, chances are good that the visitor will feel as though he or she has stepped into a gutter, and in a certain sense that is exactly what has happened, for the valley functions as a conduit for the passage of fouled water and air. Owing to the recent closure of mills on both sides of the river, air here has cleared up a little, but when I first moved to Steubenville the prevalence of vaporized metals in the atmosphere made your eyes burn. In addition to blast furnaces that produced iron, hot-strip mills that converted steel slabs into coils, and related factories that produced metal food containers, industrial concerns in the Steubenville-Weirton area included a coke factory, where coal was charred and made ready for metallurgical use, and two world-class coal-fired power plants—the kind that burn five train cars of coal per hour under boilers fired by flames that reach 100 feet in height. Hence the air in Steubenville was, and to some extent still is, a witch's brew. It had and has traces of benzene and zylene and tuolomene in it, all of which give air an acrid edge, and large amounts of sulfur dioxide, which becomes acid rain after it oxidizes, and even a dollop of hydrogen sulfide, which smells approximately like rotten eggs. In the summer, when the area's numerous slag heaps perspire and temperature inversions trap valley gases, that smell can be strong.

Bad air, of course, does not necessarily ruin a town. On the contrary, it can serve as a kind of salt that helps you taste a given city's pluck and grit. In the case of Steubenville, though, there is no pluck or grit. Its once-grand Ft. Steuben Hotel now caters to elderly gentlemen who carry brown bags instead of briefcases. Except for entrepreneurial ventures like Save-A-Lot and "da Cookie Jar Club" on South 7th, the business district is boarded up, and theaters that once showcased Judy Garland and Stan Kenton have been razed. There's a jail and a sewage treatment plant where a park ought to be, and its once-thriving neighborhoods have been replaced by long stretches of vacant lots and townhouses called "projects." Weeds grow in the pavement. Jefferson County Courthouse, scalped since 1952 when a winter snowfall brought down its domed roof, has still not been awarded the funds necessary to replace that roof.

Thanks to its suburbs the town does have a tax base, but a pattern of graft instituted during the Prohibition era has made it difficult for significant amounts of money to be channeled toward civic improvement. In 1997 the Steubenville police department was second in the nation to sign a consent decree with the federal government owing to an excessive number of civil lawsuits, and in the same year the entire office for the local branch of the Environmental Protection Agency was dismantled owing to charges that office members received kickbacks from the industries they were supposed to be regulating. Can it be possible that fast-rising Franciscan University on the ridge above "Stoney Hollow" will inject missing civic spirit? Time will tell. Right now that institution's principal contribution to Steubenville life has been to facilitate the transition of the city's substantial Catholic population from an identity built on ethnic boroughs to one built on Spirit-driven, "charismatic" experience and varying degrees of membership in apparitionist sects. The new divide goes like this. If you don't take instruction from Marian sects based on apparitions, you are probably an Italian, Irish, or Polish parishioner whose real passion is football. If, on the other hand, you think of yourself as a card-carrying member of such a sect, you probably spend your waking hours worrying in earnest about Freemasonry, the possibility that bar codes could be the "mark of the beast," and whether or not Black Hawk helicopters will soon be deployed to hunt down people who are objecting to a forced imposition of world government orchestrated by the U.N.

I was stupefied, contemplating this sort of cultural division, and as time passed I even grew estranged for principled reasons. There is a gnostic side to Marian visions of the End, seeing as how they are premised on insider knowledge not available to ordinary, allegedly unenlightened people who rely "merely" on common sense, and it was saddening to have to explain such faith-based pathology to my kids. But there it was. And when I noted this kind of pathology alongside the economic, cultural and topographical damage on view during drives to the river, it began to seem as if a condition of un-housed-ness had been raised in this region to such a high power that one could almost hear life-spirits leaving. Doublewides with hazmat trucks parked in the driveway, failing clay block foundations that would hold an expansion bolt about as long as a shoe box, hunters in jack-o-lantern orange washing down Krispy Kremes with Mountain Dew before fanning out into badlands to bag deer with trophy "racks," yard displays featuring inflated Santas or plastic ducks wearing sweaters, craters passed off as fishing holes, broken farmsteads, pre-designed ranch-style home kits featuring vinyl siding, pressure-treated decking, and trusses rather than attic space, abandoned rail yards, fouled streams, corrupt municipal machinery, fields dressed with broken glass, ragweed, burdock, and spiky mullein—this was no promised land. Think, rather: dump, vacant lot, potter's field. Think: cosa vieta, paese guasto, or—switching to English now—*low pressure area*. Think: place from which one exports coal in order, next, to bring in municipal waste and prisoners, place where a killing gets done, place so poor that even its principal city's name, "Steubenville," turns out to be a salute to a Prussian con artist who needed a job and so invented an identity for himself that would win him that job. (The man who drilled Washington's regulars at Valley Forge somewhat spectacularly called himself "Baron Frederick William Augustus Henry Ferdinand Von Steuben.")

Just the place for a Berkeley carpenter, yes?

Play that funky music, white boy, play that funky music right.

This song, which topped the charts in 1976 around the time of The Commodores, was put together by steakhouse manager Rob Parissi and his band Wild Cherry at Mingo Junction, just south of Steubenville, and after I got my bearings in eastern Ohio it tended to ring—for obvious reasons—somewhat painfully in my ear. In fact, I would venture to say that it rang only slightly less painfully in my ear than it did in the ear of my cabinetmaker friend Larry Mader, who was a founding member of Wild Cherry and left the band just before "Play That Funky Music" became the third single ever to go platinum. Over time, though, the pain in my ears subsided, and though I would like to say that the reason was an aversion to priggishness and self-pity, in fact I just got lucky. Part of the reason pain subsided was that I learned Larry's band was named after cough drops, not a tree, for that news kind of broke my petulance some. Any group of musicians with that kind of flair for titles deserves an unbiased hearing! But the main reason pain subsided was simply that I started to wonder less about my own displacement and more about what caused the damage I saw all around me.

❧

Time to look at my wrist. Five o'clock. It will soon be dark, yet the crew change is still an hour away. Ought I not to be up in the wheelhouse?

Passing through a steel locker, I find my way to the bunkroom assigned me. I remove the watch cap, padded coveralls, and down vest that have been protecting me from the cold, unpack my ridiculously heavy duffel-bag full of books, and warm my hands by holding them close to a hot (and freshly enameled) water pipe. After feeling returns to numb fingers, I stop for a minute to warm my mind by reviewing, with approval, the books now lined up on a little shelf above my bunk: *The Whiskey Rebellion* by Thomas Slaughter, *Albion's Seed* by David Hackett Fischer, *Notes on the State of Virginia* by Thomas Jefferson, *Errand Into the Wilderness* by Perry Miller, *Democracy in America* by Tocqueville. It's a strong list and I look forward very much to reacquainting myself with each of these books over the course of this trip — hopefully at the same time that I re-read Lincoln's two inaugural addresses and Frederick Jackson Turner's *Frontier Thesis*, copies of which lie flat on the little desk under the porthole. Where, though, are Kerouac's *Dharma Bums* and Snyder's *Back Country*? Concerned, I rummage through my duffel for a third time, and this time—praise God—I find them. Rest assured: I don't plan on sifting these latter two books for insights. Rather, I have brought them along simply for their talismanic value. But enough. It is time to splash my face with cold water, steal a quick look out the porthole (night has already come), and head for the ladder-like steps leading to the wheelhouse.

As previously indicated, this wheelhouse is 35 feet above the water, and you get there by climbing a set of stairs that is only a little less steep than the ones leading to a conning tower on a sub. You pass through two decks, on your way up, and when you reach the top you find yourself in a small, 12 by 12 room with walls made largely of glass. There's a desk full of nautical charts that has a laptop and a printer and a fax machine sitting on it, a water dispenser in a far corner, a high, couch-like seat for visitors, and a steersman's chair with controls in front and an excellent view over the tow. The pilot, John, is talking on the phone. He has long graying hair knotted loosely at the back of his head, and he is wearing blue jeans, a tee shirt, and running shoes. Raising an eyebrow in welcome, he motions with his head to the high bench at the rear of the cabin, and, getting the message, I make a beeline for the couch. Outside snow has started to fall. There are windshield wipers with de-icing fluid on them swishing back and forth as regularly as the radar device on the boat's roof keeps silently revolving, but here in the wheelhouse it is warm, and the various instrument panels glow like purple, orange, brown, and green embers on a quiet hearth. In addition to a screen showing radar images of approaching tows, there are screens showing how deep the water is at any given moment (lots of silt below dams), the tow's "swing" relative to its sailing line, and (thanks to real-time GPS) the boat's actual location on Army Corps of Engineer navigation charts. Captivating though these monitors can be, however, you don't stare at them all that much. Why should you? Depth finders, swing meters, VHF radio hardware—these are supplementary aids, and, as such, they are off to the side. In this room, the primary focus is the river itself, along with the engine throttles and "sticks" that control the flanking and steering rudders and, thereby, the course of the boat. Where is the river leading, and how do I get there? Those are the questions John in his role as skipper silently asks, and I now make bold to ask them too.

One's first instinct when attempting to summarize the kind of devastation on view in east central Ohio is to depict the area as archetypically exploited. For example, one can argue that the tri-state area has been "used," and then (because used once) used again and again in order that the rest of the country, Berkeley citizens included, might prosper or perhaps even satisfy craven needs. There is a disadvantage to this kind of approach, however. Even if "they" (the usual, notoriously vague term for the people charged with exploitation) turn out in the end to include (at least partially) "us," one is still at all times thinking in terms of good guys v. bad guys, and that fact, in turn, means that one is without access to more structural explanations. Accordingly, I began over time to adopt a different approach, which was to think in terms of an explosion that no one person or group of persons set off or even planned.

If you get hold of the relevant 7.5 minute U.S. Geological Survey topo maps for this area and fit them together on a wall, as I have done, you see some interesting things. Each map, called a "quad" because it shows a fourth of the latitudinal and longitudinal distance that a larger 30 minute map shows, is about 18" wide by 22" high, and if you tack up fifteen of them in correct, contiguous order, you wind up looking at a kind of mural that shows a geographical area measuring roughly 37.5 miles, going from west to east, and 22.5 miles, going from north to south. Given that the distance between Cadiz and Weirton is about 25 miles, the amount of area shown is perfect for getting a read on damaged areas in the entire tri-state area, and thanks to the 20-foot contour intervals employed by the 7.5 series maps, you get the added benefit of seeing all that land in surprisingly sharp, human-scaled topographic detail. There is green shading to indicate the presence of woods as opposed to meadows or fields, and, of course, there are also black lines indicating railroads and highways, and blue lines indicating rivers and creeks.

I used to study quadrangle maps for hours when I was planning routes in the mountains, and I was always amazed at the power of these things to hold one's attention. Is it their reliance on contour, which is in fact (referencing Isaiah here) a level road leading to water? Whatever the appeal, looking at, say, the "Mt. Challenger quadrangle" whetted an appetite for actually walking in high country, and I experienced some of the same pleasures while looking at the Weirton, Steubenville, and Flushing quadrangles once they were all fitted together. For example, I could see that this entire area was in fact, as guidebooks had said, a "dissected plateau": nearly every ridgetop featured the same elevation. Also, I could spot migration routes: in several places, tributaries emptied their waters into the Ohio River directly across from each other, and, lo—the names of the creeks matched, indicating that the original settlers thought of the creeks as trails. (One set of creeks, the one that the Norfolk and Western railroad follows, is even called "Cross Creek.") Finally, I could see that the Ohio River, too, "meanders." You wouldn't know it, driving north along Rt. 7, but thanks to my trusty wall mural there it was, plain as day: parts of Toronto and all of downtown Weirton used to be river channel.

Unlike the topos I was used to studying out west, however, these eastern Ohio topographical maps also showed strip mines, and that particular feature complicated the revelatory potential of the maps. Indeed, when considered singly the maps tended to frustrate viewers more than intrigue them, and for the simple reason that when it comes time to "map" a mined area, draftsmen switch to a rosy, pointillistic pattern to indicate the *unavailability* of contour lines—which is to say, the loss of the very same reference points that topographical maps depend on to provide the kind of information you buy them for. Given that terrain in a stripped area no longer makes sense, mapmakers in effect throw up their hands and give up when it comes time to chart a surface mine. Consequently, the viewer of an eastern Ohio "topo" often finds himself or herself looking at, well, nothing. But if you put that map on a wall—if you fit the map to other, adjoining puzzle pieces—at that point everything changes. Suddenly the troublesome maps become resplendent with sense, for at that moment you find yourself looking not so much at randomly-occurring, red smudges as at a concentrically organized roseate bloom. Which is to say, you find yourself looking at an explosion. You see this entire region going up in flames.

Just what was it, one wonders, that detonated here? What kind of flames were these? Did they sear minds as well as land? What, in other words, was the extent of the concussive force? And what kind of circuitry could have enabled explosion in the first place?

This book is my attempt to find answers to these questions.

Starting from the assumption that the firestorm, if there was one, had to have resulted from a combination of local or at least localized ingredients, I assembled, over the course of about four years, a list of seven distinct, tri-state-specific key events—call them tipping points—that, either singly or together, could have triggered a destructive impact when they made their appearance. Now, in the ensuing chapters, I propose to examine and weigh each of these tipping points in roughly chronological order so that I can then, after cross-checking my findings against the books lined up above my bunk, assess the nature and extent of their combined impact. I plan to start by zeroing in on Thomas Hutchins' Enlightenment-based 1785–87 land survey of federal lands in eastern Ohio—the so-called "Seven Ranges" whose eastern border the Ocie Clark is now tracing. That survey, which for the first time portioned land according to a grid-like pattern of "section and range" to make it ready for commercial sale, served as the prototype for virtually all national surveys conducted thereafter; indeed, its *imprint*, as it were, is still plainly in view during transcontinental flights. Next, I plan on turning our attention to revivalism and the second "great awakening," which, after being seeded by Moravian missionaries who came through eastern Ohio in 1761, broke out in "camp meetings" all over this land—most famously just across the river in Kentucky at Cane Ridge (1801), but originally at Red River, a little further south, under the direction of one James McGready, who was schooled six miles east of Steubenville. And in the fourth chapter I hope to focus on General George Armstrong Custer of 7th Cavalry fame, who (my neighbors take enormous pride in this) grew up on the ridge I look at every morning when I water our animals. I could have picked Steubenville native Edwin McMasters Stanton to illustrate this era in eastern Ohio history. After all, Stanton directed the War Department under Lincoln and is famous for moving 20,000 men across 1,200 miles in less than a week, thereby enabling Ulysses S. Grant to relieve Rosecrans' forces (after their loss at Chickamauga) and eventually defeat Braxton Bragg's (Confederate) Army of the Tennessee. For our purposes, however, Custer is the better choice: his career invites us to scrutinize not just the war against the Confederacy but, as well, the wars against Mexico and the subsistence-based traditions on view in the Ogallala and Lakota Sioux.

Not surprisingly, I expect to end that chapter with questions rather than answers; therefore, in chapter 5 I will probably continue to focus on the Civil War era, this time to reflect a little on whether the Civil War could have been focused as much on the substitution of universal suffrage for tradition, as the default means for steering our ship of state, as it was on eliminating chattel slavery.

There is a sudden, loud burst of static as marine VHF channel 13 comes to life. "Sarah Nicole. Just a mile below Weegee Mine. A full tow here. About 6.2 right now. One mile, headed for north-bound tow." John casts an eye toward the radar screen, sees the approaching barges, and then reaches up with his right hand to pull down a mike with a tightly spiraled cord. "Roger roger, Sara Nicole. Ocie Clark here. We mark you on our screen and will hang until we have you in view."

The river channel, here, is only 300-feet wide.

Within a few minutes a blue light marking the head of the Sara Nicole tow appears on the far side of a spit at the end of a point, and a couple minutes after that, the boat itself is 50-feet off our port bow, making waves. The pilot on the Sara Nicole pulls once on his whistle chain to confirm port-to-port passing logic, and John answers with a blast from his own. Then the downbound boat is gone.

John turns to me and smiles, a little mischievously. "It's close, but it's not like it is in Baton Rouge going around Sugar House Bend." I nod, remembering that in Louisiana there is ocean-going traffic as well as brown-water traffic, and then, drawn inward by the even sound of Ocie Clark engines and the sight of John smoothly manipulating four rudders to negotiate the same bend the Sara Nicole materialized in, I gradually return to the river road that I see in my mind's eye.

The commodification of land, the arrival of revivalist energy flow, and the devaluation of tradition—so far I have been talking about bomb parts. In the second half of the book, I plan on widening the focus to include damage. In chapter 6, after noting how eastern Ohio farmland served as a laboratory for the invention and deployment, by Consolidated Coal in collaboration with Bucyrus Erie, of "monster" draglines now in use all over the world by the kind of coal companies that aspire to load two unit-trains per hour, I plan to ask how it is even possible to think of stripping continuously inhabited land on this kind of scale. In chapter 7, after noting that my new hometown was also home to Ohio Congressman John A. Bingham, the man who drafted the equal-protection clause of the Fourteenth Amendment, I intend to think about the implications of his decision to frame that clause in such a way as to make it suitable for use by railroad corporations seeking protection from hostile state governments. And in chapter 8, after asking how those of us who have enabled detonation can continue to claim (as east central Ohioan Americans regularly do) that we are, in the main, bearers of uniquely civilizing light, I will consider whether our strenuously consistent maintenance of this claim could itself be a clue to the postulated firestorm's size and character.

It's a big undertaking, a journey like this, and it is entirely possible that I will fail in my efforts to describe the damage I see. Nevertheless things could be worse, for in an important sense I did not choose to write a book with these kinds of absurdly rich themes. On the contrary, the twists and turns in the road ahead have come into view slowly and unexpectedly and sometimes even annoyingly, much as evidence does; therefore, if I do fail it won't be because I tried to imagine too much. Rather, it will be because my mind wasn't big enough to keep track of this region's rich history and crack its code. Consequently, I go forth strangely heartened and even hopeful that I might succeed in my attempt to describe and perhaps even explain the hill country presently looming off our port bow.

2

Geographer's Line

The practice of facing a tow, rather than pulling one, began on the Ohio River. Was this a "bright" idea, like the invention of the wheel? Perhaps it was, but I suspect the practice began because the river demanded it. None of the Ohio is tidewater. There is always a current, and though the Ohio is, except for a three mile stretch near Louisville, free of falls and fast water, it does cut through hill country along much of its 982-mile length. Therefore, in addition to being naturally shallow in late summer and autumn it winds a lot, and its channel is often narrow. It must have made almost instant sense for towboats here to have flat bottoms and a squared-off head with tow "knees" high enough to make good contact with a barge's rim, whether that rim was low to the water (because a barge was heavily loaded) or nine feet up (because the barge was empty). The trick would have been to steer the thing.

Upon first glimpsing a loaded 15-barge tow threading its way upriver, ocean-oriented spectators typically seize on a picture of, say, a flattened cargo ship negotiating a narrow channel without the aid of a tug. And that kind of analogy is helpful. Yet it is also misleading, for in the case of a 15-barge tow there is no keel, no guarantee that boat and tow will act as one. What is it like to not have a keel? When I put that question to Jack, the Ocie Clark captain, he puts a pencil on a flat navigation chart and asks me to press the nail of my index finger against the pencil's eraser so as to push the sharpened end along the depicted riverbed. It is a difficult business, but I succeed. Then the captain tells me to factor in current. He asks me to consider that bank suction can draw you sideways, that moving water on the other side of a spit will swing your head quicker than you can blink, that traveling downstream on a swollen river is like driving down an icy hill, that empties skid on water and don't respond well to flanking maneuvers, though even if they do one can always lose a wheel (propeller) if a log gets jammed in it, and then you're down to one rudder rather than two. At this point my smile departs and I wear instead an expression of sobriety. Clearly, river pilots face a challenge or two, and thus it should come as no surprise that they reach, hungrily, for every small advantage they can get. One such advantage is a kort nozzle, which is a cylindrical casing that fits around a boat's "wheel" in such a way as to increase thrust on rudders to such a high degree that heavy, flat-bottomed vessels become maneuverable in ways that pilots used not even to dream about. But the main advantages are well-aligned barges and tight rigging. If you get those two things right, chances are good that boat and tow will behave as a single unit and permit you at least partially to "steer on the tow."

The critical point is the place where the towboat attaches to the barges. When current pushes the head of a tow in a direction that a pilot has to fight, the entire tow acts as a lever, and if face wires aren't tight or if a two-inch locking line fails, then either of the two corners on the boat's prow can become a fulcrum, and that is a situation devoutly not to be wished. Hence, the first mate and his deckhands work hard to secure and maintain that connection. They run a locking line with a hydraulic winch from a giant kevel (or cleat) on the foredeck to a kevel on the central fronting barge and then back again to a capstan. (Crewmembers stand in a metal locker while this capstan is in operation, owing to the danger of this line snapping.) Then, using slightly smaller winches, they lock in the corners of that same barge, this time going from more kevels, to thick steel buttons. And after that, assuming of course that one is securing a tow that is three barges wide and not just one, the crew runs two more sets of wing wires, one a three-part steel wire running via timberheads from the central kevel on each outlying barge to a point about twenty feet back from the boat's bow, and the other a much longer wire made out of synthetic fiber called spectra that runs from each outlying barge's corner to manual winches set forty feet back from the bow. "Dog it down," John kept repeating yesterday over the crews' VHF radio channel, as the Ocie Clark proceeded east out of the Willow Island Lock. "Dog it down." By "it" he meant a heavy steel toothpick that advances teeth past a ratchet's paw.

Well, the Ocie Clark deckhands must have done a good job because this evening the entire 1150-foot tow is still squared-up, wing-wire cocked, and line-string straight. The boat is steering well—well enough, at any rate, for the first mate to have assigned routine maintenance chores. This means we are all of us free to muse and think and, in general, get our personal bearings, and I for my part can't help but journey in my mind to a time on this river when diesel-driven tows were nowhere in evidence and all one could see were manually propelled flatboats floating on what Thomas Jefferson called "the most beautiful river on earth."[4]

※

After the Treaty of Paris got signed in 1783 there were a lot of boats plying these waters. King George III had banned settlement west of the river in an effort to appease Pontiac, but now, thanks to Washington's success at Yorktown, British authority was annulled, and many of the 95,000 Moravians, Dunkards, and (chiefly) Scots-Irish who had emigrated between 1763 and 1776 to the Virginian Piedmont and southwest Pennsylvania from Donegal and Antrim were following the bold few who had sparked Pontiac's resentment in the first place.[5] They came via the river from Pittsburgh, these immigrants, and they traveled in an assortment of boats that was every bit as varied as the localized fiddle tunes audible on these vessels' decks.[6] Prospective settlers came in standard flatboats with fortified cabins on them and sometimes even barnyards that were built with lumber that could be re-used as housing once a boat reached its destination. They came in broadhorns, which were flatboats with long-sweeps instead of oars. They came in pirogues, which was French for dugouts. They came in keelboats that could sail (or be poled) upriver as well as down, and a few immigrants even travelled in bona fide schooners if water was high enough. That made for a busy waterway, given that there were already freighters on the river carrying ginseng, furs, whiskey, and salt, and that's before even considering the addition, in 1783, of ferries. Scots had first settled this region in the 1770s, about the same time that Spanish settlers from northern New Mexico arrived on Ohlone land in Berkeley, and by 1783 there were clearings and a cabin on nearly every creek bottom north of the Muskingum River. The cabins were crude—just a single room with a fireplace and a clay-and-wattle chimney plus a piece of mica for a window—but they functioned as homes, and owners were inclined to defend them as such.

Starting in 1785, though, there was a war declared on these same owners, and it wasn't prosecuted by Mingos or Delaware braves. Rather, it was prosecuted by First American Regiment regulars from newly built Ft. Hamar at the mouth of the Muskingum River, and that particular circumstance put Ohioan pioneers in an awkward position.[7] How could the new settlers raise firearms against the very same army many of them had just served in? By and large they couldn't. Instead of resisting the soldiers, the pioneers stood by and watched homes burn on every bottom from Sandy Creek to what would become Marietta, and in consequence they turned their backs on the river and emigrated deeper into the Ohio woods along Moravian and Mingo trails to a set of ridge-tops that would eventually become the site of current-day Cadiz, Ohio.

Why had the soldiers come and why did they burn the homes? The answer to those questions is simple. The soldiers were there to enforce a piece of legislation passed by the Continental Congress that defined the homesteaders who had staked Lockean claims on the west side of the river as squatters. Its name? The 1785 Land Act. That title makes the legislation sound routine but in fact the ordinance turned out to be highly significant. For it didn't just permit the burning of some cabins; additionally in one fell swoop it enabled (a) the formation of a vigorous (still operant) strain of contrarian sentiment, (b) the privatization of an American version of the medieval "commons," (c) the establishment, in the Northwest Territory, of a Jeffersonian bias in favor of decentralized power, and (d) the USA's path-breaking commitment to a grid system for identifying, marketing, and selling real estate.

Let's start by discussing the ways in which contrarian identity in Harrison County hill country became a firmly established fact, as opposed to just a leaning, for that discussion leads naturally to the enclosure issue and puts us in excellent position to weigh the significance of both Jefferson's hope and, as well, the technology that was destined to undercut that hope.

֎

I'm not sure I would ever have learned about this region's ultimately contrarian identity if I hadn't puzzled frequently over why the men who platted the seat of Harrison County called their new town "Cadiz." This is Scots-Irish (Presbyterian) and occasionally German (Mennonite/Lutheran) country. There are virtually no Spaniards here. Wherefrom, then, the name, "Cadiz"?

Then one day it dawned on me that this area's principal market, in the late 1780s and early 1790s, was Spanish New Orleans and that the Washington administration had delayed the procurement of formal rights to trade with New Orleans until it was certain of its own control over the trans-Allegheny West. Might it not be possible that platters were saluting a time when future Harrison County citizens stood ready to declare de-facto allegiance to Spain rather than to the United States, so as to fulfill a genuinely secessionist impulse? Pulling down an encyclopedia from library shelves, I looked up "Cadiz, Spain." Bingo. Cadiz, Spain, turned out to be

Geographer's Line

the seaport that endured a multi-year blockade and near constant bombardment (between 1797 and 1798) by a British force (commanded by Rear Admiral Nelson) that bore striking parallels, in its actions, to the American force (commanded by Washington) that waged war on "squatters" in Ohio and (to the extent that pioneers had staked Lockean claims on land already purchased by speculators like George Washington) southwest Pennsylvania. Though it is of course possible that the men who platted the seat of Harrison County were thinking, in a generally patriotic sense, about the heroism of fighting a war—any war—against the British empire (as per Chamber of Commerce circulars), it makes far richer (and more exact) sense that platters were remembering a time when local farmers—already hostile to federal control after having been expelled from their homes in a manner that was consistent with what their forefathers had experienced during the Galloway Leveller Revolt[8]—declared potentially treasonous solidarity with their ideal trading partners.[9]

Given that the quickest and easiest way to get coal, lumber, lye, salted meats, and especially rye whiskey to a place where one could convert them to cash was simply to float them down the river, why had Washington and point man John Jay dragged their feet when negotiating trade terms with the Spanish viceroy? To residents on the upper Ohio that slowness was tantamount to betrayal, and when Jay later presumed to also levy an excise tax on the production of whiskey, as he did in 1794, resentment matured into outright revolt. Hence the name, "Whiskey Rebel," which accurately describes virtually all of Cadiz' original population,[10] given that the town was founded by people who looked favorably upon secession as a means for shipping whiskey to New Orleans and was "grown" by refugees who had publicly refused to pay Jay's excise tax, in consequence of which they had to flee a "Watermelon Army" that numbered 13,000 and was led by President Washington himself.[11]

Can it really be argued, though, that the 1785 Land Act was an American version of Britain's Enclosure Acts?

Let us back up for a minute to note two things—first, that the Land Act was conceived in a 1784 report written by Virginia's delegate to the Continental Congress, Mr. Thomas Jefferson, and, second, that Jefferson's report was submitted at the exact same time that Congress rather desperately needed cash.

After the War for Independence had been won, Jefferson had holed up at his Monticello estate to devise a plan for instituting a common currency. Once that task was accomplished, he turned next to the problem of how to create new states out of the huge Northwest Territory that would soon (thanks to the largesse of New York and hopefully also Connecticut, Massachusetts, and Virginia) belong to the federal government. Perhaps because it was winter, Jefferson gave a lot of thought to this latter challenge, and by the time his cherry trees bloomed he had in his hands a fully-fledged solution that was as meticulously detailed as it was boldly conceived. More on the stunningly ancient, squarely pre-modern philosophical biases to this plan later. Right now it will be sufficient to note simply the legalistic particulars: statehood eligibility once population reached 20,000, equality of statehood regardless of whether a state was new or descended from one of the original thirteen colonies, no slavery, allowance for public education, and (thinking in terms of geography now and not social justice) a grid of state lines anchored to a meridian that passed through the falls of the Ohio. Jefferson even gave names to the states he visualized. One was to be called "Metropotami," another "Saratoga," and still another "Pelisipia." The plan sounded fanciful, and thanks to a bias in favor of the new metric system the plan was also abstract. In another sense, though, Jefferson's plan cut right to the point, for Congress was $45 million in the hole after the war against Britain and needed very much to sell the land Jefferson was subdividing. Hence, while Jefferson tinkered with his plan so that it would feature a grid of townships as well as states, Congress moved swiftly and expeditiously to ready assets for sale, first by hammering out the agreement whereby Virginia would cede its lands west of the Ohio to the federal government, second by zeroing in on which land should be auctioned off first and how that auction might work.

Should Congress start by selling lots along the entire length of the river, and then, good salesman that it planned to be, work its way inland? Eventually it was decided that it was best simply to work from east to west. Congress would hire a surveyor to run a "geographer's line" straight west from the point where Pennsylvania's western border intersected the Ohio river, and then, at markers placed every six miles, a perpendicular north-south line, thereby creating an extendable grid that would facilitate the creation of lots sized for sale. Jefferson, charmed by the fact that the ancient Anglo Saxon land division known as a "hundred" punned well with a square measuring 10 km by 10 km, wanted to use the metric system when laying out these markers, but Rufus Putnam, who was used to working with surveyor chains that divide evenly into a distance exactly one mile long, wanted to use an approximately equivalent six-mile interval as a foundational unit of measurement.¹² Congress sided with Putnam. Did the unbidden picture of hauling chain up and down hillsides begin to act as a kind of brake at this point on Congress' ambition? Initially Congress had visualized lots above and below a relatively infinite geographer's line, but now, as push came to shove and the sheer immensity of the trans-Allegheny West started to sink in, Congress decided to run the key horizontal line exactly 42 miles west, thereby making it possible to initiate exactly seven controlling meridians, each of which would drop straight as a plumb bob toward the Ohio River and in the process establish borders for seven tiers of townships that would be subdivided into farm-sized parcels. Lawmakers called these successive towers of townships "The Seven Ranges."

The ordinance was promoted as a means of empowering the common man. Rules for bidding were slanted against speculators, and it was hoped that the clarity of the rectangular parcels offered for sale would discourage fraud. But to families living on the west side of the Ohio the ordinance looked (for obvious reasons) as if it had been designed to *diminish* the power of the common man, and though it is probable that homesteading families were not entirely right in this assessment, it is undeniably true that the 1785 Land Act was manipulated to serve moneyed parties intent on slowing down, redirecting, and ultimately owning western development.¹³

Easterners had a lot of capital tied up in the west! New Englander attorneys like clergyman Manasseh Cutler, Philadelphian financiers like Robert Morris, New Yorker Federalists like William Duer, and Virginia tidewater elites like George Washington all had portfolios featuring either large speculative holdings in rural western land (Washington himself owned about 63,000 acres thanks to a spectacularly successful 10-year gamble on veteran land rights, and, too, a sharp, surveyor-trained eye for potentially valuable land¹⁴) or shares in companies whose object was to develop those lands, be it through the construction of canals or the founding of a town like Marietta or the construction of a canal that would link the North Branch of the Potomac to the Cheat, whose waters flowed west to the Ohio. Hence you can imagine the alarm and the concern generated in 1784 when one visitor to southwest Pennsylvania observed that western settlers stood "on a privet" in such a way that "the touch of a feather would almost incline them any way"—for example, into the arms of Spain rather than the United States.¹⁵ That observer was George Washington, and he knew whereof he spoke, having just returned from a conference with a whole crowd of Miller's Run farmers who were annoyed to discover that land they had cleared and begun to farm had been bought, years before (courtesy of a land agent), by the war hero from Mt. Vernon. "I will have this land as surely as I have this handkerchief," Washington told the crowd from his perch in a saddle, but the remark did not appear to chasten his hearers as much as the speaker would have liked.

After that fiasco, Easterners moved with alacrity to protect their investments.

They had done it before, when threatened by excessively high English taxes, and now they did it again—first by stalling negotiations with New Orleans, second by chasing off squatters and passing a Land Act so that land could be sold rather than simply claimed, third by turning around and exploiting weaknesses in the Seven Ranges survey to secure permission to start and then aggressively shelter a rival, privatized model for land sales that would more directly benefit large-scale speculation. American officials had been wary of opening the Mississippi River to trade with New Orleans ever since 1779, when Robert Morris, who helped to finance the war for independence, argued that opening the river might encourage western pioneers to turn their backs on an East that was already geographically distant owing to the presence of the Allegheny Mountains. Thereafter Washington decided that Secretary of Foreign Affairs John Jay should use river navigation rights as a bargaining chip rather than as an end in itself when negotiating with his Spanish counterpart, Don Diego Maria de Gardoqui y Arriquibar. "The navigation of the Mississippi at this time ought to be no object with us," Washington wrote to his friend Henry Lee, in 1786.[16] "Until we have a little time allowed to open and make easy the way between the Atlantic and the western territory, the obstruction had better remain." In the meantime, western development as defined by easterners should continue and even increase.

Construction began on a third fort (in addition to Forts Hamar and McIntosh) to be situated on a bend in the river just north of "Mingo Town" in order to house troops assigned to protect the Seven Ranges survey team, and at upscale Bunch of Grapes Tavern in Boston at the corner of King and Mackerel Streets the well-tailored and urbane pastor from Ipswich, Manasseh Cutler, met with revolutionary war heroes Rufus Putnam and Benjamin Tupper to conceive the Ohio Company of Associates and lay out the future Federalist town that was destined to become Marietta. Within just a few months they sold 250 shares at $1,000 a pop, and after formally incorporating the Ohio Company of Associates at Cromwell's Head Tavern on School Street Cutler visited New York to capitalize on the glacial slowness of the Seven Ranges survey and Congress' mounting frustration. Wouldn't Congress rather just cut a deal with the Ohio Company and put some instant cash in the bank? During the fall of 1786 and the spring of 1787, while Ohio Company representatives Israel Ludlow and Winthrop Sargent conveniently showed up to help with (and monitor) the government-sponsored

Seven Ranges survey, Cutler designed a deal whereby the Ohio Company of Associates would pay 66.66 cents per acre in depreciated Continental Army land warrants (8 cents "specie") for 1,500,000 acres between the 7th and 16th ranges, and (after a July 20, 1787 prompt from Treasury Department officials) an option on 3.5 million acres more.[17] The closing date was set for one month, almost to the day, after the public auction of Seven Ranges land, and when those latter auction results proved disappointing (the auction netted $117,108), Cutler's deal went through, thereby ensuring good demand for Ohio Company lots as well as Congress' relinquishment of development reins to private, speculative concerns. Why weren't sales of Seven Ranges land parcels more robust? Washington explained that the land was "too hilly," but in truth asking prices had been set a little high ($2/acre) relative to the means of farmers who had shown an interest in living there.[18]

To former Scots-Irish squatters, therefore, the passage of the Land Act must indeed have looked, at this point, not a little like the edict Henry VIII used to confiscate the "wilderness" of monastic lands so that it could be "enclosed," which is to say, cut off from rig-based agricultural use.[19] The ostensible reason for Henry VIII's seizure (as opposed to Congress') was that corruption was rampant in England's roughly four hundred monasteries, but in fact King Henry (like Congress) simply needed cash to (in Henry VIII's case) counter leverage that Spain had recently gained owing to the importation of gold from South American colonies, and the quickest, easiest way to get that cash was to sell off land that had been owned by the church and used as a de-facto commons where peasants could farm narrow strips of land in fields where other peasants also farmed according to their whims and needs. Note, too, that should a Scotch-Irish squatter see a parallel between the Continental Congress' actions and King Henry VIII's, that squatter would be on relatively safe ground, because Henry's seizure of church lands coincided with the advancement of modern survey methods to almost exactly the same degree that the 1785 Land Act did. Witness the 1538 publication of a pamphlet by Sir Richard Benese in which the good knight tells merchants who were aspiring to be lords how to calculate the area of enclosed fields.[20]

But there is a problem with interpreting the 1785 Land Act as an American version of an Enclosure Act, and that problem is not small. It is this: in the case of the 1785 Land Act, small farmers wound up *owning the land*.

It happened fairly fast, in the space of about ten years, starting in 1794. That was the year Anthony Wayne finally trapped Tecumseh's Wyandot, Delaware, and Miami warriors in the Great Swamp near current-day Toledo that used to protect Lake Erie from agricultural run-off, and for this reason the standard explanation for the sudden surge of purchases in eastern Ohio is to view that surge as a consequence of Wayne's victory and the following Greenville Treaty, which secured a new peace. But the real reason for the surge of purchases had to do with the coincidental presence of a "Watermelon Army" consisting of 12,950 men over in Pittsburgh that injected cash into an eastern Ohio economy already primed by forts built along the river.[21] Washington's intent, in sending that army, was to put down the aforementioned Whiskey Rebellion that occurred when 7,000 disgruntled farmers gathered (1794) in Braddock's Field, the place where the French and Indian War was begun and Carnegie sited his first mill, and though in one sense the Watermelon Army invasion was a failure (the most serious insurgents vanished, as we've said, into the hills of eastern Ohio and couldn't be found, let alone charged) in another sense the operation was a success, because it created a market for the very same goods that Whiskey Rebels had staged a war to protect—namely, flour, salt pork, and whiskey. Yes, these rebels fled into Ohio hill country. When they got there, though, they had cash in their pockets thanks to Watermelon Army quartermasters, and they used that cash, these rebels, to buy land. Almost overnight squatters became landholders, and given that the region already had an informally founded but fully functioning town called La Belle that had grown up around Ft. Steuben to service soldiers garrisoned there, the economy of the entire Seven Ranges region began at that point to cough, sputter, and grow. What explains the *speed* at which the former Whiskey Rebels executed their purchases? How did the entire region come to life so quickly? It came down to just one thing: Seven Ranges land had been surveyed in such a way as to make it almost hyper-ready for sale.

One mile north of my property's southwest corner, in some brush on the other side of railroad tracks running beside the creek that my springs feed, there is a chiseled, four-foot long piece of sandstone set in the ground like a tooth. It's got a flat square top, this tooth, and inscribed on that top there are two wobbly, yet clearly perpendicular, grooves. Given that most of the obelisk is underground (below the freeze line), you have to be looking to see it, but once you catch sight of the thing it's hard to look away, for the stone is old and it serves as a monument in more than one capacity. It indicates, first of all, the exact location of a corner that separates four different pieces of property. Secondly it serves as a reminder of the original Seven Ranges survey, for this stone was installed sometime in the 1790s at a spot formerly occupied by one of the posts installed every mile by Winthrop Sargent, the surveyor who ran the fifth meridian from the geographer's line to the river. But that is not all this stone indicates. This stone also serves as a marker for something much, much bigger—something so big, in fact, that you literally have to get up into the air to see it.

Have you ever looked out the window of a jet cruising at 35,000 feet above, say, the Texas panhandle and noticed the pattern made by pivot irrigation systems used to grow alfalfa? The ground, at that point in a transcontinental flight, looks like a board game consisting of precisely contiguous squares, each of them featuring a circle or semi-circle that perfectly grazes each of the square's four sides. One half hour later you fly over Albuquerque, and now you notice that the pattern formed by major streets and even bulldozed tracks on the desert floor outside the city limits seem to be cut from the same pattern that determined the placement of the wells at the center of pivot irrigation systems. Can this sort of regularity just be coincidence? To an airborne traveler whose eyes have been opened, patterns on the ground in the Midwest, the deep South, and the far West seem almost to indicate the existence in this country of some sort of ideal or immaculate rectilinear grid that governs the placement of nearly every road, city block, and agricultural field outside of Kentucky, Tennessee, and the coastal Atlantic states. Well, that is exactly what we have here. Indeed, we Americans are oriented to a grid that organizes our built landscape so effectively that it winds up organizing, as well, the ways in which we identify, sell, tax, and even understand real estate.

Where does it come from, this grid, and what is its name? It's called the "Public Land Survey System," and it came into existence and started to grow on the very same day that US Geographer Thomas Hutchins crossed the river just east of present-day East Liverpool and drove a stake into the earth to define a "point of beginning" for the Seven Ranges survey on the west bank of the Ohio.

ある

Western farmers, moviegoers who like Westerns, and to a certain extent people descended from farmers and moviegoers who like Westerns know all about the land survey system, of course. They are used to hearing phrases like "the back forty" and they know, most of them, that such a phrase refers to one quarter of a quarter section. They probably even know that pivot irrigation systems are the size they are because they fit, exactly, into the square that *is* one quarter of a quarter section. The rest of us, however, are liable to be in the dark on this issue; hence, I now take the liberty of stopping for a few moments to nail down the logic behind its key components—to wit, "section" and "range."[22]

As readers may or may not remember, "range" is the term Congress used for a strip of six-mile square townships stacked one on top of the other. Those strips ran vertically, on the north-oriented map lawmakers used, and they appeared to "hang" from the "geographer's line" above them much as rectangular pennants with torn bottoms might hang from a long, perfectly horizontal herald's trumpet. The real organizing principle, though, is a square. Just as the geographer's line, so called, is intersected every six miles by a perpendicular meridian running north-south in order to mark the western and eastern borders of each range of townships, so too is each meridian intersected, every six miles, by a perpendicular horizontal line running east-west to mark the northern and southern limits to each township. And the grid-like aspect doesn't stop there. In addition to lines marking six-mile square townships there is yet another set of lines marking one-mile square, theoretically farm-sized "sections" of 640 acres each. I say "theoretically" because, though Jefferson and the rest of Congress imagined that 640 acres would be about right for a prosperous farmstead, it turned out that hoi polloi families were able to make a go of it on 160-, 80-, even 40-acre parcels. Hence, on many occasions property lines in section-and-range country form rectangles or "L" shape pieces rather than squares. Overall, though, the impression remains one of evenly-sized squares. No matter how minutely a given piece of western land gets divided, when you consult an up-to-date map or look down from a plane toward the fence lines dividing one rancher's property from another's you see graph paper, and so too, by the way, do the oil exploration companies who are now busily perforating eastern Ohio crust so they can tap oil and liquid gas trapped in shale formations one mile deep.[23] The standard size for the "unit" of land that is required to support each multi-million dollar deep well? Six-hundred and forty acres.

Has there ever, anywhere, been a better system for speedily identifying and transferring real estate? Prior to the adoption of section-and-range logic in this country, property was defined via land grant histories or a "metes-and-bounds" system that depended on topography and customary usage for referents. It was hard to get a handle on where boundaries were, and even if you followed a deed's specifications carefully you still ran the risk of disputes with other interested parties. Once section-and-range logic came into play, though, those problems disappeared, and land searches became relatively easy. Indeed, we are still reaping rewards from the switch to section-and-range logic. If you walk into a recorder's office in Illinois tomorrow and ask for the location of a certain tract, all you need to know are its section, range, and township numbers relative to the ruling meridian and baseline axes in that geographical region. You say "southwest quarter of section 10, fifth range east of the 3rd principal meridian, 4th township north of the baseline" and you're done. That might sound complicated, but if you break the code you see that it is in fact simple, and in the days before computers the power conferred by that simplicity was miraculous. Ask a homesteader who staked a claim in Nebraska in the 1850s. Thanks to the reliability of the American Public Land Survey System, Nebraskan farmers who staked a claim in advance of a survey team tended to be right when they spotted the probable locations of section lines; therefore, they were able to shop around, as it were, for the instantly sellable, neatly commodified "quarter section" that would best suit their needs.[24] But the chief advantage of the Public Land Survey System was not so much that it enabled you to anticipate the future and so get a jump on other, less ambitious competitors. Rather, it was that it enabled you to act decisively as a buyer. Thanks to section-and-range logic you knew what you were buying when you bought a given piece of land, and therefore you could act swiftly, without fear. That's what the Whiskey Rebels learned, and given that the survey "machine" roughly kept pace with the development it facilitated, pioneers who came after the Whiskey Rebels were able to confirm those rebels' surprising experience, again and again and again.

Surveying, now—both the sort used to map or "read" a given landscape and the sort used to establish or confirm property lines—is done via lasers, GPS equipped theodolites, and aerial photography. Indeed, thanks to the presence of Navstar satellites launched in the 1980s the discipline has become so advanced that triangulation maneuvers now refer to the center of the earth rather than merely to a particular place on the earth's curved surface. The principles, however, have not changed. Surveyors still need some sort of yardstick, an axe for clearing lines of sight, a device for determining vertical and horizontal angles, and a compass to determine true north. And when they get to work, that work still consists of locating "known points" (points whose latitude, longitude, and elevation above sea level are already recorded), getting "control" (establishing distances and elevation differences between known points), and then either relating prominent topographical features to known points or installing monuments at prescribed spots on the earth in relation to those points. The only real difference between then and now is the degree of precision afforded by the instruments, and of course the speed at which maneuvers are accomplished.

Thomas Hutchins, for his part, arrived in Pittsburgh in early August 1785. He had been here before, first as a British soldier stationed at Ft. Pitt and then again as a cartographer. In 1766 he had even mapped the entire

Ohio River. So Hutchins knew the area well. This time, though, he had been hired to do something new, which was to inscribe a grid on the continent. In addition to saws and axes, his surveyor-specific toolbox consisted of a "circumferator," a sextant, a Gunter's chain, and of course a field notebook for recording salt licks and possible mill seats, in addition to mathematical data. The circumferator, used to establish angles relative to magnetic north, was essentially a large, two-foot diameter orienteering compass on a tripod. The sextant, by which one could determine the height of the north star above the horizon, was for confirming latitude, and the chain (named in honor of the English mathematician who invented it) was for measuring distance. I say "chain" but lest that word continue to conjure up images of heavy steel links attached to nautical anchors I should say that this particular "chain" looked more like a series of interlinked eyehooks. Designed in 1624 to measure at once acreage, mileage, and the amount of land one man can work in one day, that chain was exactly 66 feet long. This was in one sense inconvenient, because you needed to pull the chain tight no less than 80 times just to mark off one mile. In another sense, though, the chain's length was perfect, for in order to ensure the accuracy of physically determined horizontal measurements you need to hold a chain level, and anything longer than 66 feet would have been too heavy. So Hutchins had a reasonably full kit of field-tested tools. All he lacked was men—men and enough flour, salt, pork, beans, dried fruit, coffee, sugar, and tea to supplement game and keep men alive while they were in the woods.

Hutchins expected to find one surveyor from each of the thirteen states waiting for him when he arrived in Pittsburgh, but when he got here he counted eight. Given that he also needed axemen, chainmen, teamsters, and a cook, he had to do a fair amount of waiting, but eventually he got the men he needed and finally, on September 30, 1785, he crossed the river, located the "point of beginning" 1,500 feet west of Little Beaver Creek, and began running a baseline west. He was 40° 38' 2" north of the equator; visibility would soon be excellent, as trees were beginning to lose their leaves; and he had a company consisting of 38 men.

The job took him two years.

This was a long time by everybody's measure, not just superintendents,' therefore Hutchins took some flak on this score. But Hutchins faced some challenges, and given that those challenges would have stopped a lesser man cold, it appears in retrospect that Hutchins did rather well.[25] Consider, first of all, that his job description was ambitious even in the best of circumstances. His instructions were to clear a line of sight, establish a target, then "walk" a chain along seven 80-mile range lines and fifteen 40-mile township lines, all the while setting mileposts as markers for section lines, constructing witness trees at every township corner, and periodically correcting for error via astronomical readings. Then, as if all that weren't enough, Hutchins was supposed to subdivide every other township (thereby creating a kind of checkerboard pattern visible at the time only to hawks, or men in baskets suspended from balloons) into sections. Consider, too, that the land being imprinted by Hutchins was both heavily wooded (the dominant species, at that time, was white oak) and rugged (the terrain features steep hillsides and tortuous ravines). Last but not least, consider that this same land was *occupied*.

Hutchins ceased his survey efforts and retreated to the east side of the river on several different occasions between 1785 and 1787, and though it is possible that (to use a tired and not very helpful expression) Indians-on-the-warpath was a cause, it is far more likely that Hutchins pulled back after encountering resistance from settlers who perceived him and his men as trespassers. Field notebooks do make mention of "stolen horses" and "moccasin tracks" and "missing" survey stakes.[26] But Shawnee braves left eastern Ohio shortly after the end of the French and Indian War and these notebook entries were made in November 1786, the same month that homesteaders southwest of Pittsburgh dressed up like "Beezlebub" in order anonymously to scare off federal representatives trying to register distilleries. Thus, it might make better sense to conclude that recently dispossessed homesteaders engaged in similar antics to scare off surveyors. There is no proof for any of this, of course, but given that the homesteaders in question were descended from a Scots-Irish culture that made a *tradition* out of "pulling up the ways,"[27] it is at the very least reasonable to assume that Hutchins was challenged by violently inclined homesteaders in addition to difficult terrain and a tall work order.

Hutchins himself, in any case, found it difficult to take pride in his achievement. He began the survey in good spirits, noting in his log for example that soils, at 46 chains and 86 links west, were "remarkably rich with a deep, black mould, free from stone," but thereafter Hutchins appears to want the job over and done with. The more the survey progressed, the more Hutchins withdrew from the public eye, and when the venture concluded he applied for a job with the Spanish. But this doesn't mean that the survey failed. On the contrary, it succeeded, for Hutchins had built what might fairly be called a land-imprinting machine.

One year after Hutchins went "south," 23year-old Israel Ludlow took the system he had learned while laying out the fifth and seventh ranges west of the Ohio River and applied it to the Symmes Purchase, where he had smartly bought land, thereby laying out the future city of Cincinatti according to section-and-range logic. By 1793 Ludlow had worked his way up the

Miami River valley, and in 1794, after platting the town of Dayton, Ludlow ran the Greenville Treaty line that came to serve as the baseline for section-and-range surveys northeast of the First Principal Meridian, also known as the Ohio/Indiana state line. At this point Ohio Company director Rufus Putnam took a few turns in the driver's seat—perhaps as a kind of victory tour during which he celebrated congressional rejection of Jefferson's bias in favor of the decimal system—but after transforming the Moravian Reserves along the Tuscarawas River into sections and ranges he tired of the job.

Which is when Jared Mansfield appeared.

Mansfield not only shared Jefferson's vision of a land-sale system slanted in favor of small farmers; he also shared Jefferson's passion for precision. Therefore, when he was appointed to the office of "surveyor-general" in 1803 (following Putnam's firing by Jefferson's Secretary of the Treasury, Albert Gallatin), Mansfield zeroed in on how the Public Survey System could be improved to the point at which it almost guaranteed clear, lawsuit-free title. Hutchins, Putnam, and Ludlow had all of them approached surveying in a can-do spirit that, while meritorious and perhaps even necessary to get a whole system started, often sacrificed accuracy. Separately surveyed sections and townships didn't always line up. Baseline latitudinal readings were sometimes off by 25 seconds or more, and corrections for true north were occasionally skipped. Additionally, accounting for the convergence of longitudinal lines (owing to the spherical shape of the earth) wasn't even in the playbook. After Mansfield took over, though, those sorts of errors disappeared. Meridians started to jog 40 minutes, every six miles. Latitudinal lines started to curve slightly, in order to be the circle they ideally were. The numbering system got streamlined. Mansfield made it his mission to align the grid that surveyors would thenceforth be burning into the ground with the immaculate grid he saw in his mind, and when he was done, when his tenure as chief geographer was over, the Public Survey System pretty much drove itself.[28] It was *self-replicating*.

Meridians and associated baselines had appeared in Michigan, Illinois, Arkansas, Iowa, Missouri, and the Dakotas by 1815. Between 1819 and 1833 similar crosses appeared in the deep South thanks to the placement of the St. Helena, Choctaw, Tallahassee, and Chickasaw meridians. In 1851 the Mt. Diablo meridian and its associated baseline appeared in northern California at the same time that the Willamette meridian appeared on the French Prairie at the end of the Oregon Trail. And so on. It wasn't just Ohio that was being covered now. Rather, it was (except for Tennessee and Kentucky) the entire trans-Appalachian United States.

What happened here? What does it mean?

Sailors had been trying to use a coordinate system for centuries in order to determine their whereabouts. But, prior to Hutchins' survey, land maps almost always deferred to prominent local characteristics rather than to an abstract grid to orient a viewer. Take Cassini, the foremost cartographer working on the European continent during the 1770s and 1780s. Though Cassini's map of France (1791) studiously avoided the kind of accuracy conveyed by mythic maps so as to be able to favor a different, more practical kind of accuracy, his 1791 map makes no use whatsoever of the rough coordinate system that navigators had begun to employ starting in 1765, thanks to the development of a chronometer ("Harrison's timepiece") for judging longitude. Rather than employ a grid, Cassini depended on realistic *drawings* of mountains and correct visual scaling in relation to those drawings. Hence Cassini's map signaled the end of a technological era rather than the start of one. Hutchins' survey, by contrast, was unprecedented in the degree to which it abandoned old frames of reference, and that abandonment had an impact. After Hutchins' use of a meridian and a baseline, for example, grids started to come to the fore in American land-mapping efforts—so much so, in fact, that they started to facilitate detail, not just extend it. Consider, too, that General John Wesley Powell's revolutionary development of contour-based topographical maps for the US Geologic Survey nearly a hundred years later in 1881 was based (squarely!) on Powell's extensive experience as a public survey engineer. It is not accidental that US Geologic Survey quadrangle maps cover the same amount of land as a public survey "quadrangle" measuring six townships by six townships.

In other words, this switch to grid-based land maps was a big technological advance. You might expect that the insertion of a grid between one's eyes and the thing one is beholding would obstruct vision in some way. In fact, grids enable us to see and understand objects in ways formerly closed to us. Think of muntins, which form the wooden lattice into which small glass panes are set on window sashes. Far from complicating vision, muntins can help us see a garden or a "wild-scape" to a degree that is just not possible if one's only view is through a sash with an undivided light. Is it the contrast between the rectangularity of the grid and the organic forms of the greenery? Perhaps it has more to do with framing a particularized view in addition to a general one. Whatever the reason, grid lines increase visionary power, and, of course, there's the rub. Grids help us to see what we want to see just as much as they help us to see what is there, and sometimes—as when we comb a piece of land for mineral deposits, or timber, or perhaps even suitable sites for pre-industrial farms—they enable the eventual sacrifice of what is "there" in order to bring what is visualized to life. Such, at any rate, may have been the case when Lockean blank slate logic was unwittingly employed in 1785 to legitimate the imprinting of an "empty" wilderness with a checkerboard pattern of sale-ready lots, thereby predisposing American citizenry to countenance the eradication of Native American cultures.

What, though, does the section-and-range concept mean in the context of deliberately American, constitutionally embedded ideals? Here the picture changes, and a more meritorious dimension to the 1785 Land Act comes into view, for owing to Thomas Jefferson's authorship this legislation signs and to a certain extent enables an entire agrarian vision in which land ownership and attendant responsibilities are distributed in such a way as to ensure political freedom.

If you frame Jefferson's agrarianism in terms of Federalists versus Republicans, the viewpoint can appear dreamy, impractical, and even dangerous, given the way trust in "the people" can be used by demagogues. How can a vision based on virtue possibly compete with Hamilton's more hard-headed one? John Adams called the St. Croix-born Hamilton a "bastard son of a Scotch peddler,"[29] and, well—Hamilton good naturedly and winningly acted like it, hustling his way with considerable dash clear to a post in Washington's cabinet and marriage to the daughter of General Philip Schuyler, who stood about as close to aristocratic status as it was possible to stand in these officially classless United States. Jefferson, on the other hand, can seem aloof, hypocritical, and roughly as cautious on the field of physical battle as he was brave in the world of letters. Born to a prominent family in Virginia that was in turn descended from English gentry, Jefferson inherited (at age 14) a considerable number of slaves, along with 5000 acres of gently rolling fertile land near Charlottesville, and when he set about building the eventual seat of that estate, after passing the Virginia bar, he went into debt so as to increase that enslaved workforce to about 150 souls—all the while consistently condemning the institution of slavery in print. Twelve years later he abandoned the Governor's office in the face of Benedict Arnold and Cornwallis' dragoons, and in 1789, after sampling cheeses and wines in Provence while maintaining support for radical factions that were soon to hatch a Reign of Terror, Jefferson left his post as minister to France to serve in New York as Washington's Secretary of State.[30]

Additionally, Jefferson disdained land speculation, and though he would no doubt have successfully defended this disapproval by describing ways in which absentee ownership compromises an ability to define and defend liberty, it might also have been the case that Jefferson did not want to introduce a crass, commercial instinct into a garden that was designed for more leisurely pursuits. Who, an observer might reasonably ask, was Jefferson to judge Putnam's or (implicitly) Washington's commitment to the health of the trans-Allegheny West? At least those fellows actually toured the country, smelled its ferns, and slept on its ground in the rain.

The fact is, Jefferson was a Romantic. How could he not be, given that his heroes were Locke and Newton? Romanticism and Enlightenment aren't opposites; they are simply two different mutually reinforcing results of the European turn away from Christian belief, and Jefferson, immensely talented post-Christian man that he was, lived both dimensions to the full. He was a violinist, a classicist, a man of reason in the mold of the French philosophes, a horticulturalist, even—at least potentially—an eroticist. (Though Jefferson apparently drew close to his mistress Sally Hemmings while she was on French ground and therefore technically "free," she remained his slave.) Given Enlightenment credentials like these, it was all but inevitable that Jefferson would also have a strongly romantic disposition, and, indeed, this was the case. "I am but a son of nature, loving what I see and feel without being able to give a reason, nor caring much whether there be one," he wrote in one letter posted from Aix-en-Provence.[31] And fifteen years later, while serving as President of the United States, he made a point of governing from Washington rather than New York, riding to work on a horse rather than in a carriage, and trying regularly not to wear the sort of wig his peers wore. Clearly, this was a man who was as liberated from "artifice" as he was enlightened by "science."

Yet there was also another side to Jefferson. A lot of what Jefferson wrote came from a deeper, decidedly pre-modern place, and that attribute makes a lot of his writing uncannily prescient as well as brave. Witness, especially, Jefferson's post-1776 statements about "ward" (nursery) "republics" as on view in letters written between 1813 and 1816, and too in *Notes on the State of Virginia*, which was written in early 1784 during the months he was conceiving a plan for, well, the Seven Ranges.

Jefferson was a "states' rights" man, meaning that he favored a seriously equal division of power between the several states, on the one hand, and the federal government, on the other. Thus, when the Adams administration successfully pushed for the passage of the Alien and Sedition Acts (1797), according to which the federal government was granted a right to censor localized opinion, Jefferson cried foul. In this day and age, of course, the original meaning of "state's rights" has become so intertwined with racist overtones that it is practically unusable. Nevertheless, the original meaning can be recovered, and until someone comes up with a less loaded code name ("federalism" is misleading) we will have to make do with asterisks and qualifiers. To Jefferson, at any rate, "states' rights" meant any right or power not expressly delegated by the Constitution to the federally united states, or denied by the Constitution to the several states, as per the Tenth

Amendment, and his point in the Kentucky Resolutions was that the federal government had assumed a kind of "constructive" power that would result in the eventual loss of a particular region's ability to handle its own affairs and define its own character, within the bounds set by the nation's first and second charters. "Handle its own affairs" and "define its own character"? How quaint those hopes sound to us now, in this age of massively centralizing, technology-driven forces and a federal government so gargantuan (in relation to the sum total of state governments) that you'd need a scale arm 30 million miles long just to start the balancing action. Nevertheless, localism was Jefferson's hope, and even more amazingly he didn't stop there. On the contrary, he conceived a way to *institutionalize* decentralized power by granting townships and small family farms key, officially sanctioned roles in the apparatus of government.

"Lay off every county into small districts of five or six miles square, called hundreds," Jefferson wrote in *Notes on the State of Virginia* in 1784, and one year later, upon the passage of the Land Act (with its provision that one section per township should be reserved for educational purposes), that idea became law.[32] But he didn't thoroughly explain the political importance of his sectional idea until the legislative, executive, and judicial branches of the federal government had all grown in power relative to more localized government. Writing in 1814 to one Joseph Cabell about the state of Virginia, Jefferson confided that he had "long contemplated a division into hundreds, or wards, as the fundamental measure securing good government," and two years later, in 1816, while writing to the same correspondent among others, he provided details.[33] "Let the national government be entrusted with the defense of the nation and its foreign and federal relations; the state governments with the civil rights, laws, police and administration of what concerns the state generally; the counties with the local concerns; and each ward directs the interests within itself." What would those interests be exactly? Writing to fellow Virginian Sam Kercheval, Jefferson explained that township-directed interests ideally included choosing, installing, and supporting an entire array of services currently under the direction of more distant authorities—to wit, justices, constables, a military company, a patrol, a means for educating the young, maintaining roads, and caring for the sick and the poor. "It is by dividing and subdividing ... republics from the great national one down through all its subordinations, until it ends in the administration of every man's farm by himself ... that all will be done for the best," Jefferson explained. The key? "Distributing to everyone exactly the function he is competent to," "placing under everyone what his own eye may superintend," and thereby forming "a gradation of authorities, standing each on the basis of law, holding everyone its delegated share of powers, and constituting truly a system of fundamental checks and balances for the government, where every man is a sharer in the direction of his ward republic."[34]

The Seven Ranges, in other words, were specifically designed to be a zone where power is distributed to the maximum possible extent. Projected townships in the region were designed to function as mini-*republics*.

It was a bold move to think of dispersing power to a degree like this, and it resonated well with ideas crafted long before the Age of Enlightenment. There was, first of all, a Greek aspect to Jefferson's plan for a grid of small, independently owned farms.[35] Pre-Athenian, polis-based Greek society similarly featured a pattern of small, equally sized and therefore equally influential land parcels (read "sections") which were owned (and defended) by the same yeoman farmers who tended the figs, leeks, olives, and grapes growing on them, and when new land was appropriated (claimed from wilderness-status) it tended to be divided up into small, eleven-acre rectangles in such a way as to form a grid, thereby reinforcing ruling egalitarianism. Secondly, Jefferson's idea of a "gradation of responsibilities" dovetails seamlessly with the Catholic (premodern) principle of subsidiarity, according to which ownership (and therefore responsibility) should be distributed to the maximum possible extent so as to ensure the integrity of social fabric.

In pre-Norman, which is to say pre-baronial England, a "hundred" was the primary jurisdictional division. It was a German import meaning "100 households," and though this unit of measurement derived from relatively qualitative considerations like agricultural production and military strength and self-sufficiency, the unit was nevertheless frequently subdivided. In densely populated regions, for example, there were "half-hundreds," "tithings" (10 households), and "hides" (enough land to support one family and no others). There were, of course, other Anglo-Saxon terms for land —one thinks right away of "hurst" (wooded hill), "den" (pasture), "worth" (homestead), and "burn" (stream)—but Jefferson tuned in mainly to "hides" and "hundreds," for he had his eyes on political liberty that could accrue should property be widely distributed and local institutions prosper much as they evidently had in England when lands were surveyed for the Domesday book in 1086.[36]

The problem with Jefferson's agrarian vision—and this problem looms now as an almost tragic flaw, given that vision's increasing relevance—was that he tied it to a system of ownership that undercut and ran counter to the very world he was trying to create. One of Jefferson's primary objectives, in pushing for section-and-range logic, had been to reduce land-sale fraud and to de-rail absentee ownership, and when Congress went ahead and abandoned the metes-and-bounds system with its quit-rents, that objective was in large part realized. Thanks to the adoption of fee-simple ownership, farmers were able to buy land as effectively as speculators, and consequently a relatively large portion of American small farmers west of Tennessee and Kentucky wound up owning land. (In the southern Appalachians, where section-and-range logic was absent, almost 75% of the land was sharecropped.) Moreover, Lincoln's 1862 Homestead Act, which enabled small farmers to stake a Lockean claim on a quarter section with no money down, would have been impossible without a public auction system designed in accordance with Jefferson's Seven Ranges vision.

However, the turn away from the metes-and-bounds system also came at a cost, for that turn made possible the commodification of land at the very same time that it reduced fraud. Owing to its reliance on universally applicable (therefore unvarying) units of measurement, standardized parcel shapes, and fee-simple ownership, section-and range logic was the perfect vehicle for conceiving and then treating land as a commodity, and therefore when the system became law it introduced into the mind of the farmer a kind of alienation or abstraction that was not unlike absentee ownership in the way it facilitated a use-and-discard attitude toward land rather than a custodial one. Worse yet, the institution of section-and-range logic also neatly undercut even the possibility of townships that functioned like Anglo-Saxon "hundreds" inasmuch as fee-simple ownership was *by definition* anti-feudal.

The distinctly, even dedicatedly anti-feudal character of fee-simple ownership is apparent in two ways.

First, it involves the replacement of feudal notions of worth with modern ones. When people surveyed land and assessed its worth in feudal times, their units of measurement were labor, yield, and quality, not meters or grams.[37] A land's worth was the number of people, animals, and crops it could support, and you calculated that worth by determining whether it consisted of meadow, wasteland, or ploughland, if it was open, and if it was wooded whether it produced fence posts, firewood, and masts. In order to make a sale you of course had to use a measuring device that recorded volume or area or physical weight, but that device was typically *altered* to account for differences in quality. Scale weights were adjusted, paces lengthened or shrank, and bushels grew larger or smaller, depending on what was being sold. Modern methods of ensuring fairness upend all that. By switching to constant and universally applicable measures like pints and sections, quality wound up being defined strictly on the basis of a varying *price*, and as a result it became easier to agree on who was cheating who, and harder to think in terms of fertility and the long-term common good, in addition to personal gain. So, that is one way in which fee-simple ownership is inherently anti-feudal.

The other distinctly modern aspect to fee-simple land ownership is the way it disables feudal notions of *obligations* relating to land occupancy. Just as peasants and nobles both had rights to use a given piece of property (nobody flat-out owned land, in the modern sense), so too they both were obligated to respect other people's rights in respect to that property, and that meant using the property in such a way that the property would still be there, in relatively good working order, for the other users' purposes. Property, in short, meant "fief," or mini-kingdom. By living on it, everyone paid "fealty," which is to say person-on-the-line allegiance, to the common good that this fief, in effect, was. Needless to say, this made ownership in the modern sense complicated. It was as though every piece of property had an endless series of conservation or agricultural easements attached to it, and this made buying and selling difficult. Hence the gradual appearance, in the late Middle Ages, of legal instruments called "quit-rents," which enabled aspiring landowners to buy their way out of encumbrances like medieval easements. The wave of the future was "de-fealtization," and when the option of literally fee-simple land ownership came along as a way to avoid even quit-rents—see, especially, the 1785 shift from metes-and-bounds logic to section-and-range logic—that dismantling of medieval convention was complete. Starting in 1785 it was possible for land ownership to have zero obligations attached to it. The land was yours to use as you, the purchaser, saw fit.

In other words, Jefferson's plan for the re-creation of "hundreds" was doomed from the moment he set down his pen. The plan was couched in terms that undermined the very vision he was trying to uphold; therefore, his project was, in effect, *destined* to fail.

Ought we to be surprised?

Probably not.

We are the rattlesnake nation, the nation that says don't-tread-on-me, as much as we are the amber-waves-of-grain nation. Defiance is written into our genetic code, and that particular stance—indeed, the very word itself—means "de-fealtization." To defy is to "throw down the glove"[38] or release from fealty.

3

Rock and Roll

It is a new day, and by the time I climb up to the wheelhouse the front watch is already half way through its morning shift. Dennis (engineer) is re-wiring a thermostat, Captain Jack is studying the annotated chart for upcoming Hannibal Lock ("good draw to the wall at 41 feet"), and deckhands Bradley and Dave are preparing to walk out onto the tow with walkie-talkies to serve as the captain's eyes when the Ocie Clark comes up on Hannibal's lower wall.

The tow is afloat now on a pool that is 602 feet above sea level. But the further the boat advances into the continent's interior, the more the neighboring elevation rises, and inbound vessels have to rise with that ground. Hence the Ocie Clark will soon switch to a pool that is 623 feet above sea level.

New Martinsville, WV, is coming up on the eastern side of the river, and details on Hannibal Locks and Dam are starting to be visible. Captain Jack, all business now, is pushing the tow just hard enough to beat the current, so that he can gently bring his 1,250 feet of freight up alongside a guide wall that positions a vessel correctly for entrance into the lock proper. The ship's engines sound capable, reassuringly strong, perhaps because they are on a kind of idle broken only by brief displays of moderately sized power. The captain doesn't want to hit the wall, yet at the same time he needs to be within a foot or two of that same wall, along the entire length of the tow. Think parallel parking, extreme version.

A marine radio speaker crackles, and suddenly we can hear Bradley out at the tow's head, on the starboard side: "Forty feet wide, ten feet down the flat." A minute later he pipes up again: "Twenty feet wide, 450 feet down the flat." And then it becomes non-stop, a kind of running commentary: "Everything still easing, nice and slow . . . seven-foot wide now, head at six . . . four and a half on your head, about five foot on your stern . . . fifty feet to pin, six inches to the wall . . . sixty feet to bull nose, five inches to the wall." When he says the word "wall," Bradley drags the syllable out a bit. The man wears a tattoo on his arm that says United States Marine Corps, but on this occasion he sounds like a stoned, very competent auctioneer. At this point Bob, who has been on the port side watching the approach of the short wall that defines the lock's actual chamber, chimes in: "One hundred feet below, looking at the inside of the flat." The captain takes a quick look at the depth gauge. Bradley again: "Medium wall, two wide . . . six inches wide . . . touching the wall . . . starting to crack out a little bit." Bob: "Right at the bullnose, thirteen wide . . . looking good, forty-five to the stripes . . . on the flat now . . . one foot wide on the gate . . . half way through the gate." Bradley: "In the chamber."

The ship is now in its berth, and within a few minutes two massive hydraulic-powered gates close behind us. Water starts to flow into the newly formed chamber, and the Ocie Clark begins to rise, along with fifteen coal-laden barges. The boat rises exactly twenty-one feet, and when I look back toward Willow Island, it is like looking off a cliff. The sun is bright there, in the mist, and so I shield my eyes. But I don't look long. Upper pool gates are already open, and Ocie Clark propellers, furiously churning waters astern, are pushing us out of the chamber and onto an unfamiliar body of water.

New elevation, new pool.

In the last chapter we examined the section-and-range technology that was birthed here in The Seven Ranges and concluded that the implementation of this technology on a national scale favored the commodification of land at the same time that it discouraged fraud commonly associated with land speculation. Additionally, we noticed that implementation of section-and-range technology resulted in the overthrow of medieval mindsets that had firmly and securely tied usage rights to land stewardship.

In this chapter I want to turn our attention to a completely different, but no less important, change in conceptualization habits that appeared here in eastern Ohio—namely, the establishment (if you will) of what I have taken to calling bi-polar energy flow. This latter change was sparked by the preaching of one James McGready and camp meetings deriving from that preaching, but the consequences of the change are by no means limited to that context, for they turn out to have ramifications in political, societal, and economic contexts as well as religious ones. What is this religiously derived bi-polar energy? Is it something new? Or is it simply, as David Hackett Fisher suggests, a kind of re-vitalization of the Christian faith from which it descends? My hunch—prompted though it may be by our recent passage through Hannibal Lock—is that it's something new.

※

This was ugly country in 1803. When Meriwether Lewis floated by Steubenville on his way to Oregon, he described the town in his journal as "a small, well-built thriving place" with "several respectable families living in it,"[39] and though it is of course entirely possible that Steubenville did in fact give this impression it is also possible that Lewis was inclined toward optimism at this stage of his journey, for other travelers saw things differently. Most people saw "broken country" distinguished by mud, blackened stumps, stone coal, and girdled trees, and when they ventured deeper into the country they found themselves journeying toward fire on darkly lit, heavily rutted roads. Lodging was cramped, inn water was often less drinkable than poorly made whiskey, and nourishment consisted of gruel flavored with bear grease. "Oct 19. Roads extremely rough, weather drizzly, buildings indifferent," ran one journal entry.[40] "Log cabins, ugly women, cornfields in the woods among dead trees." And the tally of bleakness didn't stop there. If a traveler was from New England or the more settled parts of New York, for example, Cadiz was ugly on account of mountain-based cultural "impoverishment," in addition to war-zone scenery. After all, the Scots-Irish who lived here, the folks who would later become famous for using kerosene as a cure-all, planting fence posts on the full moon, and building rockers out of bent hickory twigs—these people were uplanders. That is to say, they were people whose liberty was not ordered to an end that Puritans or Virginians or Philadelphians could respect. As David Hackett Fisher has taught us, Harrison County residents ate sallet, poke, clabber, and pork rather than roasts, apple pies, and pudding. They sang songs about killings or rape rather than sea-faring or courtship, and they fiddled—no recorders. Their clothing accentuated sexual differences rather than downplaying or hiding them, they equated authority with a gun wielded by an equal, and rather than speaking in Latinate complexities or Hampshire dialects, they spoke a more purely Elizabethan English that was peppered with words and phrases like "honey," "scoot along now," "tickle-cunt creek," "yourn," "ourn," and "hisn," "little shits," and "he didn't have none."[41]

But the ugliest aspect, to an educated Easterner, was probably not so much this land's scenery or its mountain ethos as its increasingly frequent displays of unseemly open-air revivalism. Like the Moravians before them, people here spoke in tongues. They fell down as if dead after violent convulsions and then stood up again, sometimes hours later, in an apparently right yet strangely new mind. Racial barriers were on occasion ignored. Observers spoke of ecstasies that looked a lot like sexual experience, and licensed ministers were often nowhere to be seen. Was this "democracy"? Whatever it was, it was time to call the cops.

It is said that Ralph Waldo Emerson's essay, "Self Reliance" (1839), is the real American Declaration of Independence, and to a certain extent this is true. Emerson was a new Adam, and he deliberately proclaimed a new Heaven and a new Earth. Leaning on nothing but orphic speech and a confidence in direct revelation, this former Unitarian minister invited hearers to chuck prejudice to the winds, see the world for the stunningly present mystery that it is, and then walk out over a deep that only fearless people can cross to an unconventional, always original life. Though Emerson stood squarely in the European romantic tradition, writing within earshot both of Wordsworth's "Lyrical Ballads" and Beethoven's Ninth Symphony, Emerson was stubbornly American in his cockiness, his insouciance, and his readiness to judge men vastly more learned than he could ever hope to be. More to the point, he didn't just see an absence of tradition when he looked at "the woods." Rather, he saw an apocalypse that all of history had been pointing toward—a kind of *wildfire* that philosophers somewhat lamely call "meaning." Gothic churches with their stained-glass windows and soaring ribbed vaults? According to Emerson, that architectural achievement was not so much an instance of "grace building on nature" as an instance of established religion gesturing toward the mystery that is a grove of trees, and by and large Emerson made good on his implied promise. Emerson was tremendously popular on the lecture circuit, and when you thumb through "The American Scholar" or "The Divinity School Address" you see why. Reading Emerson you practically reside in a promised land. True, from time to time you have to come down to earth. But that is just to buy lunch or get some sleep. After those needs are met, you are free to go right back to where you were, for in Emerson's brave new world there is no force pulling you elsewhere that you need to be "saved" from. All is bright; all is mega-text; you can come or go as you please.

But I question whether Emerson is all that indicative of mainstream American energy. It seems to me that real American voltage, the kind that lights up whole cities and makes possible the cultural colonization of an entire globe, has more to do with revivalism—the phenomenon that shows up first in a small Moravian sect, then in the preaching of Jonathan Edwards, John Wesley, and George Whitefield, and, more finally, in the preaching of southwest Pennsylvania's James McGready and ensuing festivals at Red River and Cane Ridge in 1801, just across the river in Kentucky. That is where the turbines really started turning, for that is where the requisite polarity lay waiting to be tapped. Emerson? That seer *transcended* Calvinistic duality, and to this very extent he was a sideshow. But Cane Ridge? There Calvinist principles got crossed with a frontier ethos in such a way as to enable a form of conversion so violent that it actually generated a hugely powerful, still-functioning reversing current. *My lord what a morning when de stars begin to fall. You'll see de worl on fire, you'll see da moon a bleedin. Shout, shout—we're gaining ground. O glory hallelujah! We'll shout old Satan's kingdom down.* Looking for America's coming-out party? Your search is done. It happened at Cane Ridge, on the very field those stars shined upon.

The Calvinist root to the Second Great Awakening, as Red River revivalism came to be called, is easy to see. Scots-Irish settlers were by definition Presbyterians, or "rednecks," and Presbyterianism, in turn, was purely Calvinistic theology that had been, in effect, systematized by Scotsman John Knox and made ready for adoption by both Puritans and Presbyterians. Perhaps because the Massachusetts Bay colonists arrived on America's shores first, most of us assume that Puritan separatists were closer to Calvin, chronologically and therefore energetically, than the Scots-Irish were, but that is incorrect. The real line of descent works like this: (1) Protestantism as a general movement shows up in England in the person of John Wycliffe, whose book of provocative theses, "De Civili Dominio" (1376), anticipated virtually all Reformation emphases, from "sola scriptura" to the dismantling of monasteries; (2) the movement breaks out in force with direct challenges to papal authority by Luther (1517), Henry VIII (1519), and then the Zurich-based Swiss rebel Zwingli, who ups the ante (1519) by challenging not just papal authority but also the tradition of corporeally representing divine life through sacraments; (3) Anabaptists (Amish and Mennonite) make an entrance (1525, in reaction to Zwingli) by speaking up in favor of adult baptism and aligning themselves with a peasant-based rebellion; (4) Calvin introduces the idea of an "elect" and then starts building (in Geneva) a Swiss state modeled on this principle (1541); and, (5) John Knox substitutes "presbyters" for Episcopal structure and builds a new "purified" Church of England after studying Calvin's model in Geneva (1554) and serving as Calvin's chief minister (1556–1559). It is only then, after "Presbyterianism" becomes the norm in Britain, that the folks who eventually became known as New England "separatists" appear.

How, then, should we characterize this twice-distilled Presbyterian Calvinism in which future revivalists were raised? Given the oscillatory aspect to the swings between sin and grace that were to mark America's Second Great Awakening, it is tempting to defer to the fact of an overall Protestant bias in favor of direct revelation and against sacramentalism—which is to say, the idea that spiritual realities are best understood through intermediary, material realities that sign them—so as to neatly and efficiently explain the appearance of a revival movement that dramatized a war between spiritual and bodily realms. But the truth is that, though Calvinists use extrinsic logic to separate grace from nature to the limit of what a Christian faith founded on Incarnation and sacramentality can allow, Calvinists also believe, ultimately, in a Word "made flesh" every bit as much as Catholics, the presumed guardians of sacramentality, do. And, for the record, Catholics have for their part (over the centuries and particularly in Christological debates between Antiochine and Alexandrian "schools"[42]) separated nature from grace to the limit of what a Christian faith founded on Incarnation can allow every bit as much as Calvinists have. My point is that twice-distilled Presbyterian Calvinism is recognizably Christian. But Red River revivalism? That phenomenon, as the following history will show, is less easily categorized.[43] Yes, as Dave Hackett Fischer (in *Albion's Seed*) and Leigh Eric Schmidt (in *Holy Fairs*) both suggest, Red River revivalism descends from and to an important degree signs the Scottish "holy fair" tradition that arrived with Scotch settlers. But, unlike United Kingdom holy fairs, which wound up reinforcing sacramentality through an exclusive focus on communion, Red River revivals depended more on *maintaining* bi-polar energy flow and to that extent de-valuing the sacramentalism that Fisher and (to a lesser extent) Schmidt claim they reinforce.

The story begins in 1733 when young, recently installed Congregationalist "scholar-pastor" Jonathan Edwards started experimenting with the repellent aspect to the Calvinist nature-grace opposition in Northampton, Massachusetts. Perhaps because he had studied Sir Isaac Newton's *Principia Mathematica*, Edwards was fascinated by "optix." Also, owing to an equally absorbing interest in pronouncedly mechanical Lockean psychology, Edwards thought a lot about "shocks of sense" and "hard pellets of sensation."[44] Hence it is possible that during sermons when Edwards slowly and deliberately brought the specter of sin close to the availability of grace, he was literally conducting an experiment on a rapt, intensely credulous congregation. In any case Edwards was a very skilled orator, and—perhaps because he kept his eyes fixed on a thin bell rope at the back of the church while speaking of sinners temporarily suspended (by an angry God) over a sea of perdition[45]—he, Edwards, used those skills to maximum effect, for within the space of just a few years he upended an entire town, ruined more than a few marriages, and got himself expelled from the pulpit. Had the Spirit stirred in the Pioneer Valley? A lot of people thought it had, and they may well have been right, for only five years later similar waves of religious "enthusiasm" began to break across England and all thirteen of its colonies, thanks to the open-air preaching of Anglican priests John Wesley and George Whitefield. Wesley and Whitefield both credited Edwards as their guide in this new business of revivals, but in fact their preaching had deeper roots in the Wycliffe-derived Moravian tradition under whose auspices Wesley felt his heart, in 1738, "strangely warmed." When Wesley first met the Moravians on a ship bound for Savannah, they were just beginning to make serious inroads into the American continent—they were only in Georgia and hadn't yet made it into Pennsylvania or North Carolina—but in a certain sense the Moravians' job was already done the second they met Wesley, for Wesley quickly embraced their emphasis on instantaneous conversion and made it the centerpiece of a brand new, "Methodist" church.

The thing that made Wesley and Whitefield so successful was that, in addition to speaking well before large crowds (Whitefield was apparently a boom-voiced entertainer who could keep a crowd of five thousand souls spellbound), they emphasized a "personal" decision for or against Christ. The Savior merited allegiance not so much because the gospel was true or because the sufferer had integrity or because tradition prescribed it as because the Savior knew you just like he knew Bartholomew under that fig tree, and if you turned away it would be like turning down a dearly bought, life-saving offer from a loyal friend. Finely crafted arguments meant nothing here. A Whitefield sermon came down to just one question: What are you, John Doe, going to do? This was a galvanizing question, given that it empowered people who weren't used to tasting power; therefore, Wesley's and Whitefield's sermons had enormous impact.[46] The two preachers first gained notoriety in England when Whitefield incurred the disapproval of the Anglican hierarchy by preaching to coal miners in open-air venues rather than in a church, and seeing as how the dispossessed state of coal miners was not too different from his own, Whitefield's movement picked up steam. Soon Wesley was imitating Whitefield, and in 1739 they took their act on the road, preaching first in Georgia to an audience of slaves, and then at every possible stop thereafter on a route that took them clear to Maine. The tour was a sensation. Large crowds turned out to hear them in town after town—crowds big enough to get observers like Ben Franklin thinking about the possibilities of revolution. But the biggest audience was still to come. It was the one Wesley and Whitefield never met, the one that lay waiting on the other side of the mountains. Thanks to their outlaw status, Wesley's and Whitefield's act played particularly well to frontier-based rednecks, and once the American frontier started to become settled, as occurred in the 1780s and 1790s, itinerant preachers trained in Wesleyan methods stepped right up and almost effortlessly "accepted" 50 percent of the Scots-Irish trans-Allegheny west into the Methodist church. In Cadiz, where ground had been prepared by Moravian missionaries in addition to long-haired Wesleyan circuit riders carrying hunting knives, a Methodist circuit was almost instantly established when Whiskey Rebels arrived in force after 1794.

Enter, now, Presbyterian minister James McGready, steersman for the revival that Cane Ridge was modeled on.[47]

McGready was born in 1763, about halfway between Wheeling and Pittsburgh. When he was a boy he moved with his father to North Carolina backcountry, but a visiting uncle spotted verbal talents crossed with a God-fearing disposition, and in 1785, the same year as the Land Act, James returned to southwest Pennsylvania with the uncle to study at a small school run by frontier-based Presbyterian minister John McMillan. That school, located a few miles east of Steubenville, became what is today Washington and Jefferson College, but when McGready attended the institution it was just a log cabin. After obtaining a license to preach from the classically learned McMillan, McGready gravitated once again to Smoky Mountain uplands, but after getting into trouble with presbytery officials there owing to an allegedly too zealous assumption of duties, he kicked dust from his feet, said a prayer for disgruntled brass ("O Jerusalem, Jerusalem, thou that killest the prophets and stonest them. . ."), and hit the road (1796) for the wilds of Kentucky, where he pastored three small congregations on the Gaspar, Red, and Muddy rivers.

This was rough country. Methodist circuit rider Peter Cartwright was later to call it "Rogue Harbor." But McGready felt at home there, even going so far as to have the members of his congregations sign a covenant in which they mutually pledged to pray that God would bless them with "an outpouring of His Spirit" and "open the spiritual door at Red River," so as to stir up a revival that would "shake the nation and eventually the world." Pray they apparently did, for two years later strange things started happening after a communion service overlooking the Clear Fork Branch of the Gaspar River. "How dreadful is this place," McGready said when congregants shared the communion cup. "This is none other but the house of God, and this is the gate of heaven." McGready was quoting Genesis, marking the spot where Jacob sees a ladder with angels going to and fro, but somewhere in the middle of McGready's service hearers evidently took the preacher at his word and got so distracted that fields were left untended for an entire critical week. *That* news got around, and thus it came to pass (one year later) that several hundred people convened at Red River for a three-day vigil, thereby kicking off the nation's first "camp meeting."

The date was June 13, 1800, and it is remembered for the large numbers of men, women, and children who fell down as if "slain" over the course of the vigil. That was the word that Red River observer Barton Warren Stone employed to describe what he saw, and this use is the source of the contemporary phrase, "slain in the spirit," which is now common in Pentecostal churches across America and around the world as a label for that moment in an altar-call when congregants fall down after the laying-on-of-hands and become a kind of turf where cosmic forces do battle. At Red River, though, the event was not at all routine, and observers like Barton Stone were astonished. "The scene was new to me and passing strange," he later wrote. "Many, very many fell down as men slain in battle, and continued for hours together in an apparently breathless and motionless state, sometimes for a few moments reviving and exhibiting symptoms of life by a deep groan or a piercing shriek, or by a prayer for mercy fervently uttered."[48] No less amazingly, congregants also rose. They "shouted deliverance" and "declared" the wonderful works of God in tones that were "solemn, penetrating, bold, and free."

Can this account be true? Of course. Can it be trusted as a complete account? No.

Though he appears to be an honest recorder, Stone's commentary is lacking in that he never notes the violence of the images that were employed to encourage hearers to faint with terror. Writing for the Cumberland Presbytery office in 1835, the Rev. John Matthews remembered James McGready as a preacher who had "a talent for depicting the guilty and deplorable situation of impenitent sinners," and this fact cannot be unrelated to the force with which participants at the Red River revival fell and rose. Indeed, it goes a long way toward explaining that force, for just as Calvin discovered that floating the idea of "an elect" required a doctrine regarding "total depravity," so too, by the same token, preachers like McGready were learning that you could start off with the conviction that you were damned and then discover a truly soaring experience of "election," or release, upon merely glimpsing the possibility that, owing to the lack of an opportunity to meet Jesus, you might have been wrong in your assumption that you were not one of the elect.

It is possible that Barton Stone himself never really found a use for this dynamic. Stone was uncomfortable with the doctrine of total depravity, and he signed the Westminster Confession with explicitly stated reservations. Therefore, he very probably would not have enjoyed touring the sights suggested by a concept like eternal damnation. Hence it is ironic that Stone, of all people, should be the one most firmly linked in our collective memory to the revival that took place the following year just south of the Ohio River at Cane Ridge between August 7 and August 12, for that revival explored the possibilities inherent in wild swings between "elect" and "damned" states like no other revival before and maybe even since.

Thanks to a meeting house that could seat five hundred people, and an alertness to precedents like communion "appointments" at Red River and similar, subsequent ones at Concord and across the river in Ohio, Stone had encouraged people to attend his carefully planned Cane Ridge meeting from very far quarters, and—lo! They came. All told, twenty thousand people showed up—a stunning number for a site in the middle of what was then nowhere—and, naturally, Stone quickly lost control of an event he had hoped to guide.[49] Before anyone knew what was happening there were not just two or three but multiple stages manned by who knows how many ministers, some of them real and some of them a purer breed of entertainer, and after people started to "fall" even the official ministers started taking cues from what they saw around them rather than from the ends their sermons were directed toward. Think of the gathering, if you will, as a large ship illuminated by torches and driven by who knows who. Everyone had heard of this vessel, thanks to reports of what had transpired at previous ports of call, and therefore (owing to the exciting nature of those reports) people had got on board, but now the huge boat was slowly and implacably turning toward a new kind of night and a new kind of day. Perhaps it was the whiskey. Perhaps it was the suggestive aspect of young women falling. Perhaps it was the moaning of whole groups that were about to fall. Perhaps it was the exhilarating aspect of the presence of a crowd after months of solitude. Whatever the reason, the still present Red River dynamic shifted slightly to accommodate a second set of poles. Whereas in Red River the poles had been ideas about sin and grace, now the poles could also become sexual experience and spiritual dalliance above a time-chained earth, and as a result some of the congregants began to enjoy access to the same sort of maneuver preachers enjoyed—that of bringing bodily desires close to heavenly ones not so much in order to integrate them or change the one into the other, but, instead, to accentuate (and better taste) the *differences*. At Cane Ridge it became possible for everybody to "feast" in this way.

Well, this fact got a few people in trouble. Unmarried women grew big with child, James McGready found himself disciplined by a Presbyterian synod for fanning revivalist spirit, and Barton Warren Stone was flat-out expelled. And given that in some fashion all Presbyterians were on trial after Cane Ridge owing to the fact that the "love feast" occurred at a Presbyterian meetinghouse, Presbyterian Church leadership formally denounced emotional forms of revivalism and even the idea of camp meetings.

Methodists, however, sensed an opportunity. Rather than disowning camp meetings, they started under Bishop Francis Asbury's eager and elaborately sober direction to champion them, and as a result Methodism practically exploded across the trans-Allegheny west, growing from 65,000 members in 1800 to 274,000 just twenty years later. Around Cadiz, Methodism grew almost exactly in proportion to camp meetings.[50] Eventually, of course, the Methodist camp meeting got systematized and began to function less and less as a portal for the entrance of genuinely Pentecostal, shouter-grade fire. In addition to camp guards with arm bands and curfews for women, there were "mourner tents" and "anxious seats" and segregated seating areas for blacks. Sermons ran on a schedule just like vaudeville acts, ministers got classed according to whether they were "eight o'clocks" or big league "eleven o'clocks," and in some regions camps themselves started to function as mini-businesses run by "camp meeting associations." In effect, the meetings became rather like the country version of the urban revivals staged later (in the 1870s) by Dwight L. Moody, evangelist, and Ira D. Swankey, singer/composer. (Moody got his start in Chicago, preaching to lake freighter crewmen and gamblers, but after his house burned down in the Great Chicago Fire of 1871, he joined forces with Sankey, the "sweet singer of Methodism," and did "inspirational" shows at baseball stadiums, thereby anticipating Billy Graham.) However, the original phenomenon from which the Methodist camp meeting was descended stubbornly persisted in collective memory if not in deed, and by 1905, after a series of Holiness Promotion revivals orchestrated at their peak by Cadiz-born Methodist bishop Matthew Simpson, it was back—this time courtesy of a new eastern Ohio/southwest Pennsylvania catalyst.

Let us back up for a minute to note that ten years after Cane Ridge and the disciplining of McGready and Stone, a southwest Pennsylvania resident named Thomas Campbell split from his local Presbyterian community and founded a new faith group on a saddle ridge just north of Buffalo Creek, a couple miles east of the Ohio River. Campbell's name for this new community was "Brush Run Church," and the idea behind it was that members (thenceforth to be known as "Campbellites") would by and large dispense with formalized creeds so that they could focus better on the Lord's Supper and the habits of an early Christian "apostolic" church. Later, after striking an agreement in 1832 with Barton Stone's similarly creed-free "Christian" movement, Brush Run Church moved to Bethany, West Virginia (which is inside the Steubenville-Weirton metropolitan area), and reopened as "Disciples of Christ," thereby inaugurating a church that, after a long and somewhat tumultuous career, is still with us today. Though Disciples of Christ does not appear to have been an especially crisis-driven church any more than Stone himself was, the church's emphasis on apostolic times was pronounced, and this fact, in turn, concentrated the energies of its most illustrious early member—to wit, faith-healer Maria Woodworth Etter.

Sister Etter, as this congregant eventually became known, was born in 1844 near Lisbon, Ohio, in a county that straddles the very first portion of Thomas Hutchins' west-running "geographer's line." She experienced a strong conversion in a local Disciples church at age 13, and after marrying, starting a small farm, and bearing six children, she quickly lost five of her six children and then the farm. (Eventually, years later, she also lost her husband.) This was a woman who knew a thing or two about loss, and perhaps for this reason she also knew a thing or two about faith. Rather than dwelling on her misfortune, Sister Etter focused on ways in which she, thanks to her emptiness, could serve as a vessel—if you will—for the outpouring of heavenly graces, and starting in 1871, after leading nine local revivals in which it became apparent that the "Holy Ghost" could not only convert people but also heal people's physical ailments, this astonishingly resilient woman invested in a circus tent and a railroad pass, thereby initiating a traveling ministry that played in nearly 48 states for 48 years. Everywhere she went Sister Etter healed people, and whenever people talked of how they experienced a "cooling of nerves" or a "tingling warmth" when she laid hands on their head, Sister Etter always pointed skyward to indicate that "the power," as she called it, came from a realm that was drawing nearer, day by startling day.[51]

Unlike Millerites, who were interested in physical cataclysm and tried to predict the world's end on the basis of things like geological evidence, Maria Woodworth Etter was interested in the dawning of a new age whose approach could be measured by spiritual signs and wonders, and given that the healings that occurred under her tent's roof were indeed remarkable, an entire nation of people began to think in terms very like her own. That is to say, they began to conceive of healings and conversions as "latter rain," thereby referencing the Book of Joel, where sympathetic readers could find scriptural nuggets like "in the last days I will pour out my Spirit on all people," and "your sons and daughters will prophesy, your old men will dream dreams, your young men shall see visions." Consequently, Sister Etter's audience switched from thinking in terms of Christ's risen life shining through otherwise ordinary circumstances to thinking in terms of Christ's imminent *return* from a place that, presumably, was *far, far away*. Moses' idea of getting to a promised land? That justice-tinged conceit began to recede a little. In its place there was a different one. Thanks in large part to Ohioan Sister

Etter from the Seven Ranges, "sanctification" now meant opening one's palms to greet a final sun that was rising whether you deserved it or not. Hence, when the relatively dormant (since 1801) phenomenon of tongues started to re-appear in St Louis in 1890, and then again between 1895 and 1905 at scattered Holiness churches that were themselves descended from Methodist camp meetings, it could seem (to committed believers) less like a puzzle than a confirmation. Bees were humming because there was sweet honey in the rock, right now.[52]

Modern-day Pentecostalism had arrived.

Whereas before homegrown American churches might best be described as a kind of Red River potency, now—thanks to the addition of this ordinariness/lastness difference to the more standard, by now well-established suite of Cane Ridge differences like sin/grace and earth/spirit—there was a sudden, instantly available increase in polarity-based electrical power that enabled such churches actually to grow, and grow they did. Self-appointed missionaries who had, as it were, surfed vocally on waves of mercy fanned out from a Holiness church on Azusa St. in Los Angeles (city of angels) to the Pacific Northwest, Liberia, China, and the Philippines with a force and an energy not seen since the coming of the Holy Spirit as described in the Book of Acts. At the same time, a Carolina backcountry Holiness church called Camp Creek morphed into the "Church of God," later to become famous throughout Appalachia for its snake handlers and strychnine cocktails, while newly energized, "sanctified" churches sprouted up in African-American communities all across the deep South. And in Hot Springs, Arkansas, after a California-based "World Wide Camp Meeting" presided over by Sister Etter herself, some 300 representatives from Pentecostal communities in 20 different states gathered at an old opera house to certify the new outpouring of divine spirit and inaugurate a new church called "Assemblies of God." That founding occurred on the eve of World War I, in 1914, and after the partnership was ratified the new church numbered perhaps fifty thousand souls. Today the Assemblies of God federation numbers fifty-eight *million*, and it has a firm foothold in countries as various as Haiti, Mexico, Kenya, Poland, Ireland, Vietnam, Great Britain, Romania, Nigeria, Japan, Ecuador, Switzerland, and Samoa, in addition to the United States.

Indeed, Red River revivalism became so strong that it even showed up—courtesy, once again, of events that transpired in or near southwest Pennsylvania—as a worldwide movement within the Catholic Church as well as the Protestant one. Like southwest Pennsylvania's James McGready at his Red River post, students at Duquesne University in downtown Pittsburgh had gone on a kind of retreat, in 1967, to reflect on, and make themselves available to, the same Holy Spirit that had rained down with power on the original twelve apostles, and on February 18—the date is now written on untold numbers of figurative stones—those students allegedly did discover, like McGready's congregants, a "risen, glorified life." They spoke of coming into an awareness of "God's personal love," they described that love as "completely undeserved" and "lavishly given," and they reported that upon coming into contact with that love they ceased to be afraid. Additionally, they (like Azusa St. Pentecostals) found themselves given over to the "charismatic" form of praise known as tongues. You would think that the Catholic Church's long-standing bias in favor of formally incarnational logic would not mesh well with a polarity-driven phenomenon like Red River revivalism, and, indeed, when the Catholic experience of tongues is sacramentally based and bee-hum is conditioned by the presence of a censer, it cannot help but be qualitatively different from a purely emotion-based experience. Nevertheless, it is also true that (as previously indicated) the Catholic Church has long wrestled with what might fairly be called a Gnostic temptation, and because the experience of tongues confers upon initiates a kind of insider's knowledge that people do not ordinarily possess, charismatic experience can exert the same kind of appeal that Pentecostalism does. In any case the charismatic movement started to grow.[53] By 1975 the movement was strong enough to attract some 10,000 pilgrims to an International Catholic Charismatic Conference in Rome, and from that point forward, thanks to a crucial assist from literally tent-based revivals staged by Duquesne's institutional neighbor, Franciscan University of Steubenville (this school, in a continuing nod to the church's scholastic bias, calls its festivals "conferences"), the movement grew exponentially to the point where there are now charismatics in every diocese on every continent. It is of course sometimes hard to spot members, but when I first arrived in eastern Ohio it was easy. Charismatics were the ones who lifted arms with such abandon that the palms of their hands curled like leaves on a burning tree.

What, you might well wonder, *is* this thing? What do we call a revival that starts out with a "slaying" in the trans-Allegheny wilderness and becomes a world's fair? It is of course possible that the event has a divine origin, as participants claim, and in this case the answer to our question comes clearly and swiftly: we're looking at the Second Coming, and woe to the person who turns back for a hat. But just in case the event does *not* necessarily have a divine origin—in case, that is, the event can also be satisfactorily explained via historical causes—what in that case does the event add up to? Here too an answer lies ready to hand, for the Red River event has manifested in secular quarters as well as more overtly religious ones, and in the secular quarter people have already given a fair amount of thought to the question of what this thing is.

They call it rock and roll.

People mistakenly think that rock and roll came into existence when Scots-Irish mountain music merged with African-American delta blues. According to this line of argument, hill country fiddling and the "high lonesome sound" of Ralph Stanley are the direct expressions of a distinctly Appalachian culture that existed in isolation from the kind of African-American plantation-based culture that is associated with guitar-based, call-and-response, 12-bar Charlie Patton blues. Then, in 1954 at Sam Phillips' Sun Records studio in Memphis, these two separately evolving traditions all of a sudden met, and—voilà—rock and roll was born. It's got a nice clean story line, this argument, for Memphis is located halfway between the Mississippi's delta and the mountains of Tennessee. Also, there's a kind of Whitmanesque appeal, for the argument appears to confirm our deepest beliefs about who we are as a unified people. But you can't hold onto this "merge" interpretation for long. There are just too many holes in it. In the first place, fiddles were as prominent in early twentieth-century juke joints as they were in Appalachia, and the black artists who played those fiddles frequently played reels and jigs. They were comfortable with the genre. Muddy Waters, grand master of Chicago blues, cut his teeth playing Gene Autry. And as for country artists, they for their part knew something about the blues. Jimmie Rodgers, who defined Appalachian mountain music like Muddy Waters defined the Mississippi River, got his start on WWNC in Asheville, North Carolina, with hits like "Brakeman's Blues" and "In the Jailhouse Now" (1928). In sum, the idea of separately evolving blues and country traditions is contrived.[54] Though it is unquestionably true that oil-field honky tonks descend from and "sign" Appalachian backcountry, and that crossroad juke joints descend from and "sign" African-American turpentine camps, the musical division between these two worlds is largely the creation of record company executives who realized that they could make more money if they packaged the same music two different ways. Elvis' "That's All Right (Mama)," in other words, wasn't so much the moment when two traditions fused as it was the moment when an artificial wall between "race records" and "hillbilly records" came down and a song that virtually all dispossessed Americans had been singing abruptly tightened and, well, got louder.

What, then, *is* rock and roll? How can we define the music if not by thinking in terms of regional cross-fertilization? I submit that the best option for defining rock and roll is that the music amounts to the *juxtaposition* of lowdown physicality (as expressed in blues played by both blacks and whites) against spiritual rapture (as expressed in gospel played by both blacks and whites).

Can gospel, with its soaring flights of praise, really be associated with the insistent beat and double entendres of barrelhouse blues? Yes, they both employ call-and-response patterns. And, yes, they both appeared at the same time. (Gospel, in its modern form, showed up and then gelled almost exactly when the blues did, thanks to the appearance of "southern quartet" arrangements in the 1910s and the arrival of commercially successful performers like Thomas Dorsey, Sister Rosetta, and Clara Ward between 1920 and 1950.) Outside that overlap, though, the genres appear to be pretty different. How, then, can one speak of a relationship between the two idioms? The key is that blues and gospel were linked but steadfastly *not fused*. Indeed, they were carefully and even systematically brought close to each other and then kept apart in order to facilitate a reversing current that enabled both "poles" to intensify.

Clarksdale Mississippi native Son House, for example, was a powerful bottle-neck slide guitarist and blues singer precisely because he was formerly a Baptist preacher given to "revelating." He had swung high; therefore, he could swing low. Conversely, Hank Williams started out "honky tonkin'," as he called his blues tendency, and then (1950) switched to gospel tunes like "Just Waitin'" and "A Picture From Life's Other Side." (When Williams recorded these latter songs, he released them under the stage name, "Luke the Drifter.") Other popular musicians during this era didn't so much emigrate from one side to the other as regularly oscillate between the two kinds of music. Witness Sister Rosetta Tharpe from Cotton Plant, Arkansas, who became famous as a sanctified "shouter" but privately played blues on the side. Sister Rosetta grew up on the revival circuit, where her mother had a place as a mandolin-playing preacher, but after moving to Chicago in the 1920s Sister Rosetta learned the blues, and by 1942 she was singing "Going Back to Jesus" with Marie Knight during the day and performing "Tall Skinny Papa" in front of Lucky Millinder's jazz orchestra at night. Or consider the career of Thomas Dorsey, the man who wrote "My Precious Lord" and "Peace in the Valley." This fellow penned practically every gospel standard you can think of, yet he also had a dual career as a pianist who went by the name of "Georgia Tom."[55] When Dorsey played as "Georgia Tom," he was backed by "Tampa Red" on slide guitar, and their 1928 smash hit, "It's Tight Like That," defined "hokum" every bit as well as "Peace in the Valley" defined gospel.

To some extent, of course, this blues/gospel dynamic derives from the same marketing strategies that created "race" and "hillbilly" product lines. In the case of blues and gospel, though, there is an *artistic* commitment to keeping genres separate as well as a commercial one, and the existence of that artistic commitment is not unimportant. On the contrary, it is crucially important, for its arrival portends a shift away from jazz, as a form of popular entertainment, to something that was, well, more sensational. Perhaps because of its Creole roots, jazz was comfortable with enfleshment. It could "swing" and positively brim with smoky sensuousness. By the same token, however, it did not give itself over well to the kind of sexual energies that derive from the perception of flesh as "other." It was rooted in ragtime, a form of music that indicated permissiveness and maintained an almost humorous detachment from the shenanigans that attended its birth in New Orleans brothels. Thomas Dorsey and Sister Rosetta, on the other hand, pledged *allegiance* to ecstatic experience. When these powerfully gifted artists entered a drinking or gambling establishment they sang like patrons rather than employees or staff, and as a result an entirely new form of music began to take shape.

It arrived in 1954 (my birth year), pretty much when common wisdom says it did, and, yes, it arrived in the person of Elvis Presley. But the occasion wasn't the convergence of mountain and delta-based musical traditions. Rather, it was the sudden tightening and ramping up of the blues/gospel dynamic pioneered by Thomas Dorsey. Elvis grew up attending Assemblies of God churches, and when his father moved the family to Memphis when Elvis was 13, Elvis started going to all-night "gospel sings."[56] During the week he listened as regularly to "Camp Meeting of the Air" on hillbilly radio station WHBQ, as to B.B. King on "colored" station WDIA, and on Sundays Elvis divided his time between Assembly of God services and (when he could steal away for an hour or two) East Trigg's all-black Baptist Church. Thus Elvis was a prime candidate for carrying on the tradition begun by Dorsey. But Elvis took things a step further. In Elvis the blues got so close to gospel that the poles started switching back and forth within the space of a song, not merely a day, and thanks to his Pentecostal upbringing he had the physical abandon necessary to go bodily wherever the music did and thereby *amplify* those switches. It was a new thing, musically, and at first even his peers didn't get it. Take fellow Sun Records recording star Jerry Lee Lewis. That man packed a wallop, but he didn't have a gospel side. He'd left that side of his life to first cousin Jimmy Swaggart back when they were growing up together in Ferriday, Louisiana, and as a result Lewis was in some pathological sense dependent on Swaggart's Pentecostal ministry to live fully the rock and roll promise (just as Swaggart was to some pathological extent dependent on Jerry Lee Lewis' kind of "devil music" to perform effectively as a minister). Elvis, though, had personal, uninhibited access to both poles. Elvis could go deep, then soar, and then (after holding for a minute, hips frozen, in crowd-pleasing transport) dig down and truly *know* the nit and the grit and the rut of ground. Witnesses were amazed. Even black "shouters" were amazed.[57] Presley's mid-1950s performances were electric, and the reason they were electric was that he had tapped into the revivalist energy of old.[58] Now it was the secular world's turn to undergo an Awakening—first by getting "rocked" with "a steady roll," as per Trixie Smith's risqué 1922 hit, and then by "rocking and reeling," as per the old Kentucky spiritual and the 1916 hit, "Camp Meeting Jubilee."

Jump-cut, now, to 1969 and the small town of Bethel in upstate New York. It is night, and a tethered microphone is in mid-arc. Wham: down comes the windmill-propelled guitar pick, a resulting power chord blares from twin 70-foot speaker towers in such a way as to bring crowd and band to earth, and the festival called Woodstock is off and running. Dare we keep watching this movie? I can think of a lot of reasons we shouldn't, not the least of which is that Woodstock is a subject that has been visited more than one time too many. Nevertheless, I see no way around at least mentioning the event, for the parallels to Red River and Cane Ridge are astounding.

In addition to being a gathering of anti-establishment types who were literally encamped for three days in a field in front of a stage that featured round-the-clock efforts to (in Sly Stone's words) "take everybody higher," the poster advertising Woodstock featured a dove. Artist Arnold Skolnick had in mind a gray catbird, but when people saw the poster they saw a dove, the very same type of bird that, according to Christian tradition, symbolizes Pentecost or the descent of the Holy Spirit. Note, too, that the peace festival was free and that it occurred in a town called "Bethel." Thus it to some degree confirmed McGready's hunch that people attending a "love feast" open to the poor were standing on the site of Jacob's ladder in "Bethel," the very house of God. Indeed, artists who had performed at Woodstock unwittingly provided a coda for McGready's revival just one year after their own, for Crosby, Stills, and Nash sang of "four dead"—or slain—"in O-hi-o." And then there are the many ways in which Woodstock specifically resembled Cane Ridge: widespread use of mind-altering substances, open sexual activity, jammed roads owing to high numbers of people attending ("New York State Thruway is *closed*, man"), reduced color barriers, antithetical earth/spirit dynamic. Add to all that the fact that Woodstock was facilitated by a "British Invasion" numbering the Rolling Stones and the Yardbirds, just as Red River and Cane Ridge were facilitated by a "British Invasion" numbering John Wesley and George Whitefield, and you have what most of us would call a lock. Woodstock, it turns out, wasn't really about a new, allegedly Aquarian, age at all. Rather, it was about the resurgence of a "worship service" that had been in session ever since America's westward movement began. It was, both formally and materially, a camp meeting.

The last person who performed at Woodstock was Jimi Hendrix, and when that performer walked on stage to begin his now famous set, he smiled slyly and said, "So—we meet again." Then: "Hm." Presumably Hendrix was referring to the fact that just two years earlier he had performed at the Monterey Pop Festival. But who knows? Maybe Mr. Hendrix saw further than the rest of us and meant that we, the American people, were meeting again after first meeting at Cane Ridge. Upon greeting his audience in this way, the guitarist turned to his band, nodded to set time, and began an instrumental piece whose watery melodic line slowly got lost amongst intentionally placed feedback. Noise pioneer that Hendrix was, he stayed in the cacophony for a while, as if searching for a shape that could be found in the reversing current powering his amplifiers. And then—digging low in order to then swing high—he did find something. The corrosive aspect to the sound was still strong, but in the midst of that corrosive aspect a clearly identifiable sequence of notes had appeared, and soon the crowd recognized it. The man was playing "The Star Spangled Banner."

4

Son of the Morning Star

Hannibal Pool, 1600 hours, four miles south of Wheeling, West Virginia. The oxbow at Dillies Bottom is behind us, and we are coming up now on Boggs Island with its salvage yard and the usual fleet of empties at Shoemaker's. It is now, and long has been, a busy section of river, but I am not concerned, as the captain is, about congestion and sunken wrecks. What I'm concerned about are the duck ponds that need to be skirted on my quarter-mile stroll to the head of the tow. Barge corners are rounded slightly, thereby forming empty spaces where four corners meet, and people who presume to go for a walk on a tow have to be careful to not trip over a wire, when passing near these holes. There isn't much to hold onto in a duck pond, and given that the ponds feature currents that can pull would-be adventurers down and under the oncoming part of a tow, the risk of death is not low. Therefore, I place my boots with care, and when I reach the head of the tow I stay there for a while, close by the jack staff with its mailbox, so as to safely call to mind the city that will soon be in view.

The most important thing about Wheeling, of course, is that it's the site of Capitol Music Hall and radio station 1170 WWVA, home to the Wheeling Jamboree. WWVA had a powerful signal between 1926 and 1977, and the live country music show beamed out across its waves enjoyed remarkable success. Buck Owens, George Jones, June Carter, and Tammy Wynette regularly performed there, among others.

But there are also other things about Wheeling that make it worthy of notice, and most of these other things sign the 1861–1865 event known as the Civil War.

Take this suspension bridge that will soon be coming up on the far side of the Music Hall. The bridge was built in 1849 so travelers on the National Road wouldn't have to take a ferry to cross into Ohio, and given that the structure has an elegant appearance, observers quite reasonably conclude that the bridge's story has little to do with the nature of the road it carries and lots to do with engineering prowess. The bridge deck depends from massive iron cables held aloft by stone towers that straddle the highway beneath like the Arch of Titus does in Rome. These cables are anchored deep under the corner of 10th St. and Main, and when they cross the river they travel 1,010 feet. That was a long way in 1849! In fact, at that time no other bridge in the world featured such a long span; hence, when the bridge was completed its design was quickly copied and refined—most spectacularly by Brooklyn Bridge designer John A. Roebling (who had competed for the contract to build the Wheeling bridge), and also by Roebling's son Washington (who in 1871 outfitted the Wheeling Bridge with signature wind-defying timber truss stiffeners). So, there is a lot to notice on architectural grounds alone. Yet, as I've said, there are also other things to notice, and one of them is that Pittsburghers didn't like this bridge.

The river was a public waterway, yes? Why, then, should Wheeling be allowed to obstruct the passage of tall vessels bound to and from Pittsburgh by constructing a bridge that spans the entire waterway? Wheeling was in effect *stealing* Ohio River "headship" status, and as a result the investment of Pittsburgh businesses in their region's future would in a few short years count for nothing! At the very least, Pittsburghers felt, Wheeling citizens should acknowledge the problem; hence, Pittsburghers speedily filed a request that Wheeling rebuild the bridge in such a way that steamers with high smokestacks would be able to freely pass under any and all obstructions. Indeed, they took the suit all the way to the United States Supreme Court on two separate occasions (1852 and 1856), and though in the first instance Supreme Court justices decided in favor of Pittsburgh, in the second instance those same justices decided in favor of Wheeling. Clearly, the issues posed by building this bridge were difficult, and the reason they were difficult is that they highlighted differences which were soon to contribute to an outright war.

It wasn't so much that Pittsburgh was a northern city that frowned on slavery and Wheeling was a Virginian one that recognized a right to own slaves. Rather, it was that Pittsburgh repeatedly called for federal control of interior waterways and the nullification of Wheeling's *state*-derived charter for bridge construction. When Wheeling businessmen first floated the idea of a bridge in 1844, they thought of their bridge as a missing link in a National Road. So, they petitioned Congress for the necessary funds. After

Pittsburgh lobbyists frustrated that attempt, the Wheeling contingent, now doing business as "Belmont Bridge Company," turned to the Virginia state legislature for help, and lawmakers in Richmond complied by granting the enterprise a state charter in 1847. Thereafter bridge builders moved fast, and by 1849 wagon traffic was crossing between Virginia and Ohio (the South and the North) ninety feet above water. After Pittsburgh filed suit, the Wheeling-based company defended the bridge in three different ways. First, it argued that the Cumberland Pike necessitated the bridge. Second, it argued that Pittsburghers had themselves built a bridge downriver from Pittsburgh that was 13 feet lower than the Wheeling bridge. And—last but not least—the company argued that the state of Virginia had more authority on that waterway than the federal government did. Most of the Supreme Court justices disagreed. They argued that because the Ohio River was a navigable waterway, it was essentially a zone of "interstate commerce," therefore quite definitely subject to federal intervention. Upshot: either raise the road deck or tear the thing down. At this point (1852) attorneys arguing the case for Wheeling found reasons to delay the proposed remodel while they enlisted the help of *Ohioan* legislators whose districts were already improved by the bridge, and this time—thanks to an argument based on the importance of mail routes—the Wheeling group won. In another sense, though, they hadn't, for Virginia had effectively conceded that gunboats operated by a commander like Grant—129-ton displacement, two boilers, thirteen-inch diameter pistons, 3'6" stroke, six cannons, 24-pound shot—had a right to patrol the Ohio and its tributaries. The name of the attorney who argued the case for Pittsburgh? Edwin McMasters Stanton of Steubenville—the very same Stanton who later ran the War Department for Abraham Lincoln between 1862 and 1865.

Other facets of Wheeling infrastructure besides its famous bridge call to mind the Civil War no less vividly. At the corner of 11th St. and Main, for example, there was a regularly scheduled slave auction in the early part of the nineteenth century, and in 1862 the relatively modest brick building that still stands across the street from the B&O train station served as a kind of western equivalent to Philadelphia's Independence Hall when Wheeling residents hammered out a way to separate from Richmond and create an entirely new state thenceforth to be known as "West Virginia." Additionally, one can spy out the field where General George McClellan assembled a newly formed "Department of the Ohio" and departed south and east toward Cheat Mountain in July of 1861 to initiate Union engagement with Robert E. Lee. Today, though, it is the war called to mind by the Wheeling suspension bridge that compels attention, and this bias is reinforced as I look west and catch a glimpse of Route 250 snaking up into the Ohio hills toward Harrisville, the town Confederate General John Hunt Morgan rode through on July 25, 1863, in a last-ditch effort to ignite a Copperhead/Butternut rebellion and so bring southern Ohio over to the Confederacy. Morgan was caught two days later a few miles northwest of Steubenville, near the town called Lisbon.

Why did that cavalry officer go for broke toward Lisbon, of all places? Given that local Historical Markers omit crucial parts of the story, it can take a while for a visitor to figure this out, but eventually I discovered that Lisbon was the birthplace of Copperhead leader Clement Vallandigham, who had been apprehended two months before Morgan's ride. Congressman Vallandigham was unarmed, therefore not dangerous in the usual sense, but Lincoln and his cabinet considered the Ohio congressman a serious threat because he was an articulate and unusually coherent "peace Democrat" who believed Lincoln was manipulating abolitionist sentiment to centralize power. Vallandigham argued that because such centralization undercut the American people's capacity for self-government far more drastically than southern secession ever could, the only reasonable course was to push for northern disarmament, and if that meant aiding and abetting Confederate soldiers in their efforts to disable Union armies, so be it. Not surprisingly, Union General Ambrose Burnside was ordered by Lincoln to put Vallandigham in chains, thereby setting the stage for General Morgan's equally unsurprising conclusion that the time was ripe for a foray into the Seven Ranges, the land of Vallandigham's presumed base. That the Confederate general was wrong in this assessment does not mean that localist Copperhead biases did not exist in this area, right next door to (and even amongst) abolitionist ones. Rather, it simply means that war energies in this region were at that time stronger.

Might it be possible that the issue raised by the Wheeling Bridge controversy and Vallandigham's imprisonment—namely, our country's tilt toward a centralized power structure—is as relevant to our inquiry as the issues raised by land commodification and revivalist energy? And, if so, might it not be possible that these three phenomena turn out to reinforce one another? I suspect that the answer to both questions is "yes," and I propose to test this contention by looking a short distance past Harrisville toward my hometown of Rumley so that we can consider the career of *that town's* most famous native son. Name? George Armstrong Custer, the very same Custer who fought at Gettysburg and served as the first commander of the 7th Cavalry, the regiment that was later to become identified with helicopters in Vietnam.

If you drive out today to the site of Custer's defeat, in Wyoming, you quickly find yourself on a grassy ridge, looking down a ravine toward a sparkling-clear, impressively cold stream. There are trout in that stream, and when they hold their position in the current they are hard to distinguish from gold-colored stones over which they swim. Far to the south you can see snow on the Bighorn Mountains, and to the west, on the other side of willows, box elders, and cottonwoods bordering the Little Bighorn River, there is a vast expanse of plain with a cover of greasewood, saltbush, and buffalo grass. There's a railroad track and an interstate running through that plain, and in the distance you can occasionally see a Burlington, Northern, & Santa Fe freight train. On the morning of June 25, 1876, however, things would have looked a little different. The lay of the land would have been the same, but the plain on the other side of the river would have been dotted with tipis. A lot of them. Indeed, if you superimpose the 1876 tipi encampment on a current-day urban center, the encampment would have covered fifty whole city blocks. And beyond those lodges, just visible through smoke wafting upward from approximately 950 cooking fires, you would have seen a massive pony herd. All told there were probably 15,000 people on that plain, and the dominant impression would have been one of domesticity and peace.

You would have seen children, women doing household chores, dogs, old men on their way to harvest turnips. There were warriors present, but you wouldn't have seen them, as most of the Arapaho, Sans Arcs, Blackfoot, Cheyenne, Miniconjou, and Oglalla braves who owned all the lodges were inside, catching up on sleep after an all-night chant. Custer's scouts, upon spying the village from a distant eastern ridge, were astonished by the size of the encampment, and when Custer, worried that he might lose the advantage of surprise, declared his intention of reconfiguring his 647-man force into battalions and attacking, his most trusted scout quietly gave away his most treasured possessions and made out a will. Four hours later, after dispatching three of twelve companies on supply-and-reconnaissance missions and proceeding to a point that was slightly south of the vantage point we have been using, Custer dispatched another two companies to the valley floor with instructions to engage "hostiles" at the southern end of the village and then rode north with remaining companies along a ridge that led to the village's rear. *We are the boys who take delight / In smashing limerick lamps at night / And through the streets like sportsters fight / Tearing all before us.*[59]

By late afternoon, every last man in that northbound force was dead. In a war that had so far been marked by skirmishes in which (during the Fetterman massacre) 81 soldiers at most died, the United States Army had in one very fell swoop lost five entire companies from the 7th Cavalry regiment—a total of 268 men. No less shockingly, the violence that cost these men their lives apparently continued without abatement, for after soldiers were killed their bodies were stripped by women in the camp and mutilated. Custer himself, it is said, wound up with a sewing awl in his ear—so that he might hear better in whatever world he had departed to.[60]

What, exactly, is on view in a scene like this?

The main thing you see, of course, is story. You see the components of an almost preassembled hero myth, be it Custer's battalion as The Three Hundred holding the pass at Themopylae to secure the eventual victory of Athenians over barbarians, or Crazy Horse (the man who most likely ensured Custer's doom) as David resourcefully and decisively taking down the Goliath who had threatened hearth and home. The version in which Custer is deified has historically been the most popular—America's poet laureate Walt Whitman, for example, bought it hook, line and sinker. But the Crazy Horse version has proven durable too. Just ask Neil Young. Either way, the mythic aspect is prominent. The minute you glimpse these obvious storybook elements, though, you tend right away also to see an entirely different kind of narrative called "the facts." This is the sort of story military historians prefer—the sort of stripped-down, emotion-free analysis of movement and strategy in which you learn about how, say, Crook was to head north from Ft. Fetterman on the North Platte and drive the Sioux toward an unyielding "anvil" of Montana-derived Terry/Gibbon "columns" but how Custer miscalculated and divided his forces when he shouldn't have, and the adversary therefore walked out of the "press." This story is powerful and certainly has its uses, not the least of which is learning how to ably defend ourselves should we ever discover that an attack is imminent. That having been established, it must also be said that this kind of story can't help but blur occasionally with the mythic kind, for it is hard to maintain requisite coolness when "belligerents" being driven against an "anvil" have hailstones painted on their chests, scalplocks dangling from their spears, and dragonflies sewn into their war bonnets. Also, even military historians get thrown off balance by a "last stand." The sheer finality of such an event tends to overpower professional observers just as it does casual ones.

What else is there to see besides story?

Here it is necessary to wait a bit—i.e. visit, read Connell's book, sift—but the wait isn't long, and even if the wait did tax our patience the rewards vastly outweigh the inconvenience. For example, it is possible to see and even taste and smell the texture of a certain place and time. Stare at the Little Bighorn Valley long enough, in other words, and there is a good chance that the entire June 1876 Powder River basin will materialize, completely unbidden, before your eyes: ponderosa pine, riffles, Gatling guns, whooping cranes in flight, a torch bag filled with resin, coal outcroppings, frayed hawsers on snag boats, checkerboards, coffee mills, a black bib on a meadowlark's yellow breast, percussion caps, lead, pack animals loaded with trade-able riches like pickles, chewing tobacco, tinned salmon, thread, and licorice root. And the marvel need not stop there, for one can also see people. You can see Lonesome Charlie, a college student from Illinois who went west to look for gold, got a job with a trapper, and wound up working as a guide on the upper Missouri. You can see Isaiah Doman, a black veteran who worked for the War Department as a mail courier and then for the Northern Pacific as a crewman on a survey team. And you can see Mitch Bouyer, the scout who, after being born to a French father and a Santee Sioux mother, married a Crow. Other people who come into view include surgeon James DeWolf, who wore rubber leggings to protect himself from rain and wrote his wife every day; George Crook, the flint-eyed general who said little, fought mean, and found a way to live on slippery elm bark and acorns[61] when he had to; and Crazy Horse, who took no scalps, gave freely to the poor, and prepared for battle by painting a red lightning bolt on his cheek, throwing a handful of dust across his chest, and dotting his body with white hailstones.[62]

More to the point you can see Custer, a man who, after an apparently joyful eastern Ohio childhood, became a sentimentalist who killed people because he wanted to rather than because he had to.

Custer's father, Emmanuel, arrived in the largely German town of Rumley in 1830 to work as a blacksmith after the death of his first wife, and within the space of a couple years he courted and married Maria Ward from western Pennsylvania who had just lost her shopkeeper husband. As a couple, they attended Ridge Presbyterian Church on the other side of my neighbor's woods, but starting in 1839, the year George Armstrong was born, they switched to a more lively Methodist church on the north side of the creek my springs flow into. Which came first: the joys of an affectionate marriage or the joys of emotionally frank worship? Either way, George Armstrong—or "Autie," as he was known—evidently rode into adulthood on a tide of leniency and good humor.[63] As a young boy he trained, for sheer love of pageantry, with a drunken local militia, and when he became a young man he trained, for sheer love of the feminine figure, with literate types who knew something about sonnets. Young Custer liked to see maidens blush almost as much as he liked the idea of war. Therefore, he became both an excellent horseman and a schoolteacher. He taught at Beech Point School, south of Cadiz, but after the exasperated father of a sweetheart turned to local congressman John Bingham for help, the amorous teacher found himself finally admitted to a military academy that was, luckily for him, only slightly less interesting than his current flame's heaving bosom and deeply coloring cheeks. ("Oh my heart can ne'er forget thy parting look of sorrow.") While at West Point, Custer distinguished himself by garnering an unprecedented number of demerit badges for "highly unmilitary and trifling conduct." Offenses committed by Custer at the school included "cooking utensils in chimney," "gazing about in ranks," "late at supper," "wall defaced with pencil marks," and "swing'g arms when march'g from publication of delinquencies."[64] As it happened, though, there was soon to be a war. The Union Army took every man it could get, and in that new context Custer proved himself to be fearless as well as foolish.

One morning when McClellan was in conference with senior officers, trying to ascertain the depth of a river he wanted to ford, the commander muttered that he wished he knew how deep the water was. Custer, overhearing the remark, instantly rode out to the part of the river where current was big. Turning his horse smartly, he said, "This deep, General."[65] Thereafter Custer's star began to rise, and when Gettysburg came along, Custer used newfound responsibility to impressive effect.

Like the November 1863 defeat of Bragg's Army of Tennessee at Look-Out Mountain and Missionary Ridge—a defeat made possible by War Secretary Stanton's transfer by rail of 20,000 soldiers to Chattanooga—Gettysburg was a crucial turning point in the war. Actually, given that Gettysburg preceded the surrender of Vicksburg as well as Grant's surprise amphibious landing at Brown's Ferry, it was probably *the* turning point. After victories at Fredericksburg and Chancellorsville, Lee was on a roll when he marched north into Pennsylvania toward Harrisburg at the end of June, in 1863, and upon surrounding his adversary it was within his reach to end the entire war in the South's favor. Hence Lee's decision to go all-out at Gettysburg on July 3rd and charge Cemetery Ridge. Well, that Pickett-led charge failed—as most people know. What a lot of people don't know is that the charge didn't just fail because of a deceptively quiet hilltop battery and the relative impregnability of the Union's defensive and tensely braced "fish-hook" configuration. There was also another factor at work, and that was the absence of 9,500 men belonging to Confederate Major General J.B. Stuart's vaunted cavalry, owing to a deflection caused by none other than newly appointed Brigadier General George Armstrong Custer.

Lee's battle plan for July 3rd included assaults on the Federals' eastern flank as well as the western one. Specifically, Richard S. Ewell's 2nd Corps was to attack near Culp's Hill while the faster and more mobile J.B. Stuart swung down past the pointed end of the Union "fish-hook" and then in, toward the east side of Cemetery Ridge, at the exact same time that Pickett charged from the west. Had the plan worked, Stuart might have drawn enough forces from the federal western flank to make it possible for Pickett to succeed. Stuart, however, never got close to that ridge. Three miles east of Gettysburg, two of his three divisions found themselves in hand-to-hand combat with a brigade commanded by Custer for an entire afternoon. Was it just chance that Custer was standing in Stuart's way? No. Though the Confederates were accustomed to being pretty much unchallenged in the world of horsemanship, the new Federal cavalry unit that Custer belonged to had capably engaged Stuart on June 9 at Brandywine Station, and on June 30, when Stuart took the town of Hanover directly east of Gettysburg on his way to meet up with Lee, Custer's brigade fought on foot to reclaim the town and thereby force Stuart to swing wide of his mark and miss the first two days of the Gettysburg battle entirely. Lee in effect fought Gettysburg with one arm tied behind his back, and the man who immobilized that arm was Custer.[66]

After the war, though, and even towards the end of it, Custer's resume starts to read a little differently. Though he affected a dashing manner, Custer was in truth a fastidious teetotaler who showed a furtive interest in D.C. "art" exhibits like "Oriental Princess." Also, he executed prisoners without hesitation and had men flogged for infractions that resembled the ones he himself rang up at West Point. Later, while posted on the Great Plains, Custer opined in his journal about the "barbaric" practice of scalping while at the same time showing a keen interest in the Sioux technique of preserving scalps by stretching them on a wooden hoop via needle and thread. "The dried, fleshy portion of the scalp," Custer dutifully noted, "is ornamented in bright colors. . ... In other instances, the hair is dyed, either to a beautiful yellow or golden, or to crimson."[67] Another thing about Custer was that he apparently thought law was for benighted others who needed guardrails when he himself did not. Unlike Grant and even Lee, Custer favored a highly personalized uniform/weaponry kit—red bandana to offset long yellow hair, Hussar's jacket, rakish hat with wide brim, Remington sporting rifle with octagonal barrel, and two self-cocking Webber Bulldog pistols. When Congress passed a law forbidding flogging, Custer ignored it. On an 1865 mission to Hempstead, Texas, the men serving Custer subsisted on hog jowls and maggot-infested grain; Custer, meanwhile, ate privately prepared meals featuring fresh meats, vegetables, milk (Custer called milk "Aldernay," after the British cow breed), and fruit.[68] Even worse, Custer ordered his men to wait each morning while Custer's wife, Libbie, got ready to ride in a specially prepared, spring-loaded wagon.

This kind of thing happened all the time on Custer-led expeditions. On an 1874 reconnaissance trip to the Black Hills, Custer used his regiment's hospital tent as a personal dining hall, and when a man fell seriously ill with dysentery the ambulance that could have been used to ship the weakened man back to Bismarck was unavailable because Custer had requisitioned that wagon for hunting trophies and a growing menagerie. Mail wagons bearing orders and the letters of enlisted troops to loved ones back home? Those too were hijacked, if Custer's need was great enough. In 1867, while leading the newly formed 7th Cavalry regiment stationed at Ft. Riley (Kansas), Custer commandeered a postal wagon's horses to sustain a long-distance, spur-of-the-moment ride back to base to see his newly arrived wife. Most of Custer's men hated him. They called him "Hard Ass," "Iron Butt," "Ringlets," even (Luciferic reference here) "Son of the Morning Star." Moreover, Custer's superiors by and large *agreed* with the sentiments lurking behind these monikers. After the Kansas incident, Custer was court-marshaled for shooting deserters without trial, in addition to abandoning his command, and in 1875, during the months leading up to the Little Bighorn expedition, Custer was actively barred from service by no less an authority than President Ulysses S. Grant.

Nevertheless, the man from Rumley kept finding work.

After cavalry mentor Phil Sheridan got Custer out of jail (as it were) to help with an upcoming winter campaign against the Cheyenne on the southern Plains, Custer led a pre-dawn attack on November 27, 1868 against a village on the Washita River, just east of the Texas panhandle. The pretext for this attack was that the village's chief, Black Kettle, had allegedly held a white woman hostage and negotiated terms for her release, but it is no less likely that the United States Army was finishing a job begun four years earlier when preacher John Chivington led a force of 800 militiamen against Black Kettle's clan when it was encamped on Sand Creek, a stream on the eastern Colorado plains. On that occasion, Black Kettle's village flew an American flag as per instructions from officers at Ft. Lyon, 40 miles to the south, who had promised him that by flying the flag he would be left in peace. But after a night of drinking, Chivington and his Colorado Thirders ignored the flag and massacred the 163 women, children, and old men who had gathered under it while able-bodied Cheyenne warriors were off hunting. Now, after being re-located to a reservation on the Washita River in western Oklahoma, Black Kettle and approximately 50 potential warriors were in their homes, keeping warm under a foot of snow, along with 200 women, children, and older men. Black Kettle had just returned from a meeting with an Indian agent during which he confirmed his intention of relying on food provisions and staying south of the Arkansas River, away from the war, but 150 young men from villages south of him had other ideas, and Custer's scouts picked up their trail. The encampment's dogs were killed during the time it took for the 7th Cavalry force to take up positions at opposite corners of the village; next, soldiers moved through the village firing at anything that moved. Nobody knows exactly how many people died, but witnesses agree that soldiers fired at both women and children before using 54 more of them as shields upon retreating.

Custer's next major (and perhaps chief) accomplishment was the 1874 Black Hills Expedition in which Custer led five reporters, a U.S. Geological Survey engineer, a photographer, a handful of miners, and 1,200 soldiers on a summer stroll through land that had been explicitly reserved for the Lakota Sioux under the terms of the Ft. Laramie Treaty that concluded the Red Cloud War in 1868.[69] Some of Custer's soldiers were musicians, and Custer made sure that sixteen of these men were outfitted with white horses in addition to brass instruments so that the show they put on, under the direction of Chief Musician Felix Vinatiori, would be a feast for eyes as well as ears. Custer's party entered the reservation from the north, when wildflowers were in full bloom, and when the revelers got near its heart—well, they behaved like tourists. They noted the variety of scaffolds erected to offer up the remains of fallen warriors to the four winds, home to eagles. They shot a great white swan in order to measure its wingspan. Custer tracked a grizzly and posed for pictures beside a downed elk with a fine rack of antlers. The party collected rattlesnakes, petrified tree trunks, even a live hawk. And then, when the party arrived in a meadow with a stream running through it, Custer and five others made the first ascent of the region's highest peak. The proud climbers called this Black Hills mountain "Harney Peak," in honor of a military commander previously based in the Dakotas, but to the Lakota, most notably a nine-year-old boy named Black Elk, the mountain meant other things.

Unbeknownst to Custer and his party, this future medicine man had stood on this same mountain peak just one year before (perhaps even that very spring) while recovering from a fever, and when he had "looked out," he had discovered that the mountain was "the high and lonely center of the earth." *They are appearing, may you behold!*[70] "We were going east," he later told John Niehardt in 1931. "I looked ahead and saw the mountains there with rocks and forests on them, and from the mountains flashed all colors upward to the heavens. Then I was standing on the highest mountain of them all, and round about beneath me was the whole hoop of the world." When young Black Elk looked west, "yonder," he could see "frightened swallows," and also his own people "running about, setting the smoke-flap poles and fastening down their teepees against the wind, for the storm cloud was coming on them very fast and black." Additionally he saw "twelve black horses all abreast with necklaces of bison hoofs." But when Black Elk looked down from the height of the mountain he saw hoops. "I saw that the sacred hoop of my people was one of many hoops that made a circle, wide as daylight and as starlight, and in the center grew one mighty flowering tree to shelter all the children of one mother and one father." Did Custer see anything like that? If he did, he never spoke about it, and in any case it appears unlikely, for the first thing Custer did upon descending from the mountain was to check out rumors that gold could be found in a creek near its base. The rumors turned out to be true! Slowly it became clear that miners panning for gold in the Black Hills could clear $150 per week, and once *that* fact got in focus Custer immediately sent word of the find to Ft. Laramie, via courier, and thence to the entire world, via telegraph. Result? Deadwood, South Dakota, a town that quickly became notorious for brisk trades in women, gaming, and opium—in addition to shovels.

Thus we come, once again, to Custer's last and most famous extravaganza, the attack on the Native American encampment beside the Little Bighorn.

When we last looked out over the village we noted its large size. Now we know the reason for that size. The Lakota were angry about what was happening in the Black Hills, and warriors had begun drifting in from reservations in Montana, the Dakotas, and Wyoming to decide how and where to draw a line, thereby swelling village numbers. Given that General Crook was supposed to be arriving soon from the south with 1,200 men (in fact Crook was waiting for reinforcements 40 miles away after having collided with Crazy Horse a week earlier on the upper Rosebud), given too that Gibbon and Terry would quickly be approaching from the north with 1,000 more, given finally that Custer's orders were to locate the village, swing wide of it, and then approach from the south in order to merely *test* the village's strength, why did Custer try to capture the village? It is hard to say. Yes, he had been given permission to depart from orders if there was "sufficient reason." But on what basis did Custer conclude that a full-scale assault was reasonable? Perhaps he really did think that the village's warriors were at that moment absent and had left the village unguarded on the assumption that only a very large, relatively immobile, easily detected force would dare to attack. Custer's last words were "Hurrah boys, we've got them" and it is possible that this statement was a logical conclusion based on visual analysis. On the other hand, perhaps Custer knew he was taking a large, potentially suicidal risk yet saw no alternative, given his need for exoneration after being publicly chastised by Grant and placed on parole.

Still another explanation is that Custer simply had a train to catch so he could be home in time for the Centennial Exposition in Philadelphia and then the 1876 National Democratic Convention.

Whatever the reason, Custer decided to attack, and when he put men in motion he used a battle plan that was reminiscent of the one he used in

Oklahoma, along the Washita. First, he dispatched Reno to the valley floor with orders to open fire on the village from the south, where it faced open plain. This meant that, when fighting began, women and children would move to the back of the village, where an approach by cavalry would be difficult owing to the steepness of nearby hills. Next, Custer himself drifted along the ridge with five nimble companies toward exactly that spot, and if it hadn't been for the sheer numbers of warriors who were available to surround him, he might very well have secured the human shields he sought and succeeded in his effort to take the village. Who knows? Perhaps he might even have nabbed or killed twelve-year-old Black Elk, who was present in the village at that moment with his parents.

All told, it is a depressing picture, and—switching to confessional mode here—you need not be a Sixties-based practitioner of New Western History to ask whether tracking Custer's career and bringing it into rudimentary focus is a wise investment of time and energy.[71] Upon asking this question, though, you instantly see three things. You see, first, that Custer fought against the Cheyenne and the Lakota Sioux as well as the Confederacy. Second, you see that Custer served on the Great Plains only two years after the conclusion of the Civil War. Third, you see that Custer's first job on the upper Missouri was to protect railroad survey teams. Can the picture be any clearer? The truth is that Custer unwittingly fronted something much larger than himself, and he served in that capacity, at key intervals, in an astonishing variety of circumstances. Thus his career provides a kind of window onto forces that would otherwise be obscured by the originality and brilliance of their agents. Looking at Custer, you find yourself pondering the appearance and then the advance of a juggernaut that ran on coal (the North had a 38:1 coal advantage over the South[72]), furthered the interests of companies like the Northern Pacific Railroad, and warred against nomadic Plains Indians with as much dispatch as it formerly used against a "feudal" South. Can it be possible that the Union army's telos had as much to do with destroying tradition-based cultures and securing access to fossil fuel as it did with enforcing and to some degree delivering enlightened principles?

Here we all are, locked in on Custer's "defeat." We forget that Custer successfully executed orders to irritate the Lakota by violating the terms of the 1868 Laramie Treaty and create an excuse to annihilate the Sioux as a people. Previously the objective of the United States military was forced re-location, as in the 1832 Indian Removal Act, which uprooted Cherokees from North Carolina and sent them to Oklahoma along with Choctaws, Seminoles, Creeks and Chickasaws. But over the course of the Civil War, and especially in 1864, Sherman and Grant learned a few things. Thresholds were crossed both in the Shenandoah Valley, where Sheridan burned farming infrastructure, and in Georgia, where William Tecumseh Sherman famously razed community infrastructure, and these acts, in turn, allowed Union generals to start thinking in terms of "extermination" rather than simply forcing an enemy to concede defeat. "We must act," wrote Military District of the Missouri head Sherman to Grant in early 1867, "with vindictive earnestness against the Sioux, even to their extermination, men, women, and children. Nothing less will reach the root of the case." Hence the decisions to destroy the buffalo herds on which the Sioux depended for food and send Custer with a team of reporters, surveyors, and miners to the Black Hills in 1874, where the Lakota (since the 1868 Ft. Laramie treaty) had been living in relative peace.

This latter move was a truly brazen one, given the explicitly stated terms according to which the Lakota had ceased their Red Cloud-orchestrated hostilities. "No persons except those designated herein," the treaty read, "shall ever be permitted to pass over, settle upon, or reside in the territory described in this article." However, Custer's insouciant, sauntering gait had the desired effect. Within three years Crazy Horse was murdered (knifed in the back upon turning himself in, to a fort) and the Lakota Sioux—driven literally to the ground during attempted escapes to Canada and the Black Hills—were broken, as a people. And what happened after "the natives" were vanquished? Why, at that point (1877, the year of the B&O railroad strikes and the opening of Carnegie Steel) the prospector-driven brothels of Deadwood, South Dakota, flared up, burned brightly for a few years, and then burned (literally) to the ground, thus making room (in Black Hills lore) for the real gold-mining that was destined to take its place—namely, the 8240-feet-deep Homestake Mine at nearby Lead which served (until 2002) as the nation's largest producer of gold and then (starting in 2003) the site of its "dark matter research," to say nothing of the hugely important gas wells and surface coal mines in the Powder River basin a few miles to the west.

It used to be that the center of strip mining in this country was the area around Cadiz, where Custer got his start. Now, thanks to the relative exhaustion of surface deposits there, the center has switched to central West Virginia, where mountain top removal is practiced, and (until very recently) the area between the Bighorn Mountains and the Black Hills. The Appalachian coal seam in Ohio was about 4 feet thick, but the seam in the Powder River basin is 70 feet thick, and this seam is now being mined 24 hours a day, seven days a week, 365 days a year by approximately seven different multinational coal companies. Gillette—with its motels booked solid and its dirt air strips busy—looks like Cadiz did during its boom years, and the design for the earth removal equipment at work on the other side of its city limits—shovels, preparation plants, over-sized trucks—literally *comes* from

Cadiz. Cadiz is where the equipment was designed, tested, and made ready for export. I'll have more to say on that in chapter 6. Here let me just point out that coal trains leave the Powder River basin for eastern power plants on an *hourly* basis. At the Black Thunder Mine, which is currently the nation's biggest (it is the second largest strip mine in the world), there are 60 two-story trucks ferrying 300 tons of coal apiece to tipples that load one train car every 40 seconds. If Black Thunder were to stop suddenly, the United States would instantly lose 9 percent of the coal in its delivery system. That's a lot of energy. And it comes to us (like the West Virginia coalfields) courtesy of the Union army (which secured the area for industrial use) and of course the National Park Service, which maintains 60-foot busts of Washington, Jefferson, Lincoln and Teddy Roosevelt over at Mt. Rushmore to celebrate, sanction, and to some degree bless the activities carried out beneath the four presidents' beneficent gaze.

Mt. Rushmore was carved in the Thirties, right as mining started to accelerate, and it stands just a few miles north of Mt. Harney, which Custer and Black Elk both climbed. In fact, it is the very same mountain that Black Elk was standing on when he was invited to "go the distance" and see further. The Lakota medicine man called the peak "Six Grandfathers" in honor of the ancients who spoke to him there and called him by name. But times have changed, and perhaps it is better now to think of the mountain as Mt. Rushmore, for clearly the land visions driving Washington's land speculation, Jefferson's section-and-range technology, Lincoln's Homestead Act, and Roosevelt's National Park Service have triumphed. Moreover, there is a poignancy about the monument, for the institution of Roosevelt's plan for national wilderness-flavored (Lockean blank-slate) "parks" implicitly required the re-location of longstanding native residents who would otherwise belie the very idea that wilderness is essentially different from civilization.

It is time to head back to the galley for tea. Rising with difficulty from my sitting position near the jack staff at the tow's head, I stretch my arms and set off toward the Ocie Clark. Nearby duck ponds look dark as well as deep, but eventually I make it back to the boat and find my way to a sheltered spot on the port side where I can sit on an upside-down bucket, lean against a wall, and raise closed eyelids to the last of this day's winter sun. My body is cold but the sun is warm, and thanks to a steaming cup of China Black tiredness recedes and I find myself able to turn a corner (briefly!) toward analysis.

Let us suppose that the more cynical among us might be right, should anyone ever claim that 1877 is the year Americans stopped pretending the Civil War was about emancipation. The Union army gave up enforcing reconstruction efforts in that year, in addition to honoring the 1868 Ft. Laramie Treaty. Hence, it is possible that the cynical view might have truth to it. If that were to be the case, though, what was the Civil War really about?

This is a place I don't particularly care to go.

Indeed, I am uncomfortable even posing the question, for I believe that the Civil War was a crucible. I am a "hewer of wood" and a "drawer of water." How can I not stand with Lincoln and the rest of the North against apologists for chattel slavery? In an 1837 speech on the Senate floor, John C. Calhoun even went so far as to declare that civilization *depended* on the enslavement of one people to ensure the comfort of another, and in 1858 fellow South Carolina senator James Hammond, speaking with uncanny directness across the years to someone a lot like me, punctuated Calhoun's point. "In all social systems," he said,

> there must be a class to do the menial duties, to perform the drudgery of life. That is, a class requiring but a low order of intellect and but little skill. Its requisites are vigor, docility, fidelity. Such a class you must have, or you would not have that other class which leads to progress, civilization, and refinement. It constitutes the very mud-sill of society and of political government; and you might as well attempt to build a house in the air, as to build either the one or the other, except on this mud-sill.[73]

Excuse me? If the world is to be divided into classes like these, I make haste to stand with slaves—both the legally recognized sort and the northern Proletariat sort depicted by one Civil War era Alabama newspaper as a rag-tag assemblage of "small-fisted farmers" and "greasy mechanics."[74] More to the point, I pledge allegiance to the overall case for the North, as scripted by Lincoln at Gettysburg, four and a half months after Lee's failed attempt to demolish the Army of the Potomac.

Though justifying the war according to the terms set forth in the 1861 First Inaugural Address was a stretch (Lincoln conveniently omitted the fact that the federal government had over the years breached the original contract every bit as much as seceding states), the alternative justification discovered at the Gettysburg cemetery (where Lincoln steered clear of constitutional issues and focused on a "new birth of freedom" rather than a "more perfect union") has proved durable. Indeed, it has proved strong enough to serve as a creation story that is every bit as powerful as the Declaration of Independence to which it alludes. Look into your own mental habits and see if this isn't true. Thanks to Lincoln's brief remarks we now know that Southerners and Northerners comprise a "nation." Furthermore, we know that we are a nation to the extent that we follow through on a joint dedication to a "proposition," which is that "all men are created equal." What does it mean to say that all men are equal? It means that no one individual or class is fit, by nature, to be sacrificed in order that another individual or class might live. And—last but not least—we know that this kind of dedication is historically unique and of enormous worth. How do we know that? By acknowledging and remembering and saluting the sacrifices made by soldiers who fought at Gettysburg to ensure—for Southerners as well as Northerners—that "government of the people, by the people, for the people, shall not perish from the earth." It's a rousing story, this, and so far as I can tell it is also—in the big sense—true. Which is to say, it matches the historical record and it orients us so that, like a milled board that is straight and therefore "true," we tend toward our proper end.

So, that is one thing that makes me reluctant to question the official storyline regarding the Civil War.

Another is that I admire Lincoln.

How can one not admire a man who, upon being asked whether he planned to go to heaven or hell, said he intended to go to Congress? Lincoln told stories well. He knew Shakespeare and the King James Bible backward and forward. He could hold his own amongst rough company on a flatboat bound for New Orleans. Additionally, he was a highly skilled (and very successful) attorney. Hence he exhibited an almost inimitable blend of lawyerly detachment, sincerity, wry amusement, and vision. At Trenton Lincoln called America an "almost chosen" nation. Add to that his courage (when he gave his first inaugural address sharpshooters were positioned on nearby rooftops to protect him), his understanding of loss (he lost one son prior to leaving Springfield and another, aged 10, while serving in the White House), and his ability to actually carry the weight history put on his shoulders while at the same time tending to mundane yet crucial detail (he wrote the Gettysburg Address on the back of an envelope just a week after pacifying his perpetually disgruntled Treasury Secretary, who had threatened for the third time to resign, while at the same time pacifying his, Lincoln's, wife, who had refused to attend any and all receptions organized by the beautiful daughter of the Treasury secretary[75])—add all that up and you have the makings of a genuinely great man. Had I been around when Lincoln, bound for his first inaugural, passed by on the railroad tracks below my house on February 11, 1861, I would unquestionably have been standing beside the iron rails to salute him, and I would also have been present when his casket went by on its way west, toward Springfield.

Lincoln's friends and enemies, though, make me nervous. They tend to either idolize or demonize the war president, and this fact (in turn) suggests that there may be more to Lincoln's actions (and those of the ship he steered) than one would at first suppose. Hence I am inclined to go ahead and follow through, if cautiously, on the sorts of questions that come into view upon studying Custer.

Okay. In what ways can it be said that the Civil War was *not*, ultimately, about ending the institution of chattel slavery?

The first and most obvious answer is the one I hinted at earlier when I mentioned the speed with which the Union army abandoned attempts to enforce integration—namely, that the Union army and its boosters were not particularly interested in freeing the African-American people. Racism was rife among Union soldiers. Black enlisted men received less pay than whites, in addition to being assigned the dirtiest and most back-breaking chores, and white soldiers on more than one occasion expressed fear of blacks by raping and debasing black women. Indeed, there was strongly racist sentiment across the entire North. How could there not be? Jonathan Edwards owned a slave, and Rhode Island used to be known as Rhode Island Plantations, owing to the fact that it consisted of plantations staffed by black slaves. Moreover, the ships that brought Africans to the American continent belonged, largely, to New England sea captains. Note, too, that the Emancipation Proclamation was largely thought of as a tactical measure that enhanced military advantage, in 1863, rather than as an altruistic one.[76] To the soldiers and functionaries who implemented it, and even to a majority in Lincoln's cabinet if not to Lincoln himself, the Proclamation meant the same thing that it meant to southern planters—that Union forces had now made it their mission to destroy the antebellum South and replace it with something of their own devising. Thus it can be convincingly argued that when African Americans, via Jim Crow statutes, wound up as segregated citizens starting in 1877, the event was consistent with northern objectives and not a contradiction at all.

A second reason for concluding that the Civil War was not, primarily, about freeing slaves is that secession was an immensely threatening issue in and of itself, regardless of which reasons Southerners supplied to justify their attempted withdrawal from the Union. As mentioned in chapter 1, Whiskey Rebels too had posed a secessionist threat, and when they had organized themselves, federal troops instantly appeared in overwhelming numbers to suppress the insurrection. Note that this was in 1794, well before tensions regarding slavery co-opted national discourse. Given that precedent, it is possible that Lincoln's call for 75,000 militiamen was successful simply because Confederate batteries near Ft. Sumter had challenged federal authority. In other words, Lincoln may have tapped a deep-seated collective need to protect hard-earned collective identity and to function as a coherent nation with a recognizable head, let alone a nation dedicated to a specific, if controversial, end. "The Union," Lincoln boldly asserted in his March 21 address, "is unbroken." Five weeks later the new president asked for help in the business of "holding," "occupying," and "possessing" the "property and places belonging to the government," and—presto—that help came. Volunteers poured into Washington, and all of a sudden there was a war on.

Third—and here we get into the "big" reasons for claiming that the Civil War was not just about ending slavery—industrial interests were very strong in 1859, and almost all of those interests were located north of the Mason-Dixon line. I call this the Charles-and-Mary-Beard explanation, in honor of the Columbia University professors who popularized (in 1927) the thesis that our Civil War was driven, and caused by, industrialization.[77]

The argument goes like this. After first appearing on the timeline of world history in, well, 1776 (Manchester cotton mills, the fuel-efficient Watts steam engine, and the United States of America all appeared at the same time!), the industrial revolution gathered force to the same degree that factories driving it did. Wherever possible, the business of manufacturing became mechanized, and when iron-makers discovered the puddling process (which vastly increased the speed at which large quantities of wrought iron could be produced from pig iron) at the same time that railroads (thanks to Watts' engine) started to connect factories to each other as well as to rivers (the Liverpool and Manchester Railroad and the B&O both started up in the early 1830s), there was no looking back. Hence the stage was set, in America, for a show-down between agricultural and industrial sectors that had formerly commanded roughly equal leverage owing to the dependence of Lowell textile mills on southern cotton. And, given that the industrial sector had an impetus to develop railroads at a far greater pace than the agricultural sector required, it was an almost foregone conclusion that the industrial sector would press its advantage and provoke a kind of economic war. Railroad power was not yet monolithic in 1860. The holding company had not yet been invented, and the federal government had not yet subsidized railroad construction on the scale made possible by the Pacific Railway Act, passed in 1862. Hence railroad financial interests were as variegated as they appeared to be, given the simultaneous, scattershot emergence of unconnected local railway lines. Nevertheless, each railroad in the country faced the same set of challenges. When they saw a way to make money, they tended to raise their voices in unison; therefore, when they spoke up they functioned as a most effective lobby—for themselves and, too, for the manufacturing concerns that they depended on and serviced.

Consider the 1854 Kansas-Nebraska Act, which nullified the Missouri Compromise regarding the prohibition of slavery in the Louisiana Territory north of the 36th parallel and turned Kansas into a war zone well in advance of the Civil War proper. The principal reason that Act passed was that Douglas needed to appease railroad lobbyists who needed southern consent for the northern location of the proposed transcontinental railway route.

Even better, consider the Republican platform Lincoln stood on while running for the Presidency in 1860. During the spring of 1861, Ohio Senator John Sherman (brother to General Wm. Tecumseh Sherman) characterized the platform as follows:

> Those who elected Mr. Lincoln expect him to . . . secure to free labor its just right to the Territories of the United States; to protect . . . by wise revenue laws the labor of our people; to secure the public lands to actual settlers . . . [and] to develop the internal resources of the country by opening new means of communication between the Atlantic and the Pacific.[78]

That meant: extend the factory-friendly system of wage labor, install a high tariff on imported goods needed by the South in order to shield northern manufacturing concerns, pass a Homestead Act to encourage the development of railroad traffic and ensure the sale of land soon to be owned by railroad companies, and subsidize the construction of a transcontinental railway that would pass through northern states. It was an aggressive platform, to say the least, and if times had been normal an elected official might justly look forward to scoring one or two *compromises*, thanks to the bluff of such a lop-sided agenda, let alone a victory. These, however, were not normal times. Thanks to the possibility of southern secession and a consequent lack of "nays," the North stood a chance of actually achieving these objectives, and, needless to say, when that chance came they took it. Welcome to the 37th Congress, which amounted to a kind of field day for Republican legislators.

In the space of just two years, from March 4, 1861, to March 4, 1863, when representatives from southern states were absent, the United States Congress enacted legislation that permanently achieved every single objective listed by John Sherman, along with other, similarly pro-North acts that radical Republican legislators hadn't even dared dream about. The Morrill Tariff, according to which duties on imports increased by 70 percent, became law on the very last day of the Buchanan administration, hours after

Southern senators vacated their seats. This legislation was followed by the 1861 Revenue Act, thanks to which we now have a federal income tax, and then, almost two years later, by the 1863 National Banking Act, thanks to which we now do business with "greenbacks" rather than state-derived currency. (Secretary of the Treasury Salmon P. Chase floated gold-yielding war bonds that could be bought with greenbacks.) The real watershed year, though, was 1862—the year in which Congress passed, in quick succession, the Homestead Act (May 20), the Pacific Railway Act (July 1), and the Morrill Colleges Land Grant Act (July 2).

Note the apparent sequence. American farmers look west, then government facilitates their emigration by granting pioneers the right to stake a claim (as per Jefferson's quarter-section logic), get products to market via rail, and educate their offspring via a system of federally designed, state-rooted colleges. The actual causal sequence, however, reads differently, for corporate attention to profit was the deciding factor here, not farmers' need for land. The Pacific Railway Act authorized the release of truly enormous pools of capital ($16,000 to $48,000 per mile of track laid) to the Union Pacific Railroad company run by Charles Durant and the Central Pacific Railroad company run by Charles Crocker, Mark Hopkins, Hollis Huntington, and Leland Stanford. (I remember these names because streets in Berkeley, which is one town north of the transcontinental railroad's western terminus, are named after them.) The idea was to cover the cost of constructing a railroad that would run all the way from Omaha to California, but given that at least one of the two construction companies hired to do the work was in fact a sketchily defined subsidiary of Union Pacific, accountability was compromised. Railroad company directors were able to both over-estimate costs and manipulate events to ensure timely rises in the worth of Union Pacific stock. Thus "profit" was realized before the railroad even got built. Congress, however, had determined that "construction costs" meant what they appeared to mean, and consequently lawmakers arranged to bestow upon railroad companies millions of additional acres of federal land (6,400 acres per mile of track laid) as a kind of incentive to get trains running. The idea here—and it turned out to be a very good idea from the railroad companies' point of view—was that railroads would be able to cover costs by selling rural acreage to ranchers, as well as lots in towns that would be sure to grow up beside regularly positioned terminals. How, though, could the railroads be sure that significant numbers of people would actually want to live on an arid prairie subject to high winds and sub-zero temperatures? They couldn't, and for this reason a Homestead Act was passed to lure settlers who otherwise might vault prairie and mountain states altogether by committing to fertile valleys in California and Oregon.[79]

Here we all are, learning in grade school about homesteaders welcoming the railroads as signs of advancing civilization, but in fact railroad companies created "homesteaders" just as they created "cowboys" when long-distance herders became necessary thanks to the appearance of rail yards in Oglalla with direct links to slaughterhouses in Chicago.

What about securing endowments for colleges via land grants? Schools descended from the Morrill College Land-Grant Act include the Massachusetts Institute of Technology and the University of California at Berkeley. Surely an act that resulted in the founding of schools like these was a good thing. That the ordinance was magnanimous is certain, for any time a school gets founded, students eventually show up who have the smarts actually to learn something and become schooled, be it in business administration, the fine arts, or sciences. Whether or not the magnanimity is pure, however, is another matter. After all, Southerners had consistently voted against the land-grant act because it favored engineering schools and therefore manufacturing. Given the sorts of things for which Berkeley and MIT are famous today (nuclear research, robotics, computer science), those Southerners' assumptions appear to have been correct. Also, it is possible that the legislators who approved Vermont Senator Justin Morrill's land-grant idea needed a cover for awarding, just one day before, enormous sums of money to a project in which many northern congressmen had a financial interest. It wasn't just that many of these men were attorneys who had served as counsel for railroad companies and got paid in shares of the companies they represented. It was that, as lawmakers, these men had gained a kind of insider's knowledge about where and how a railroad might succeed, placed distinct bets, and then (naturally) used their role as public servants to influence events so that those bets proved successful. How could they not? Even Lincoln rode in private railcars for free.

In short, there were other things going on between 1861 and 1865 besides a war prosecuted by bayonets, cannonballs, and gunboats. More to the point, it is now clear that the war against the South was at the very least entangled in, and sometimes even indistinguishable from, attempts to "grow" an industrial economy. Thus it is possible that the Charles-and-Mary-Beard thesis, so called, is in its own limited way correct. Yet we should also note that such a thesis can never exhaustively explain a puzzle like the Civil War, because economic determinism—as a viewpoint—has limits. Yes, it can handily detect and perhaps even define acquisitiveness. When it comes to actions based on sacrificial ideals or fear or culturally informed biases, however, the viewpoint (due to intentional blindness) has relatively little explanatory power. Therefore the Charles-and-Mary-Beard thesis would in an ideal world serve chiefly as a supplementary explanation that fills out and provides texture for different, perhaps equally persuasive, but ultimately more encompassing explanations.

This brings us to the fourth angle that can be employed to understand the Civil War, and that is the degree to which Northerners were bent on centralizing power and altering the constitutionally embedded balance between state and federal governments. Odd though it may seem to us now, prior to 1860 the United States of America was a federated polity. This does not mean that our country had a strong "federal" government. On the contrary, it means that we were a federation of small states that had made a compact to achieve common ends. Northerners thought this way every bit as much as Southerners did. When Jefferson and Madison floated their Kentucky and Virginia Resolutions in order to remind citizens and lawmakers not only that powers not expressly delegated to the national government were reserved to the states, but, as well—this was a stretch—that states could judge, for themselves, the constitutionality of national government decrees, Massachusetts and New Hampshire strongly *seconded* the founders' motions. Clearly, it wasn't just Southerners who were "strict constructionists" (and therefore inclined to uphold inconvenient constitutional language regarding state power) in the early years of the republic. Nor was it just Southerners who believed that southern states had a right to *secede*.

Though they were sickened by the prospect of secession, almost all lawmakers (radical Republicans like future Supreme Court Chief Justice Salmon P. Chase included) conceded that there was no constitutional leverage available that could prevent southern states from withdrawing from the original "compact."[80] Upon ratifying the Constitution, the several states had reserved the right to withdraw should they ever decide that membership was not in their best interests, and that was that. Arguing otherwise, in the first half of the 19th century, required that the speaker publicly commit to a diminution of state power that was literally unthinkable—indeed, such a scenario loomed as a betrayal of the very ideals that the Continental Army had fought for between 1775 and 1783. Thus when the Confederate army defended Southerners' rights to secede, it was in some sense fighting for an understanding of American polity that Northerners and Southerners had *both* subscribed to, prior to the onset of the Civil War.

What caused Northerners to reconfigure their understanding of this polity?

I think it was because Northerners' fears changed. During the War for Independence and the drafting of the Constitution the principal concern had been a tyrannical state, be it King George's kind, with its power to tax subjects arbitrarily and quarter Redcoats in people's homes, or the American kind, centered first in New York and then in Washington. Hence the relentless attention to checking and balancing centralized power. Sometime around 1848, though, a new kind of fear surfaced—and perhaps in direct proportion to the rise of "free" labor and an industrial economy. Though many still feared a tyrannical state, large numbers of Northerners began at this time to worry more about patently unjust aspects to privilege and its corollary, forced labor. Hence the growing interest in abolishing "inequality." That creating and then relying on centralized power to achieve this goal might in the end compromise hard-won, community-based freedoms that enabled the perception of injustice in the first place did not appear to bother pro-centralization Northerners much. Instead, these people turned a blind eye to such ironies, and as the sheer inconvenience of decentralized power became more and more apparent through the Southern tendency to block Northern initiatives, this group of Northerners slowly became a majority. Thus it came to pass that the North, through the election of Lincoln, parted ways both with Bostonian John Adams and Virginian John Randolph. The North put its trust in universal suffrage as a protection for the common man (rather than in simply dividing what the founders considered to be inevitably privileged powers) and disregarded the constitutional provisions for an even division of power between state and federal governments. How and in what way did the North disregard those provisions? By literally destroying any and all states that were in favor of the old power arrangement and then remodeling the Constitution via "reconstruction" amendments so that the document would conform to the new power arrangement.

The key step, in this last maneuver, was the adoption of the Fourteenth Amendment on July 9, 1868. Section One of that amendment, as scripted by Congressman John Bingham of Cadiz, Ohio (more on this later) reads as follows: "No state shall make or enforce any law which shall abridge the privileges or immunities of citizens of the United States; nor shall any state deprive any person of life, liberty, or property without due process of law; nor deny to any person within its jurisdiction the equal protection of its laws." On the surface the intent of this law was simply to follow through on the abolition of slavery formalized by the Thirteenth Amendment. Just as the Fifteenth Amendment ensured that freed slaves would be allowed to vote, so too the Fourteenth Amendment ensured that freed slaves would not lose citizenship privileges in the face of still racist state legislatures. But Bingham's "section one" also accomplished other things.

I have already hinted, in chapter 1, that wording in the Fourteenth Amendment's Section One empowered corporations as well as former slaves, and, as promised, I plan on returning to this subject at much greater length in chapter 7. Here, though, I want to point out a different benefit to the Fourteenth Amendment, which is that it empowered railroad companies as well as citizens at the expense of the very same governments that were best qualified to police and if necessary curb railroad companies. Prior to the Civil War, states had real power. Though federal power had increased in direct proportion to the interstate commerce and the war it was authorized to oversee, by and large states still commanded powers not expressly reserved to the federal government. Furthermore, it was believed that national government existed solely in order to strengthen states in their efforts to govern their own affairs. By ratifying the Fourteenth Amendment, however, we agreed to start thinking of "privileges and immunities," "due process," and "equal protection" as at risk primarily owing to incursions by state governments, and that it therefore made sense for the *United* States (i.e. the national government based in Washington) to assume control of crucially important zones formerly under the exclusive control of states and the counties constituting them—local business initiatives, land use, hiring practices, schooling, and individual mores. Federated logic was, as Laurence Tribe states in his classic, universally recognized summary of constitutional law, *over*. Politically, the country had been founded anew.[81]

Indeed, despite Lincoln's talk of "mystic chords of memory," it is possible to argue that virtually every aspect of our country was re-founded between 1861 and 1869.[82] According to Mark Noll, the Civil War wasn't only a trial that tempered us as a nation and confirmed our identity as a people. Additionally, it was a social and political revolution that overthrew a constitutional republic and gave birth to a centralized democratic polity in which the principal actors are an atomized populace and a potentially Leviathan state. Accordingly, our exposure to tyrannical power increased, and even more importantly—this is the truly revolutionary part—we grew comfortable in the face of that fact. During the Civil War years we discovered that we *liked* the idea of conceiving programs for improving our lot and then instituting them from the top down, so as to minimize idiosyncrasies and disable prejudice. Yes, intermediary institutions that had formerly helped us to withstand corrupt overlords might have to go, but given that corruption itself could be eradicated—think, here, Emancipation Proclamation—the time would soon be upon us when we wouldn't even need such institutions. Liberty, it turns out, can be *implemented*.

Well, we are accustomed to such thoughts, now. We are the inheritors of nearly 150 years of activist government. Therefore, these sorts of thoughts no longer startle us. But in 1865 they were new, and people marveled at them. And when they marveled, they felt a rising pride in what was clearly a brand new nation. After all, they had a new Capitol building, freshly enlarged after a flurry of construction undertaken immediately before, and during, the war. (The dome was completed a couple weeks after the

Gettysburg Address.) They also had new cemeteries in which to bury their dead. (Cadiz, like many another northern town, abandoned its constitutional-era cemetery in 1861.) They even had a new sacramental meal called Thanksgiving (instituted by Lincoln himself in 1863) that pointed forward to an ultimate wedding feast at the same time that it reminded everyone of their new identity as Americans rather than Virginians or Vermonters. O, glory. Hallelujah! Clearly the Lord himself had come in 1861 for *the vineyards where grapes of wrath are stored* (the tune, here, is directly descended from camp meetings[83]) were on all sides being *trampled*.

Once again: there was a little bit more going on in the Civil War than you might at first suppose.

The other arguments about racist aspects to the North, secession, and industrialism make this clear all on their own, of course, but this last argument regarding centralization is the strongest, and if you position the first three theses so that they supplement the argument about the destruction of the federated aspect to the original American polity, you wind up with a key that unlocks many, if not most, Civil War puzzles. Nevertheless, even this argument has its limits, and given the nature of those limits it should be advanced only with extreme caution. Consider, first of all, that anyone who upholds the constitutional republic as a viable alternative to the democratic polity we currently live in runs the risk of whitewashing and to some extent legitimizing the crime of chattel slavery. One has to be agile to avoid that particular pratfall, and, indeed, I am not sure that it can or should be done, given that the Constitution as originally configured implicitly condoned slavery. Secondly—and this is an even less easily corrected problem—one runs the risk of overlooking those aspects to the constitutional republic which foreshadow and to some extent pave the way for the admittedly very different centralized democratic polity that was to come. It is natural to assume that, because democracy in America was to a large degree instituted via Lincoln's seizure of dictatorial powers and the invasion of the South by Union armies, it is cut from a cloth that is entirely different from constitutional republicanism. This, however, may not be the case. It is entirely possible that these two forms of government are different only in the way that the British emphasis on classical liberty is different from the French emphasis on liberté. They could in essence be *flip sides* of a modern societal model called liberalism that arose in the vacuum created by the collapse of a medieval societal model. Therefore, it might be a mistake to assume that the version founded on limited government and property would be immune to the troubles besetting the democratic one.

What, then, to do? Is there another theory?

As it happens, there is. It's the one that comes into view when you start to think about why Custer was driven to destroy Native American cultures as well as the "feudal" South.

Look at the list of "losers" in the Civil War proper. In addition to plantation owners, they include small, subsistence-based Appalachian "Butternut" farmers from places like North Carolina and Tennessee who owned *no slaves*. These latter individuals comprised 75 percent of the Confederate fighting force, therefore 75 percent of the total number of Southerners killed.[84] Other losers included Cherokees, northern Irish Catholics, Vallandigham's Copperhead "peace democrats," and, of course, pretty much all of the Appalachian-based northern farmers who thought of themselves as Butternuts.

You would think that the Cherokee nation would have sided with the Union. After all, memories of Jackson's efforts to "remove" them were still fresh. Yet regional loyalty evidently mattered more to Cherokees, for they hitched their fortunes—with memorable clarity—to those of the Confederacy.[85] ("The war now raging," their Oct. 28, 1861 declaration reads, "is a war of northern cupidity and fanaticism against . . . the commercial freedom of the south, and . . . the political freedom of the states, and its objects are to annihilate the sovereignty of those states and utterly change the nature of general government.") Irish Catholics, for their part, became prominent as a traitorous anti-Union force when they rioted in Boston and New York rather than submit to a military draft. Ten years earlier they had defected from the United States Army when it presumed to invade Mexico in 1848 and lay waste the Catholic culture flourishing there. (The deserters were known as "Los Colorados," owing to red hair, and they wound up forming an entire "San Patricio" battalion that became feared by Winfred Scott's troops owing to a precise, quite lethal, use of artillery.) Now Irish Catholics were inclined to take a similarly contrarian position, and, as in Mexico City, their opposition was extinguished via the use of force. As for Butternuts, they were less inclined toward violence and therefore (except in the case of Ohio Congressman Vallandigham) less feared as a counterforce. Nevertheless—and here I am reiterating a point made earlier while talking about Morgan's Raiders—this does not mean that localist Butternut farmers with artisanal biases and southeast Ohio "mountain" roots did not exist. Rather, it just means that those farmers had experienced, first hand, the searing aspect to the heat that gets generated when air already warmed by patriotism blows across the white-hot coals of abolitionism and post-revival Methodist righteousness. Take the quiet, if you will, as an index of the Union army's quickly accelerating strength. By 1863, Butternuts were obliterated in spirit if not in fact. Thus, they count every bit as much in the "losers" column as do other defeated cultural groups.

Northern Butternuts, southern Appalachian counterparts, Cherokees, Irish Catholics, Lakota Sioux—needless to say these groups have a thing or two in common. They are, all of them, overtly tradition-based (custom-oriented) cultures. For this reason it can fairly be said that the Union Army waged a war against our strongest carriers of participatory, site-specific knowledge. But can it really be argued that the entire Civil War was about destroying that kind of knowledge? Here three other clues suddenly become relevant. First, the South really did manifest vestigial traces of medieval lore. Section-and-range technology was not a factor there, and the South's vaunted emphasis on chivalry wasn't entirely false. Thanks to a retrograde royalist bias, the South to at least some degree authentically signed an era when traditionalist culture reached a high-water mark and supported a life of reason in addition to myth. Which is to say, it signed a culture that stood as a rebuke to anyone who assented to the claim that rationality and custom are at odds. Second, democracy is opposed to tradition *by definition*, for it necessitates the replacement of custom (prejudice) with education (the propagation of universally accessible "truths"). Third—and this is a clue just begging to be noticed—medieval architecture became the rage in northern cities directly after the war (thanks to trend-setting architect Henry Hobson Richardson's courthouses, libraries, and churches) in much the same way that the idea of wild Mohicans became popular in upstate New York (thanks to James Fenimore Cooper's novels) after that tribe was forcibly removed from lands drained by the Mohawk River. Coincidence? Maybe. On the other hand, it could very well be that these dots form a picture very like the one Robert Nisbet came up with, out in Berkeley, when he pondered (in 1952!) the modern "turn" from medieval forms of social cohesion to bread-and-circus forms driven by a modern state.[86] Should we try to connect these new dots?

Given the nature of our current inquiry and the stake we have in completing it, I propose that we take advantage (after dinner) of the coming dark. The river and its banks will soon be invisible. Consequently, we will have nothing to lose if we cast ahead in our mind's eye to Pittsburgh, where we can get Henry Hobson Richardson's grandest achievement clearly in view. That way, we stand a chance of at least glimpsing a dimension of tradition-based culture that might be commensurate with the Union army's seeming mission to destroy it. We could corroborate this fifth and possibly conclusive explanation for why the Civil War was fought. But—I have to warn you. The project involves heights. Henry Adams, who was the first to undertake it, reported that when he tried to get the Middle Ages in perspective, relative to the Modern Age, it was like crawling out onto the ridge of a building that had two very steeply pitched roofs.⁸⁷ Moreover, he discovered that he was high—very high—above the ground. Dare we follow? I don't think we have any choice. If Sitting Bull were here, he would say *you bet!*⁸⁸

Therefore, we go.

5

Allegheny Courthouse

Etta James, the Ocie Clark's cook, has either worked on the river or been around river people her entire life. On months off, she lives in Paducah. Her son is a steersman, her father a captain. She doesn't offer any information about the father of her son. Instead she talks about her "boys," which is to say the men she cooks for. She takes pride in being a person they can confide in, and her Christmas card list is long. When she's working she's either in the pantry doing inventory, or in the dining area building menus, or in the galley proper preparing food, and when she's off (bright yellow rubber gloves fixed to clothesline above kitchen sink) she's usually sleeping. The hardest part, she says, is planning. Ingram Barge has credit at A&A Boat Store in Paducah and at Jack's Market, near Ironton, but sometimes a boat keeps getting turned. Therefore, Etta has to stock up at those ports of call so she can cook for nine people "ten days at a time." If she runs low on coffee, sugar, or charcoal she can usually trade for them when the boat she's on passes through a lock, but all other items—Jello, spam, lettuce, oatmeal, tuna, tomatoes, pie filling, sauerkraut, yams & onions & potatoes, mustard greens, beets, asparagus spears, hominy, white "shoe-peg" corn, black-eyed peas, Minute rice, Uncle Ben's long grain wild rice, cabbages, pasta, Parkway butter, pork chops, bacon, steaks, chicken fryers, sausages, flour, turnip greens, collards, Canola cooking spray & meat tenderizer, eggs, garlic, orange juice, salad dressing, cheese, apples—all that pretty much has to be on board. And, by the same token, pantry shelves need to be depleted by the time the Ocie Clark returns to base, so as to avoid spoilage. She says she wins 99% of the time, and she attributes this success to sweet potatoes. She says that though most cooks tend to "build around" pork chop, meat loaf, cutlets, round steaks, wings, or spaghetti, she likes to build "to" and "from" sweet potatoes.

Food, however, does not alone a meal make. For that to happen you need people, and on the Ocie Clark people appear via watch changes. Right now seats at the dining table are filling up as the front watch (captain, first mate, deckhand) arrives, rested, to eat just a little ahead of the backwatch (pilot, second mate, deckhand). As if on cue, Dave (second mate) and Frank Workman (deckhand) now come in from the cold to hang up gear, stow walkie-talkies on chargers, and head off to showers, where they will wash off coal and change for a dinner that will in all likelihood get underway about the same time the first mate and his man start thinking about dessert. Then Dennis (engineer) arrives. Given that an engineer's day resembles a 9-to-5 job, Dennis can let his dinnertime overlap two watches instead of one, and much to my advantage (I haven't yet heard how Dennis' cattle survive when he's on the river) Dennis does just that. John Kirvin, the pilot, isn't here yet, because he can't leave his post until Captain Jack climbs the ladder to relieve him. Six hours from now, though, the roles of these two men will be reversed, and therefore the captain wastes no time in pouring himself a cup of coffee and heading aloft to liberate John, who appears minutes later (after debriefing Jack on ship speed plus condition as per Coast Guard regulation). All told, such traffic to and fro makes for a lively gathering, and seeing as how there is also savory food present, the Ocie Clark is transformed at such intervals into a place of warmth and cheer. It's not quite on the same level as the Tabard Inn in Southwerk, where Chaucer (sometime in the 1300s) rested up before embarking on his exploration of the Middle Ages. After all, the Ocie Clark serves (to my acute disappointment) cherry, orange, and grape Kool-Aid instead of ale. Also, towboats no longer hire roustabouts right off the locks. Thus there are probably fewer thieves on board than you'd find at the Tabard. Nevertheless, there is an inn-like ambiance, and on this particular evening that hostel aspect is strong.

It's a heated, well-lit place, for one thing. Owing to the storm raging outside, warmth and incandescent light now signify just one thing—shelter. Also, we are all wayfarers. I am a transient, and the crew—they are all from, as Captain Jack puts it, "well south." (Mobile, Alabama. Muscle Shoals. Campbellville, Kentucky. South Carolina. Lake Pontchartrain.) We are far from home, this "compaignye," and though we are not headed toward a shrine like Canterbury ("the hooly blisful martir for to seke"), we are headed toward a place of proportionately equivalent darkness that most of us would prefer to avoid. (Try as I do to build Pittsburgh and environs up, this crew is unanimous in its disapproval of the region.) Laughter comes easily and stories—especially ones about this reporter's admittedly comical run-in with freshly applied engine-grade, high-heat enamel paint—abound. But the chief reason the inn-aspect is strong tonight is the supper piled high on everyone's plate. Truly, it's as though we were on the Ohio during glory years. I guess we're missing watermelon rind preserves, springhouse butter, and the smell of corn husks burning on a bed of coals, but on all other counts—chicken rolled in flour and browned in sizzling grease, mustard greens, corn, homemade cole slaw, potatoes and gravy, hush puppies, lemon meringue pie—we're good. Can one possibly dine on anything more satisfactory? I go back for seconds, even thirds, but then I draw a line and stop while I'm ahead. "Good luck with your loo-cue-bray-shuns," my newfound friends tease, for they know about the poems, speeches and histories I smuggled aboard, and upon hearing the barb I roll my eyes and shake my head to indicate approval of the decision to shoot the little dart. Bookish habits require skewering. Halfway down the hall to my room, though, I realize that this particular barb stings twice, for "lucubrare" doesn't just mean self-important disputation. It also means working at night by the light of a book—a worthy ideal that none of us Moderns are equipped to achieve. Rolling eyes now for the second time, I turn the latch to bunkroom "C," place teacup and saucer on a gently vibrating desk, and dig in my briefcase for pencil and paper. Then I see that the desk comes with a small, supplementary lamp. Should I or shouldn't I? In the end I decide imitation has its benefits, and press the button marked "on."

At the end of chapter 4 we noted that Custer and other mid-nineteenth-century Ohioan generals appear to have been prosecuting a war against tradition-based culture in general, rather than simply a war against the Confederacy, and that fact, in turn, led us to ask whether the war against the Confederacy might itself be explained as a war against tradition-based culture, given that the ante-bellum South did function, in legitimate ways, as our most committed regional guardian of America's portion of the medieval inheritance. In this chapter I propose to answer definitively that question by showing (a) that the North was held in thrall by our medieval inheritance every bit as much as the South was, and (b) that the North and the South worked together during the Civil War years to turn that medieval inheritance into a curiosity rather than a threat.

Let's begin by admitting that we Americans have a strange relationship with the Middle Ages. On the one hand we refer to the age in a pejorative sense, as when we dismiss something for being so backward, violent, or blunt that it is positively "medieval." If a mind appears isolated and in that sense undeveloped we call it "cloistered," and if an arrangement appears callous, poorly designed, or cruel we call it "feudal." After all, the "Middle" ages were "dark," yes? They featured torture racks, superstition, disease. If they had any merit it was simply to set off and call attention to the light-filled eras of classical antiquity and modern science that came before and after. Indeed, these sorts of dismissals are so vehement and widespread that an impartial observer finds himself looking with interest at the person doing the dismissing: what is the allegedly enlightened Modern trying to protect? At the same time, however, we exalt the Middle Ages. John D. Rockefeller, for example, went to extraordinary lengths to disassemble thematically related pieces of five different medieval monasteries, ship them across the Atlantic, and then reassemble them (during the 1930s) on a knoll in northern Manhattan. Today that installation (owned by the Met and known as "The Cloisters") not only displays a vast collection of medieval tapestries, stained glass, metalwork, illuminated manuscripts, statuary, and diptych-based enamels. It also (via herb gardens, porticoes, tile roofs, a bell tower, and thick stone walls) enables full ambulatory *entrance* into the very real wealth of culturally mature 12th century France. (Abbeys re-presented at The Cloisters include St. Guilhem le Desert, Trie en Bigorre, and St. Michel de Cuxa.) But the easiest way to see the American tendency to idealize the medieval era is to note the pre-Raphaelite aesthetic biases of a person like me, or simply tour public buildings built in Boston, New York, Pennsylvania, and Ohio during the late 1800s. Look at courthouses, libraries, museums, railroad stations, churches, and municipal buildings built during that era, and then take note of the stone, narrow windows, arches, and multifaceted roof systems on view there. Overall, these buildings look like variations on the 10th century Benedictine abbey of Cluny, in Burgundy. And that is precisely what they are. The architect who created the look—Henry Hobson Richardson—set out very deliberately to *recreate* the Romanesque architecture he had admired while touring eastern and southern France between 1861 and 1865.

Richardson's interest in towers and embedded turrets was apparent from the very start. The Buffalo State Asylum for the Insane, completed in 1870, looks a little more like Count Dracula's keep than an abbey, but the bell tower effect is real, and as commissions started to pour in, Richardson turned more and more toward frankly Romanesque features that he had studied in his youth. Semi-circular arches started to appear on a more regular basis, stone mass and texture became more prominent, and towers began more and more to figure as an offset to wide bases and squat columns. All these themes are apparent in the church he designed (1872) for the Episcopal diocese of Boston, on Copley Square (Trinity Church), but it was only upon completing a set of libraries (1877, the year after Custer's death and the very same year the Industrial Revolution took off), that Richardson finally had the moves necessary to create (out of local materials) a medieval abbey almost at will. (See the Ames Library, in North Easton.) This was the point at which Richardson started turning out masterpiece after masterpiece, thereby ensuring imitators for years to come and, too, the full-scale arrival of an architectural style that came to be known as "Richardsonian Romanesque." Yet in order to really "get" Richardson's vision one first has to see the Allegheny County Courthouse and Jail that he designed for Pittsburgh in 1883, for that complex represents his vision at its most mature.

When I first drove by the site, ignorant of what I was about to see, my ability to drive a car got so compromised that I had to pull off the road. I was headed south on Ross Street toward the Monongahela River, thinking about the extroverted, confirmedly ugly "Cor-ten" (allegedly maintenance-free) skeletal steel frame on the 840-foot tall, 1970s-era U.S. Steel Building I had just passed, when I realized I was about to drive under a fortified stone bridge that led to a compound with turrets and conical roofs and windows narrow enough to favor archers who might, even now, be posted inside. Additionally (looking southwest now) I saw an eight-story Benedictine bell tower at the far end of a heavy, somehow welcoming stone building with French Renaissance roofs and bands of windows that became progressively deeper as columns and arches framing them became, with each new gain in elevation, more numerous and pronounced. Okay, okay—put the car in park. Upon climbing out of the automobile to study the buildings, I learned that windows were narrow on the compound side, owing to a need to keep prisoners *in* rather than arrows *out*. Was there anything else to know? Go and see, said a guard at the entrance. Passing through what used to be a basement door (prior to the lowering of Forbes Avenue), I rounded a corner and discovered—gasp—a genuinely grand staircase concocted out of nothing but gravity-defying arches, light, and stone. Moreover the staircase led to a completely enclosed courtyard, as per the Santa Scholastica monastery in the hill town of Subiaco above Tivoli in central Italy. Yet, stunning as these features were, I found myself returning again and again to the turreted guard tower, arches, varying roof slopes, and rough stone at the southeast corner of Ross and 5th Avenue. Why was this relatively modest view so arresting? Could the answer be that because Richardson was at this point laying out the corner of a prison, he discovered here an artistic freedom (long sought) to cut back on windows, incorporate more stone, and actually reproduce the early, decidedly not showy, defensively oriented Romanesque architecture he had seen while touring Europe?

It seems probable, much less possible. Standing at the corner of Ross and 5th Avenue, you see building lines that are practically identical to the ones on view at the 10th century abbey of St. Michael in Saxony or—even better—at the eleventh century Burgundian abbey of St. Philibert, in Tournos. It's as though you had entered a time warp.

Which is my point.

There is something weird about the decision to recreate a very different culture's achievements. Indeed, it is no less weird to do that than to dismiss the medieval era as a time of relative darkness. Just as you begin to wonder about the motives of people who act as though the civilized aspect to the Middle Ages did not exist, so too you begin to wonder about the motives of people who so idealize medieval architecture that they seek to reproduce it. Is there anything going on here besides artistic achievement? Might the re-presentation have something to do with a need to create a facsimile of a reality that someone was either destroying or proposing to destroy? To what extent is Richardson's Allegheny Courthouse an equivalent to, say, Henry Ford's Deerfield Village, which recreated the small-town life that automobiles had begun to undercut? So far as I can tell, these two projects have more than a little in common, and when you consider that the Middle Ages stand to a certain extent as a rebuke to the Modern Era in the same way that the integrated aspect to small town America stands as a rebuke to automobile-dependent suburbia, the plot only thickens. Might Richardson's sort of prosthesis have been necessary to de-fang and render harmless a civilizational model that was at least as advanced, and possibly superior to, the one Richardson was born and raised in?

Feudalism began, like America, with acts of flight from hostile environments. After the abandonment of military posts along the Rhine in 406 and the consequent sack of Rome by northern Germanic tribes (Visigoths) in 410 and then again in 455 (Vandals), the western half of the Roman Empire fell apart, and as its major cities became uninhabitable, wealthy citizens began to hire bodyguards, retreat to backcountry villas that didn't show up on maps used by invading armies, and build reliable agricultural connections. At the same time, Benedict of Norcia used inherited wealth to migrate 40 miles east of Rome and set up shop as a hermit above the Aniene River in mountainous terrain near Subiaco. Solitary life suited Benedict, and soon the contemplative found himself attracting so many disciples that he no longer had access to the quiet he had retreated to the mountains to find. What to do? Rather than flee deeper into the hills, Benedict adopted a different strategy. When the number of disciples reached a kind of critical mass at twelve, Benedict organized everybody into a monastery dedicated to the preservation (via manual labor as well as prayer) of the very same interior silence he would otherwise lose, and when the next batch of disciples reached critical mass Benedict simply moved to a different ridge and started another monastery. Soon he knew what worked and what didn't, and by 529, the year he founded the monastery of Monte Cassino eighty miles southeast of Rome, Benedict had drafted a blueprint or "rule" that could be used by any number of former Roman citizens in any number of situations for the construction of deliberately *literate* agrarian communities, as well as more defensively oriented, villa-based ones. And they were used. Benedictine monasteries proliferated in Italy as quickly as strongholds with agricultural dependents, and soon both societal arrangements spread to Gaul.

Indeed, the decentralized pattern became so established that the rise of Carolingian power (secured by the ability of Frankish kings to hold back an Islamic wave) wound up *serving* that arrangement rather than weakening it. Knights who served in Charlemagne's forces were paid in land grants called "fiefs," and when the Carolingian empire devolved at the beginning of the ninth century, the mutual obligations linking peasant to lord ("breadward") or abbey were further strengthened by a new need to withstand invasions from the north (Norsemen) and the east (Maygars). Hence when peace finally arrived (courtesy of a succession of new German kings who ruled alongside the Church), it was practically guaranteed that development, should it occur, would come from the ground up. Geographically inflected nodes for cultural and economic exchange were *already in place*, and thanks to a remarkably consistent tradition of self-sufficiency (each manor or abbey grew its own food and featured stables, kitchen, refectory, outhouses, bakery, laundry, chapel, and lodgings), the nodes were of equal size and importance.

The world that we think of today as "medieval" came into existence primarily via fairs.[89] By the early eleventh century most of the villa-based "villages" that were linked to manors and abbeys had become small towns, and every town had its fair. The biggest ones—Reims, Lubeck, Troyes, Geneva, London, Paris, Cologne, Bar-Sur-Aube, Leipzeig—were on rivers deep enough for barge traffic. They played for weeks at a time, these fairs, and thanks to the fact that feast days for town patron saints occurred at different points in the liturgical year, the fairs tended to be staggered, thus making possible tours by merchants as well as entertainers. Trade exploded. But there were also two other reasons the medieval world flowered, and those were the arrival of the Cistercian order in 1098, near Citeaux, and the appearance of a middle class.

Like the original monks at Cluny, several days' journey to the south, Cistercians were Benedictines intent on recovering the spirituality that had fed their founder. In the case of Cistercians, this meant rooting out comforts that had become entwined with manorial roles and building a life around manual labor in addition to chant. Hence when Robert of Molesme looked for land on which to found a new monastery, he zeroed in on swampy areas that had not yet been cultivated under feudal rules, and when St. Bernard of Clairvaux sited a daughter house, he chose a completely wild, heavily wooded area somewhat ironically known as "Clara Vallis." Thanks in large part to the force of Bernard's example, this pattern became customary, and as a result practically all of Europe tilted toward agriculture. Working with lay brothers who joined the monasteries in return for shelter and food, Cistercians claimed lowlands, established orchards and vineyards, identified watersheds, instituted silvicultural practices designed to protect key woodland belts, ran de-facto seed banks, and, in general, increased the capital of arable land. Which is to say, they "managed"—for fertility. Additionally, they introduced technological innovations like water mills, three-crop rotations, and fish hatcheries. Last but not least they provided land-secured financing for both "public works" like suspension bridges and for riskier trade gambles undertaken by com-panies (bread-sharers) who were intent on, say, opening a trade route to Russia. (Russians stood ready to export fur.)

Where, though, did the liquid capital come from? Henri Pirenne argues that it came from burghers (or "freemen") who had begun to number riggers and craftsmen as well as merchants, thereby forming a "middle class" that to us is all but unrecognizable, owing to the installation of municipal laws that positively protected the common good. Result? Civilization, sometimes known as the High Middle Ages.

The twelfth and thirteenth centuries certainly featured violence. Disputes were often officially settled via physical combat, and on those occasions when a court presumed to decide a question of guilt, punishment frequently involved physical mutilation. Also, there was widespread illiteracy between 1150 and 1300. In most towns the only people who could read and write were clerics. (Hence the name, "clerk"; if you needed to record a deed, you had to find a priest.) Yet the overall percentage of people subjected to physical violence was comparatively low relative to other ages, and though most people couldn't read or write, during the High Middle Ages, they were literate in the most important senses. They knew, for example, that the natural world was a book consisting of symbols that pointed to—and participated in—another more just and less broken one. They read seasons and discerned therein the mystery of permanence joined to change. They understood that they were part and parcel of a creation, and that their job—if you can call it that—was to praise their maker as well as creeks, trees, and wolves did. Ptolomaic cosmology, while technically incorrect, has its advantages! How, though, can we be sure that the average peasant was literate in this way? By looking at the artistic, scholarly, and logistical achievements of persons who were formally schooled and thus able to articulate the vision afforded to everyone at that time and place.

My point is that the High Middle Ages was a learned era. Logic bloomed, and cathedral schools dating from Carolingian times (think Notre Dame in Paris) suddenly became universities. Oxford appeared in 1096, and then Cambridge in 1209. If you had academic leanings during the second half of the thirteenth century, you could choose between lectures by Roger Bacon (the British empiricist who favored Aristotle's kind of inductive logic), fellow Franciscan St. Bonaventure (who leaned toward the more vertically oriented St. Augustine), or the Dominican scholar St. Thomas Aquinas (who was busy trying to synthesize the two points of view). Alternatively, you could take a short cut and walk into any of the impossibly tall, colorfully lit Gothic cathedrals that had recently sprung up (pun intended) at Salisbury, Reims, Mont St. Michel, Chartres, and Canterbury. All these buildings were engineering marvels, and when you entered one, it was possible actually to experience the presumed link between heaven and earth.

What, though, was it like to be a serf in such an era? What was the *cost* of all these cathedrals?

Here the answer is somewhat different from the one we are trained to expect, for contrary to most persons' assumptions, serfs were not slaves. Yes, serfs were obligated by custom-driven feudal law to farm whatever estate they were born on. And, understandingly, this rankles modern nerves. (Like mine.) But serfs weren't *owned*. Though serfs were obligated to provide labor, military service, and 1/10th of their surplus livestock and produce to the master of an estate, ultimately they were working on an equal basis with that seigneur or lord because he was bound by similar obligations (providing food and shelter in times of stress, leading defensive maneuvers, safeguarding fertility) and so was no less tied to the land than they were. Each party, in other words, was compelled by the custom of "fealty" to work for *the good of the estate*. They became rich or poor in direct proportion to the fluctuating fertility of land they *both* had rights to use, and that meant they both achieved something close to a good life. Serfs typically owned a hut with a fireplace, a set of cooking utensils, some pewter dishware, a table and some chairs, and a feather-filled mattress. They had a barn, a beehive, and a chicken house. They had stakes in the village's arable land, woodlot, and pasture, and on Sundays, after Mass, they drank ale, sang, and watched their kids play a medieval version of football. (Though a leather-cased ball was not outside the realm of possibility, the game was apparently played most often with an inflated pig bladder.) Things could have been a lot worse for an agricultural laborer, and the story turns out to be much the same for other typically exploited classes like women, masons, and woodworkers.

Women were respected as per the chivalric code. This doesn't mean that they were put on a pedestal and revered for virtues most of us never exhibit. Rather, it means that they were (a) looked on as persons with sexual attributes rather than the other way around, and (b) highly skilled. The wives of medieval lords were essentially businesswomen who cut deals, hired seasonal help, and audited quality at the same time that they bore children, wove cloth, salted meat, brewed beer, maintained a garden, and supervised baking. Abbesses ran entire microstates. Women under their care included mystics, professors of literature and theology, and composers.

As for craftsmen, they too had opportunities during the medieval era that were probably unparalleled. Glassblowers, harness-makers, blacksmiths, carpenters, boat builders, masons, cobblers—all of these workers were their own bosses. They had control over what they made, when they made it, and how they made it; therefore, when they sold a product they were essentially selling workmanship. Once again, things could have been worse.

If there was a problem in the High Middle Ages it was the rapid growth of cities, for this growth seriously strained the pre-existing network of equally sized, villa-based nodes. Prior to 1100, towns in Europe typically numbered 3,000 people. By 1200 Ghent, Lille, and Bruges had each swelled to 50,000 souls, and Paris boasted 100,000. London, growing from a population of 18,000 in 1200, climbed to 100,000 by 1300. In one respect the increase in numbers was a good thing, for it financed pointed arches and ribbed vaults just as, earlier, the growth of Benedictine monasteries had financed the development of chant. But in another respect the appearance of cities was problematic, for cities tended to erode the feudal ties that had helped produce the soaring vision on view in Gothic cathedrals. Urban centers like Cologne, Reims, Delft, and Worms were, of course, the base for the entirely new mercantile class, and to the "commune" officials who were charged with allowing entrance to this new mercantile class, freedom meant securing a release from feudal obligations rather than upholding them. Given the growing power of these assemblies (courtesy of trade agreements brokered by city-based guilds), the feudal idea of freedom couldn't help but recede a little. Feudal lords, sensing a potentially lethal threat, lobbied vigorously to deny the independence of communes, but kings, sensing an opportunity to amass power currently held by widely distributed feudal lords, were quick to design and then grant "charters" that enabled cities to function, legally, as the independent municipal zones they already were. Hence clashes between the two parties became violent. In northern Italy, communes like Venice and Milan wound up becoming so powerful that feudal lords essentially became adjuncts, but in France, where feudalism was stronger, cities tended to adorn the medieval fabric even as they threatened to pull it apart.

Now: modernity. That world has just ended, and therefore its full significance is still under debate, but the dates of its beginning and end are fairly clear, and so too are its defining events. In any case, when I say "modernity" I mean the world signed by: (1) the Renaissance (1300-1550), which saw the emergence of a humanist "lay" culture driven by Medici banking, oceanic exploration, Machiavelli's "realpolitik," the discovery of perspective, Gutenberg's printing press, heliocentric cosmology, and paintings by Raphael, Michelangelo, and Botticelli; (2) the Protestant Reformation in 1517; (3) the Scientific Revolution (seventeenth century), which was keyed by the systematic use of controlled experiments, a quickly growing ability (think Kepler, Galileo, Descartes, and Newton) to describe motion mathematically, and (consequently) a dramatic increase in predictive power; (4) the arrival of classical liberalism via John Locke (1689) and then democratic liberalism via the French Revolution (1789); (5) the Industrial Revolution (1776-1876); and, finally, (6) modernity's end, as heralded by the world premiere of Wagner's complete *Der Ring des Nibelungen* (1876),[90] the collapse of Enlightenment-based epistemology, and the programmatic killing of European Jewry (1942-1945). What are the characteristics of *this* era?

As with the medieval world, there are surprises.

The first surprise is that a lot of the things that we typically think of as "medieval" are modern. Take magic. Though Walt Disney taught us to think of magic as the stock-in-trade of wizards who guided the likes of King Arthur in the sixth century, in fact magic was cultivated and (if such a thing be possible) advanced by modern-day scientists like Isaac Newton who, having bought on the Baconian equation of knowledge with power, were increasingly drawn to alchemy and (in Newton's case) a rather secretive, calculating interest in whether or not one was living at the end of time.[91] (Newton ran the British Mint.) Alternatively, take the "Divine Right of Kings."[92] That too is very much a modern concern, for the idea was hatched in order to legitimize a reach for political power that would have been unthinkable during the Middle Ages—namely, the kind of reach that becomes possible when checks like the separation of church and state are *withdrawn*. Contrary to popular belief, the decentralized aspect to medieval power was reinforced by an arduously enforced *division* of authority between the Papacy (in the person of Gregory VII) and the "Holy Roman Emperor" (in the person of Henry IV), and it was only upon *abandoning* this hard-won ideal of institutional pluralism that apologists for new (originally Tudor, then Spanish and French) "absolutist" states subscribed to a frankly monarchic "Divine Right of Kings" conceit.[93] Or take slavery. We often imagine that slavery wasn't eradicated until the Enlightenment came along and forced people to notice the discrepancy between the institution of chattel slavery on the one hand and "natural rights" on the other. In fact, slavery declined during the medieval era owing to that era's deference to the Judaeo-Christian idea that persons are made in the image of God, and then got *reinstated* in direct proportion to the devaluation of that precept and a growing interest in absolute power and the uses to which "mere" nature can be put.[94]

In sum: magic, the installation of a "Divine Right of Kings" concept, and slavery all turn out to be markers for modernity rather than for the Middle Ages. But the chief surprise is still to come. It's that modernity is best defined in contradistinction to medieval achievement.

We have already talked in chapter 4 about how modern political structure tends to self-organize in such a way as to produce centralized states and an atomized citizenry, but there is also something else to notice about this tendency, which is that it is directly opposite to the medieval tendency to produce federated power and a citizenry whose members find identity and purpose through membership in a guild or attachment to an estate. Additionally, we have talked (in chapter 2) about how Moderns tend to see tradition—be it culinary lore or a religious rite or linguistic custom—as a "prejudice" that needs to be overcome or at least set aside, if we are to access universal truths. After making that observation, we noted that people living in the medieval era tended, conversely, to look on tradition ("established usage") as a storehouse of collected and, to use evolutionary parlance, "selected" information that *ensures* access to universal truths. Hence it can already be seen that the Modern era to some extent counters the Medieval one. The surprise is that the two eras appear to be opposed on a lot more than just those two points.

Look, for example, at the two eras' contrasting views of knowledge. Whereas Medieval persons thought of theory as the fruit and very end of all technological science ("theoria" being the contemplative apprehension of teleological causes in addition to material and efficient ones), Moderns see technology as the fruit (technology enhances human power) and theory as the means for achieving that end (to a Modern, "theory" means experiment-based explanation of material and efficient causes). Accordingly, medieval persons exalted receptive, epistemologically "naïve" knowledge that was available to everybody, regardless of his or her station, to the very same degree that we, today, exalt doubt-based knowledge that is discovered and dispensed by experts. Or look at the difference between Medieval and Modern attitudes toward land. To a Medieval person, land was spirited in the same way that a body or a vocal sign is spirited. It was, shall we say, "quickened" with the breath of very life and enabled, thereby, to "mean"—to embody and to some extent reflect that which is good in and of itself. To a Modern, however, the worth of land is measured solely in instrumental terms. The whole point is to use it—be it as a scenic backdrop or as a staging ground for the extraction of timber, grain, and coal. Hence the integrity of ecological wholes was safeguarded during the medieval era to exactly the same degree that it is, now, at risk.

Yet another place where it becomes clear that Medieval and Modern points of view are exactly opposed is in contrasting notions of freedom. For a Modern, freedom is a function of autonomy. We are "free" (alive, functioning at the height of our powers) to the extent that we independently control our actions and maintain a condition of inviolability that can only be changed via our consent. To a Medieval person, though, freedom was a function of embedment in a rightly ordered community, sufferance of whatever was not goodness, truth, or beauty, and obedience to the same Holy Spirit that informed the natural world.

Many students of the medieval era, of course, will not agree that modernity is best defined in contradistinction to the medieval era. Such a student will either continue to argue that the medieval era was so benighted that there is nothing available there to even support comparisons, or that the modern era (sometimes just the Renaissance) is the crowning achievement of the Middle Ages or at least the end point toward which medieval art and society had been ripening. The former argument has of course zero merit and doesn't bear repeating, but the latter argument is potentially strong and should not be quickly dismissed. It is typically advanced by people who are interested in reconciling unregulated free market capitalism with the idea of a Christian America, but believers in human progress are also loath to see a rift between the medieval and modern eras, and so too are distinguished and very sharp "meta-historians" like Christopher Dawson, who at the end of his life was Chauncy Stillman Chair of Roman Catholic Studies at Harvard. I am sympathetic to the idea that the modern world is the end-point of medieval accomplishments, and, indeed, I would rather stand with these sorts of interpreters than with the anti-modernists gathered at the other side of the political allegiance circle—the place where the Far Left rubs shoulders with the Far Right. I have already talked about how Marxists in Berkeley idealized pre-modern times in order to justify the subversion of classical liberalism. Here I need only add that ultra-traditionalist, essentially fascist thinkers like Julius Evola and René Guénon, also idealized the feudal era—in their case by saluting the cultural cohesion, eco-vision, and place-specific biases on view in the early Middle Ages, and then using that idealized picture to justify a repudiation of the entire Modern Age.

Who in their right mind would not be grateful for widespread literacy, uniform sanitation standards, paintings by Cezanne, respect for private property, and an entire new existential zone called "inwardness"? It's fine to note the advanced aspects to medieval civilization. But would you really want to *live* there rather than here? Ale was sweet during the Middle Ages and C.S. Lewis' favorite kind of bitter (hop-laden Californian IPA) was flat-out unavailable! Given sobering facts like these, I have long thought it advisable to disavow connections to Far Right and Far Left positions regarding the transition from the Medieval to the Modern eras, and sometimes even to disavow connections to less reactionary Southern Agrarians and less radical British Distributists. Despite helpful critiques of Progress, on the one hand, and capitalist economies, on the other, it seems to me that the Southern Agrarian and Distributist camps still stand uncomfortably close to ultra-traditionalists and socialists. Consequently, my instinct is to lean all the way North and cast my lot with thinkers like Dawson who argue that Renaissance humanism and liberal democracy constitute the fulfillment of medieval energies.

However, the evidence suggests that Dawson and thinkers descended from him are wrong.

I am not just arguing that Dawson was mistaken in his belief that legally articulated individualism appearing in the early 1300s built up the "complex unity of social organisms" (Dawson's phrase) that was triumphantly on view during the Middle Ages.[95] I am saying, rather, that the transition from the Medieval to the Modern eras was a programmatic 180-degree turn, an about-face, a literal revolution that was heralded by King Edward's expulsion of Jews from England in 1290, activated by William of Occam's deft use of a razor in 1318, and then ratified by thinkers like Bacon and Descartes who systematically set out to turn the medieval world upside down in the early seventeenth century.

Sir Francis Bacon (born 1561 in London) served as England's Lord Chancellor (the same office held earlier by St. Thomas More) before being kicked out of office for taking bribes. Along his merry way this lawyer/scientist wrote several books in which he envisioned (and accurately foresaw) scientific research institutes ("machines for the mind") that were ordered toward technological advancement, and in those books—one thinks, especially, of *The Novum Organon* (1620) and *The New Atlantis* (1627)—Bacon was astonishingly frank about ultimate goals. Comparing nature to a woman, he argued that subjects under white-coated ("neutral") investigation should be teased, subjected to experiment, and physically penetrated in order to get them to "betray" their "secrets." As for the kind of purely receptive, contemplative knowing that is geared to identity and simple thereness—to hell with it. After all, what good does it do? It's "like a virgin consecrated to God" who "produces nothing." According to Bacon, the only objective worth serving is complete domination over the natural world via slow but steady advances in experimentally derived knowledge, and if two thousand years of inherited, "perennial" philosophic insight becomes useless baggage thanks to the installation of this new objective, then that inheritance has to go. But it wasn't until Descartes came along that the drama really intensified, for René Descartes was less frank than Bacon was. Though Descartes moved like Bacon to upend scholastic methods and thereby make possible previously unimaginable gains in human power, Descartes disguised these moves as service to a God he professed to worship, and to that extent he commands attention in ways that Bacon cannot.

The drama proper begins on November 10, 1619 (just one year before Plymouth Rock) when twenty-three-year-old René—alone at the time, and asleep in a snug, stove-heated loft—allegedly dreams about a tree of knowledge.[96] At the beginning of this dream, a nattily dressed man walks into Descartes' room and offers him a choice of two books. One is a dusty dictionary and the other is a rather exotic book of poetry. Hmm. Which should he pick? After deliberating for a few seconds, Descartes chooses the latter, and he is instantly rewarded, for suddenly he has a vision of a new science through which mankind will be able to *know* with a certitude that had been denied to men from previous, merely faith-based ages. Just a few years ago, Descartes' teachers at the Henry-Le-Grand Jesuit College Royal had been lecturing him about how the entire point of philosophy was to apprehend, through name-like concepts, the "mirandum of being," but now Descartes sees in a flash that the true marvel is the nearness of predictive power—assuming of course that one has the courage to turn the medieval tree of knowledge on its head, make quantitative physics rather than theology the crowning discipline, and actually cultivate a "scientia mirabilis." Upon waking, Descartes set about doing just that, and by the time he was done (1650, the year of his death) he had both invented analytical geometry and, via thought experiments thrillingly recounted in *Meditations* (1641), provided a metaphysical basis (or apology) for the entire edifice called "modern science."

What did that basis turn out to be? As Descartes himself quickly and perhaps nervously realized over the course of writing his book, it came down to just three things: distrusting custom ("prejudice") and the evidence of one's senses, abandoning incarnationalism as an organizing concept, and dividing life on the planet into a mental realm (res cogitans) and a physical realm of inert matter that can be measured and manipulated (res extensa). This new science, in other words, was predicated on a point-by-point overthrow of medieval principles. Indeed, the overthrow was so perfectly calibrated, and the leverage gained so extravagantly won, that no less an observer than Bacon would have been impressed. Clearly, it was not just accidental that Descartes decided to conclude his work with a long, if increasingly shrill, argument for the existence of God.

Where did Bacon's *Novum Organon* and Descartes' *Scientia Mirabilis* come from? Descartes may have believed that his new science came to him in a dream, but we for our part would be wise to take hint from his doubt-based science and look for historical influences that might have disposed him to turn medieval science on its head. Thankfully, more than a few people have tried to solve this puzzle over the years, most notably Richard Weaver in *Ideas Have Consequences* (1948),[97] and the consensus (among paleo-conservatives, at least) is that the most important groundwork was completed by William of Occam in the early 1300s, directly after medieval civilization reached its apex.

Occam, who was born sometime between 1290 and 1300 in heavily wooded country near a town called Southwerk that was renowned for an especially even distribution of self-governing, section-sized "hundreds," is famous for many reasons, not least the elegance of the arguments he used to dismantle Plato's theory of forms, but his signal accomplishment was to anticipate and to some extent enable modernity.[98] He enthroned dissent and was wary of external authority. He defined freedom as a "power" that allowed him to "indifferently and contingently produce an effect."[99] He accentuated God's omnipotence in such a way as to cause readers to doubt human participation in God's creative life (thus prefiguring the Protestant Reformation). He limited the concept of causality to sequential action only. He even (thus prefiguring apologists for the enclosure movement) pioneered the substitution of "usus facti," according to which agricultural tenants and members of a religious order had permission to use property belonging to another, for "usus iuris," according to which tenants and members had customary rights to use property belonging to another.[100] What really defined him, though, was his devaluation of the conceptual aspect to words, and his consequent impatience with the mediatory role that words play in the accumulation of knowledge.

Given that there was "no metaphysical reason" for degrees of similarity between individual things, any and all arguments that names indicating similarities stood in, as it were, for metaphysical "forms" were by definition null and void. In fact, if it could be said that words had a role in apprehension, Occam thought, it was chiefly that of an irritant. Owing to the common tendency to mistake signs for referents, words tend to *compromise* knowledge rather than enable it. Therefore, if one's goal is to get to the truth of things, one's first step ought really to be putting words off to the side and apprehending things "immediately"—which is to say, "without any medium between the thing itself and the act by which it is seen or apprehended."[101] Indeed, why shouldn't we jettison needless, so-called contemplative conceptual apparatus altogether? Voilà: the question had been posed. In that very instant the medieval mindset slipped from instinctive reach, and the Middle Ages were gone. From 1319 forward the implicit point of our life on this earth was to transform nature rather than apprehend it, and by the time Descartes and Bacon came along—on the heels of Gutenberg's printing press, Alberti's discovery of perspective (which made artist and viewer large at the same time that it made the world small), and Pico's new humanism—we began to accomplish that deed courtesy of the predictive sciences devised by Bacon and Descartes.

After that commitment another sort of work became necessary, which was to destroy any and all traces of medieval ways of life that had begun to function more and more as a rebuke.

⁂

Out in the hall I hear traffic. Doors opening and closing? The watch has changed. Putting down a pencil, I rub my eyes. Then I stand up and walk over to the bunkroom's porthole. Outside there is only blackness. Cupping hands now so as to shield eyes from the desk lamp's glow, I catch glimpses of phosphorescence in wake formed by the tow, also the shapes of tree-covered hills. Dare I crank the window open? After fumbling with the latch, I finally hear the sound of a weather seal breaking, and subzero air suddenly slices across my wrist and into the room. The sensation is thrilling, but that air seems dangerous. Thank goodness for two large diesel engines and a warm berth. Closing the window, I take a sip of water and return to my post at the desk. I've only got a few minutes before *my* "watch" is over and I still need to get clear about the kinds of conclusions we can draw, given the points established thus far.

⁂

Spending this much time on modernity and how it differs from the medieval era is in one sense ridiculous. Given that our subject right now is the Civil War, why am I telling stories about René Descartes? Sure, these stories are entertaining. But aren't they detours? How can telling them advance our understanding of the Union Army's destruction of the Confederacy?

By way of answering these questions, let us note, first, that America was discovered—"planted," if you will—a mere six years after Pico della Mirandola[102] penned his "Oration on the Dignity of Man" and a full 25 years *before* Martin Luther nailed a copy of his 95 theses to the door of Castle Church in Wittenburg. Hence the minds of the European men who first set foot on American soil were relatively at home with medieval cosmology. Second, the first American colonists arrived 34 years before Descartes performed the thought experiment described in *Meditations* and 82 years before the Glorious Revolution and the publication of John Locke's *Second Treatise on Government*. Hence the first American settlers, while Protestant and to that extent without access to the robustly incarnational logic that was the hallmark of the medieval era, were completely ignorant of the *uses* to which the abandonment of medieval prejudices could be put. And, third, the United States of America was founded 13 years before the French Revolution and the subsequent war in the Vendée, which together completed the European substitution of modern ways for medieval ones. Many if not most Americans had no real issue with the institution of monarchy, per se, during those years! Rather, they fought a war against England because King George had, in their minds, abused his power, and they looked on with horror, most of them, at the ruthlessness with which French men and women moved in 1789 to exterminate royalty. In other words, America was from the very start positioned on the outside of the European war on medieval tradition. At virtually every key juncture, Americans watched from afar, and given that many of them were living near forts in the middle of wilderness, they watched from posts that were not unlike the ones manned by medieval pioneers in northern Europe.

At the same time, though, modern energies found a perfect host in America. They were present in the Protestant roots to our colonies, and they got a huge boost through our wholesale adoption of Cartesian metaphysics and Lockean anthropology, our wilderness-inflected romanticism, and, eventually, our hostility to aristocracy and the leisured philosophical tradition to which aristocracy is linked. Does it not make sense, then, that we too would eventually move to root out (once and for all) vestigial medieval ways? I submit that it does and that the American Civil War was that move.

The war against medieval tradition, as fought in the United States, had five fronts.

First (as described in chapter 4) we acted to destroy supports for agriculture, and replace them with inducements toward the phenomenon that we now call agri-business. This operation had of course already begun with the invention (in New England) of the cotton gin and the subsequent consolidation of small southern land holdings in order to build plantations big enough to produce cotton on the scale these machines demanded. But between 1861 and 1865 industrial agriculture gained further and not insubstantial leverage owing to: (1) the passage of the Morrill Act (which provided for a cadre of extension agents positioned to dispense scientifically validated advice to presumably inexpert farmers); (2) the related creation of a Department of Agriculture; (3) the actual dismantling of the southern rural economy (so as to be able to re-found it, via northern capital, on coal and iron, in addition to cotton); (4) the displacement of "agrarianism" as a guiding philosophy by a more industry-friendly notion called "progress" (here the ideals were mobility, convertibility, speed, and standardization, rather than permanence, accommodation to natural phenomena, and commitment to place); and, last but not at all least, (5) the outright killing of small, family-dependent, subsistence-based upland farmers who owned no slaves and (even more incredibly) depended on access to a *commons* (think single fields to which an entire village had access, after dividing responsibility for planting, cultivating, and harvesting constituent strips called "rigs") for the cultivation of ginseng, deer, mushrooms, ramp onions, and medicinal herbs. Moreover, small Southern farmers who did survive were quickly labeled "hillbillies" by war-empowered timber and coal companies intent on mining (and privatizing) Appalachian land. Hence critical Southern varieties of horticultural and artisanal expertise were either erased or marginalized during the Civil War.

On the second front, we destroyed the *mind* of the South (to use Cash's phrase) by displacing pre-modern, realist tracery that to some extent still organized the ways in which Southerners thought. By "realist" I mean *biased toward pre-scientific, receptive, word-based knowing that is geared toward what a thing is rather than what it does*, and I call this kind of disposition "tracery," in part because evidence for this kind of antebellum disposition (outside of personal correspondence, a still operant chivalric code, and putative respect for the Thomistic synthesis of Greek and Christian world views) is slim. Indeed, the best evidence we have for a southern inclination toward medieval realism as a school of thought is merely the artistic bias of twentieth-century writers (Allen Tate, Flannery O'Connor, Walker Percy) who in some sense claimed to be "unreconstructed." Nevertheless, that body of evidence is not insignificant, for surely it is not a coincidence that nearly every American writer with a distinctively sacramental viewpoint hails by hook or crook from a defeated South. Clearly, these writers are to some extent products of that South, and if we can't see the world they came from, we can at least tell that such a place must once have existed from the fact that Southerners can (if rarely) draw strength from it.

The third way in which Americans waged a war on medieval tradition during the Civil War years was by committing to the disenfranchisement of societal members who had previously been represented by tradition—namely, the dead and unborn—and formally substituting "universal suffrage" (so called) for established usage as a means of steering our ship of state.[103] Think of such suffrage, if you will, as a kind of *coronation* for the contract theory that legitimated our nation in the first place. As noted earlier, medieval citizens were encouraged to act in the interest of past and future generations simply by allowing themselves to be guided by precedent—which is to say, by methods and patterns that had been "selected" (in an evolutionary sense) as the ones most likely to ensure their culture's survival. Lockean contract theory, though, undercut all that, and therefore over time it became clear that we would need some kind of a counterbalance if we were also to check self-interest and ensure the survival of bona fide communities. Would enhanced access to Enlightenment truths via "education" prove sufficient as a means of checking self-interest? Jefferson thought so, but in the years leading up to the Civil War the question remained unsettled.

The Land Act of 1785 facilitated movement, rather than landed permanence, and the reservation of one section per township for schools had not yet yielded consistently wise stewardship of resources. At the same time, American sympathizer Edmund Burke's argument that custom uniquely protected the interests of past and future generations won admirers in the South, if not in the North, and there was discussion, before the Civil War, about the need to redesign our charter so that past and future generations might be better represented.[104] However, Southerners also tended to advance flagrantly racist viewpoints, and for this reason otherwise eloquent arguments about the dangers of relying entirely on universal suffrage did not get the respect they deserved. Eventually, the window for debate flat-out closed, and in 1863, when Lincoln issued the Emancipation Proclamation, the United States of America effectively abandoned established usage as a means of steerage every bit as thoroughly as the French had in 1789. Rather than curtailing individual rights in an effort to enfranchise communities, we moved (for better and worse) to *extend* them, and to that very extent we implicitly endorsed full-scale democracy as the best answer to our problems. From 1863 onward, we were (outside of continued deference to a written Constitution) essentially a one-man-one-vote nation that was subject to the whims of whatever generation had its hands on the tiller.

The fourth front in the war on medieval tradition was the swing, in military contexts, toward "total war." I have already talked about how—perhaps in direct proportion to the twofold appearance of "In God We Trust" on northern currency, and the adoption of "Battle Hymn of the Republic" (in which Union victories are depicted as God's truth "marching on") as a rallying cry—Grant and Sherman increasingly felt authorized to burn farms, poison wells, and (in the case of the March to the Sea) permit the random execution of civilians.[105] Here I need only point out that this kind of strategy amounted to the overthrow of longstanding military etiquette that had reached a kind of high-water mark during the Middle Ages. I refer, of course, to the distinction between combatants and non-combatants. This distinction was first codified during the early Middle Ages, and thanks to its linkage to the concept of a "just war" it survived, on formal terms, well into the Modern Era. Starting with the French war in the Vendée, however, that distinction began to blur, and by the time of the American Civil War the concept was ripe for abandonment. Nevertheless it was not a certainty that the distinction would be abandoned, and therefore the Union decision to attack non-combatants could rightly be considered a tipping point in the modern overthrow of medieval habits.

And the fifth key front in the war against vestigial medieval ways? That was the front where we withdrew support for citizen-directed, *intermediary* institutions that perform the very same duties centralized power depends on to justify its continued existence.

As Tocqueville and other observers like Robert Nisbet following in his tracks have pointed out, town halls, small businesses, families, granges, volunteer fire departments, churches, guilds, and neighborhoods are all crucial components to any state that aspires to safeguard and draw strength from a free populace. Individuals find fulfillment through these sorts of associations to the same degree that states draw strength from them, and if they are variously rooted in social class, geographical place, and ethnicity, so much the better. That way, social articulation is assured, vigor becomes possible, and the body politic, so called, gains a readily recognizable (talking physiology here) constitution. The catch is that political power must to some extent be decentralized in order for states to become strong in this way. That is to say, governments must continually release surplus power as it is accrued so that the green belt of intermediary institutions may absorb it and then convert it, gradually, into a form that individuals can actually use. This is easier said than done. Nevertheless, the United States of America was founded on the assumption that the goal can be achieved. Thus when the American founders convened to draft a written constitution that would to some degree reflect the decentralized power arrangement already in evidence, they favored federated power.

In the time leading up to the Civil War, however, this commitment—like Jefferson's commitment to free schooling—came under severe stress. Rather than strengthening the Union, the federal ideal and its associated bias in favor of intermediary institutions appeared to threaten it, for a new generation of "strict constructionists" like Calhoun and Randolph had begun to use the idea of states' rights as a means of defending slavery. Hence Northerners were encouraged to act on the ever-present temptation to toss out the burdensome requirement that centralized government should be limited, and by passing the Fourteenth Amendment (which transferred to Congress power formerly reserved to the several states) they did so act. From that point forward, it was possible to delegate to the government in Washington duties that had formerly been performed solely by citizen-directed associations, and as a result those associations were doomed to disappear or at least become obsolete.

Now, I recognize that I have depicted these five fronts as positions adopted by Northerners during a battle against Southern ways of life. The move was intentional, for though vestigial medieval ways were on view in northern Butternut regions, they were best on view during the early nineteenth century in the South. Biases in favor of agriculture, tradition, word-based knowledge, genuinely chivalric conduct, and decentralized power were strongest there. Nevertheless, it would be wrong to assume that Southerners were not complicit in the attempt to root out medieval ways. Indeed, without Southern help the American war against vestigial medievalism may not even have been won, for if a war against something is to be successful that thing must first be falsified, and Southerners sentimentalized the Middle Ages in ways that the North could not begin to match.

Tidewater Virginians in particular thought of themselves as members of an "armigerous" elite that focused as much on obligations as it did on rights. They dressed in high leather boots, wore tunics with slashed sleeves, affected "courtly" manners, carried swords, and followed a code of conduct that compelled them to protect inferiors and behave gallantly toward "ladies" (who were later, under different circumstances, "rogered"). They favored amusements like hunting stags and racing horses. They dined on roasted meats, lived in "manors" behind colonnaded porches, and versed themselves in Latin and Greek. Obviously, these men were not knights. Rather, they were the sons of disinherited or persecuted Tudor-generated "cavaliers" who had procured American land grants and become rich thanks to a boom in tobacco, rice, cotton, and the use of slaves who were literally bought and sold as commodities.[106] Thus Southern "gentlemen" practiced a form of leisure that was qualitatively different from—and even radically opposed to—the essentially metaphysical leisure known by medieval lords, and, even more tellingly, they wound up suffocating the kind of vibrant town life that genuinely medieval manors ought, by historical precedent, to produce. How many towns did New England boast? Seventy times seventy? Virginia and South Carolina boasted two capitols and just as many ports. Hence it can in no sense be argued that the medieval world on view in Richmond and Charleston was authentic. Rather, it was a theme park, a cheap imitation, a fundamentally dishonest *substitute*, and, as such, its very existence legitimated and to some degree required the destruction of the world it so obviously failed to be. Think of it, if you will, as Richardsonian Romanesque's more destructive (less nostalgic) twin.

Falsification, then, is one way in which Southerners actively helped to prosecute the war on medieval tradition. But there is also another, and it becomes visible, this other way, simply by our looking at the terms Southerners assented to when they decided to go to war.

Let us return—just for a moment—to the defining characteristics of modernity. In addition to an interest in magic, a tendency toward absolutism, and the maintenance of slavery, we noted a tendency to specifically counter medieval ways, and in order to support that statement we noted neatly opposed aspects to differing views about knowledge, land, and freedom. As it happened, there was also another example of contrasting viewpoints that we could have used, but seeing as how our list was already long, it didn't seem necessary to include it. Now, however, we need that example. It is this: whereas Medievals depended on true opposites (being and non-being, heaven and hell) as referents, Moderns appear always and everywhere to orient themselves by similars or contraries that are mistakenly (sometimes willfully) taken to be opposites. Thanks to an inherent (Occam-derived and revivalism-enforced) hostility to incarnational logic, modern thinkers tend to show a blind eye to middle terms and consequently wind up oscillating between poles that are either similar (same substance, different aspect) or merely contrary (not mutually exclusive). That sounds complicated, but it's not. Imagine a forest on a hillside. When it's healthy, the forest functions as a sponge-like watershed, absorbing fast-moving run-off from rock-paved courses above that would otherwise be lost and then releasing it slowly (via, say, moss-paved springs) to settlements below. Now remove that forest. Instead of being watered by small, meandering streams that run year-round, farm fields on the valley floor face either severe drought, or severe erosion from periodic floods. Practically speaking, in other words, drought and floods are not opposites. Rather, they are two different aspects of destruction, and they show up, these two aspects, upon the removal of the very thing that best integrates the nourishing potential of dry seasons on the one hand and wet seasons on the other.

Well, in the modern world one can see that scenario playing out again and again and again, almost everywhere. Artists, having lost access to a genuinely common culture in which the ordinary is celebrated and "performance," as such, does not even exist, veer either toward "high" art, which equates excellence with inaccessibility, or an equally alienated "low" art, which prides itself on being easy and cheap. Theologians, having lost access to the Greek-derived, Johannine-colored medieval concept of logos, swing wildly between sola scriptura (meaning without interpretation) and nominalism ("it's just a name"). Metaphysicians, having lost access to a concept of creaturehood in which body and mind figure as aspects of ensoulment, become either rationalists, who stress the role of "a priori" knowledge and "pure" reason, or empiricists, who stress the role of sensation and observation. Statesmen, having lost access to the idea that a heavenly Jerusalem is visible in and through a broken world, envision a Kantian notion of "universal peace" one year and then unleash "total war" the next. And that's just the beginning. Other distinctively modern false-opposite sets that have appeared in the wake of Christendom's collapse include public/private, nature/civilization, leviathan state/exposed individual, is/ought, historicism/universalism, and progressivism/classical liberalism. But enough. My point is simply that such polarities are false. In each instance the so-called "poles" are in fact aspects of a middle (or whole) that was clearly in view during the medieval era but subsequently was excluded or for some other reason lost.

Okay, so what? Why do I make this observation? I make it because the American Civil War was itself an oscillatory dynamic that fueled itself on contraries that masquerade as mutually exclusive, traction-enabling reference points.

As noted earlier in this chapter, freedom in its fullest sense isn't the absence of constraints. Rather, it is embeddedness in (and allegiance to) a community of sovereign selves who are mutually, interdependently, resolved to serve and uphold the good, the true, and the beautiful. During the Civil War, however, this view of freedom was withdrawn from view. In its place we were only able to see flip sides of its *absence*—"no constraints" on the one hand, "tyranny" on the other. Thus when Southerners and Northerners actually went to war in order to fight for one or the other of these ends, they (together!) enacted modernity at its most fierce—which is to say, modernity at the pitch when it is most able to disable vestigial medievalism carried by Butternuts and the American South, modernity at the pitch when it can touch down like the polarity-driven storm it is and compel people either to join it and help it grow or die running from it.

Orestes Brownson, the immensely learned yet perpetually miscast 19th century social critic whose hugely insightful book, *The American*

Republic, was published in 1865, was alert to specious oppositions and their associated dynamics. Moreover, the ex-workingman thought everywhere in terms of a "middle term" that "conciliates" contraries by making them "dialectically one."[107] Hence his analysis of the Civil War and how it changed the course of American history stands, today, as a good starting point for those of us who might be interested in confirming the idea that the Civil War was, first and foremost, a typically modern event that instituted the very thing it signified. True, Brownson ended *The American Republic* by asserting that that the conflict between the North and the South had more to do with synthesis than annihilation. Yet he composed that ending in 1865, a time when (loyal Vermonter that he was) he couldn't help but be swayed by the charity available to victors. Two years later Brownson was singing a very different kind of tune, and I suspect that if the seer had waited to publish until this latter date his masterpiece would have been tweaked slightly and made to end differently.

But you don't have to read Brownson in order to see that the Civil War had more to do advancing modernity than eliminating slavery. All you need to do is consider that, though every other nation found a way to abolish slavery via peaceful means (Britain eliminated the institution in 1838), Americans chose to fight a war over it. Why? Was it that our commitment to industrialization tipped the scales in favor of Northern abolitionists and thus definitively alienated Southerners? No, for other nations also industrialized at the same time that they abolished slavery, and those nations, unlike the American one, avoided war. Was it that a dedication to equality was explicitly written into our charter and thus created a level of hypocrisy that was both unique and ultimately unbearable? Perhaps. By the same token, though, wouldn't hypocrisy effectively be *over* once citizens started to vigorously and purposefully try to effect change through referendums and the courts? Clearly, there was another factor at work, and that factor was our need to finally declare unacknowledged modernity—express it, enact it, recognize ourselves in it, and perhaps even (Pentecostals that we had just become) *glory* in it. How? By firmly establishing spurious opposites as per the Lincoln-Douglas debates,[108] and committing—for an indeterminate length of time—to literally *civil* war.

Can that kind of war take a toll on land as well as on small farmers? Finding an answer to that question will have to wait until morning. Right now, it is time to put away paper and pen, steal a quick glance at the stars coming into view between streaking clouds, and lie down on a bunk where the sound and shuddering force of ship engines can snugly pull us toward sleep.

6

Draglines

It's the sudden quiet that wakes me up. Half past five. Turning alarms to "off," I roll out of bed and pad over, once again, to the porthole. The world outside is still dark, but this time woods are no longer in view. Instead I see an array of sodium lights on a steel grid that is as tall as a skyscraper and three times wider. Leading to that structure there are moving conveyor belts. Above it there are blinking beacons on three impossibly tall smokestacks, and beyond, in the harsh glare of yet another set of flood lamps, there is a five-storey mountain of pulverized coal. Fully awake now, I run scalding water against the side of a noisy steel stall, temper that flow with sand-filtered cold, and shower. Then I get dressed, run a comb through my hair from front to back, and step into the hall. Drawn now by the smells of coffee and bacon, I find my way to the galley where I discover additional bounty like grits, scrambled eggs, fried peppers, and sausage. Where are we, I ask. "Cardinal," Jack tells me, meaning Ohio Power's generating plant in Brilliant, Ohio. "We're cutting the tow loose here rather than PA." Where do we go next, I ask. The captain shrugs. Dave's eyes lighten at the thought of heading south, but Bradley (as always) is unreadable. I'm hoping we head upriver. Dawn is upon us, and this new day promises to be bright.

One hour later I'm in the wheelhouse with sharpened pencils. Sunlight is pouring into the cabin through a gap in the eastern hills, leveraging vision, and no matter where I look outlines are sharp. The now severed tow, still directly in front, is cinched up against a line of twenty-foot diameter, reinforced concrete mooring cells, and out at the tow's head, on a small field of newly fallen snow, Dave and Frank are taking down the tow's jack staff and the peep light fixed there, which helps the pilot keep track of the tow's head. When the deckhands turn into the sun, the buckles on their orange vests glint. To the west, a Norfolk and Southern engine with a thermos on the dash comes into view as it hauls another engine, and the power plant itself, now miraculously present as a brick-and-mortar edifice rather than an arrangement of walkway lights, features workers with yellow hard hats, enough high voltage electric lines to power all of Cleveland, and a thickly churning plume of exhaust. Halfway down the smokestack proper I see a tiny, man-sized door that opens onto a small grated platform, and from that platform a tiny metal ladder ascends—apparently all the way to the top so that some poor soul can change a lightbulb. Toward the south there's a cooling tower shaped like a gargantuan flask, and out on the river, flying low, there is a lone bufflehead duck headed south. The duck is small, but the bird makes a big impression owing to sharply contrasting white and black wing patches.

Mainly I just look at the mountain of snow-covered coal. It's not so much that there is enough coal gathered there to blanket three whole city blocks. It's that for some reason I suddenly get how coal is just one of several different energy *forms*. Another is greenery and still another is—well, cities. Looking at that pile of coal, in other words, I can "see" Pittsburgh. More to the point, I can see that downtown Pittsburgh is simply another version of Cadiz.

As was the case in other rapidly industrializing cities, Pittsburgh was the site of accelerated capital formation in the late nineteenth century. Botanical gardens with pea gravel paths and edged lawns appeared. Concert halls. Aviaries. Carriage drives lined with plane trees from London. An entire financial *district*. Almost all that wealth is still visible today, and in order to get a read on its splendor you have only to drive through Ft. Pitt tunnel, cut left on one of the many bridges crossing the Allegheny River, and face east. For if you do that, you will see (on the other side of the river) a built landscape every bit as stunning as Yosemite National Park. Downtown Pittsburgh features fastnesses, narrow canyons, and variously situated ledges with trees sprouting on them. Steam rises from ventilation systems on tall buildings, and below, in the voids between skyscrapers that are created by streets, you can see hawks circling. Get out of the car, if you like. Walk across Sixth St. Bridge (built in 1928) and tour the city on foot. Trail maps aren't available, but if you start at "The Point" near the ruins of Fort Pitt, you can't get lost. Just skirt the Fifties-era "Gateway" Hilton, cross a pavered square in the shadow of an entirely glassed skyscraper with Gothamite spires (Pittsburgh Plate Glass), and make a bee-line for the small alley called "Strawberry Way."

First a charmingly stuffy Harvard and Yale Club comes into view, next the city's original Bell Telephone Building (which features an utterly incongruous, grotto-like cab entrance defined by limestone piers and green Guastavino tile), and, finally, Grant Street—home to the 600-foot-high Art-Deco-themed Gulf Tower (1932) with its neon-lit pyramidal top, the slightly less tall Koppers Building (1929) with its chateau-like copper roof, and (down the road a piece, opposite Allegheny Courthouse) Frederick Osterling's Union Trust Building (1915) with its absurdly overwrought and slightly over-sized Gothic "hat." These buildings are roughly half the size of the US Steel and Mellon Bank towers on the other side of the street, but the disproportion is not irksome, and if you keep walking, angling now toward the northeast, you find that the brashness of late twentieth century buildings is balanced on yet another front by Pittsburgh's twelve-storey Penn Station (1903), which comes into view at the terminus of the old Johnstown canal. And don't forget to check out the cobbled carriage "turn-around" at the entrance to the train station—Moorish arches, domed roof, rosette skylight, graven inscriptions at each of the four roof-supporting stone pillars invoking *Pittsburgh, Chicago, Philadelphia, New York*. Given that the architecture there is vaguely reminiscent of the Hagia Sophia in Istanbul, these latter place-names ring out as though they represented the four ends of the known earth, and, indeed, to a late nineteenth century American captain of industry they might well have summed up those four ends.

What generated all this wealth?

The driver was steel. True, Pittsburgh-based H. J. Heinz Corporation had an impact (Henry sold his first jar of tomato ketchup here in 1876), and so too did Westinghouse Corporation (George Westinghouse patented the first railcar air brake in 1872). Next to Carnegie Steel, however, Heinz and Westinghouse were sideshows. Andrew Carnegie opened his first Bessemer process steel mill in Braddock in 1875 (site of both General Edward Braddock's 1755 defeat by the French *and* the 1794 Whiskey Rebellion "gathering" that so alarmed Washington), and almost from the day it started the plant boomed in a figurative as well as a literal sense. Thanks to the fact that the railroad industry's demand for steel was high, and thanks to the new (Bessemer) system of mechanically blowing air through molten iron to oxidize (remove) excess carbon, production costs were low. Carnegie right away generated large profits, and he invested those profits in mills featuring path-breaking "open hearth" furnaces that enabled the creation of large amounts of high-grade structural steel in addition to train tracks. These developments, in turn, created a huge and practically endless market for Henry Clay Frick's ovens (on the other side of the Monongahela River), which readied coal for use in Carnegie's furnaces by baking off undesirable, potentially gaseous, elements like sulfur and by turning coal into "coke." And those coke ovens, in turn, created a nearly inexhaustible supply of solvents, sulfurous gases, and tars. Hence the runaway success of Heinrich Koppers' Tar and Chemical Company, which rearranged coke-oven flow lines so as to capture, manufacture, and then commodify acids, oils, and tarmac. Given this degree of company interdependence, it was almost guaranteed that capital in Pittsburgh would accumulate exponentially, and once that happened Andrew W. Mellon (the Pittsburgh native who fronted a lot of the money necessary to get all these enterprises going) became a force in his own right by forming Union Trust and helping to create the ancestors of Gulf Oil and Alcoa Aluminum. Back of it all, though, there was steel—both in the form of Carnegie's company (which eventually became US Steel), Carnegie's chief competitor (Jones and Laughlin Steel), and innumerable, relatively small upper Ohio River companies (eventually to be consolidated as Wheeling-Pitt Steel) that started out as iron foundries.

Nowadays, of course, steel is made mostly in China. Thanks to Mao's Great Leap Forward and the related if somewhat correctional implementation of capitalist biases, Chinese steel makers now make more steel than the United States, Japan, and Germany combined. At the same time, and perhaps in direct proportion to the rise of Chinese, Indian, and Russian steel, the last remaining upper Ohio River steel mills are closing.[109] The Edgar Thomson Steel Works is still in operation over in Braddock, but Weirton Steel and Wheeling Pitt's two plants at Steubenville and Mingo Junction will soon be idle.

How different this valley looked forty, even three times forty years ago! "Hell with the lid off," proclaimed a jubilant 1868 *Atlantic Monthly* contributor.[110] And that was just the beginning. By 1889, most of the foundries described in the *Atlantic Monthly* article had been upgraded to compete with Carnegie's operation on the Monongahela, and in 1895 (thanks in part to the opening of new plants in Pueblo, Colorado, and Gary, Indiana) American steel production passed Britain's, moving every bit as fast as China's is now. Plants appeared on the Mahoning River near Youngstown. A tin plate mill appeared in the old Ohio river bed at Weirton ("Holiday's Cove"), and in 1915 a new railroad bridge got built over the Ohio River to connect Wheeling Steel's newly acquired "La Belle" iron works in Steubenville to a state-of-the-art coke plant in Follansbee, West Virginia. Upstream, on the Monongahela, shipping lanes started to carry more traffic than most big city ocean harbors, and by the 1930s the entire upper Ohio River was functioning, essentially, as one big furnace. Then World War II arrived, and this same furnace burned brightly enough to be seen from interstellar space. From Pittsburgh clear down to Wheeling, poured slag made "booms" like regularly discharging howitzers.[111] There was a lurching unit-train loaded with coal or Lake Superior ore or 20-ton steel coils at nearly every railroad crossing, and ammonium sulfate, benzol, and naphtha spewed heavily from coke-oven chimneys. Streets, lawns, walkways, even gardens turned black. Downtowns stayed cheery through the use of neon, but out on the river you mainly saw searchlights. The place literally had no parallel. Compared to the Wheeling/Pittsburgh corridor, industrial zones on the Ruhr and the Clyde were fun parks.

Steel is purified iron. That is to say, it is "pig iron" (iron captured from ore) that has been refined to the point where carbon content resulting from association with fuel has been reduced to 1.5 percent or less, and the trick in making it is to remove that carbon and then either carefully reintroduce it or add some other element (tungsten, say, or manganese) to give steel its signature characteristic of malleability plus strength. If the goal is soft steel (cans, shells, nails) the product can be made by injecting air into a converter full of molten iron, but if the goal is structural steel (I-beams, armored plate, earth-mover teeth) you have to blow reheated air across entire pools of the stuff for long periods of time. Hence the "open hearth system" where oxidation is slowed and slag is used as a kind of blanket to extend the molten phase and buy time to add alloying agents, which "fix," or lock in, ferric atomic structure as per engineers' requests. Around here, mills featured ten or more 3,000-square-foot open-hearth furnaces arranged in a row, and the iron in them was kept bubbling thanks to reheated air that periodically blew like dragon breath across molten surfaces. Once the iron became steel it ran off into ladles and then molds where it was "cast" and pickled—left to soak, glowingly, in steam-forming vats—before being transformed into coiled plate at a hot "strip" mill. But the most remarkable aspect to steelmaking remains the more basic accomplishment at the front of the flow-line, which is the almost magical transformation of coal, limestone, and ore into molten iron, courtesy of a "blast" furnace.

Blast furnaces are instantly recognizable thanks to over-sized "downcomer" pipes that capture furnace exhaust and deliver it to be scrubbed, cooled, and then re-introduced as fuel for the heating of air destined (via a doughnut-shaped "bustle pipe") to "blast" (or fan) furnace fires. They stand about 100-feet tall, these furnaces, and they are the focal point of nearly every steel plant delivery system save the one that delivers scrap to an open-hearth operation (or, now, electric arc and basic oxygen furnaces). Train tracks converge at blast furnaces, and when trains are running you tend to see (waiting to be unloaded) rail cars filled with pelleted ore from either the Mesabi Range in Minnesota or (since 1995) the Itabira mountains in southern Brazil, fuel in the form of sometimes local but ideally (owing to low sulfur content) West Virginian coal that has been coked (usually at Follansbee but sometimes, now, as far away as Egypt), and flux (for drawing off impurities and converting them into easily removable "slag") in the form of Dolomitic limestone from western Ohio till plains. One by one these cars (eighty per day for a single furnace) get switched onto tracks that deliver contents to screening stations, and thence to skip cars that carry "charge" ingredients up the side of the furnace (via a kind of cog railway winch system) to the furnace's throat. Those skip cars run up the side of the furnace nearly every minute (during a charge interval) for as long as three years straight, because once a blast furnace is lit, it stays lit, and inside the cavernous casting house, which sheds rain and snow, the furnace contraption looks like a rocket ship that is perpetually starting to launch. Blue flames flicker here and there around its base owing to carbon monoxide build-up, and through various peepholes you can see an intense variety of gold (thanks to already smelted iron). There is also an ever-present roar as compressed air flows steadily through melt-proof copper nozzles called "tuyeres" that penetrate lower furnace walls like spokes on a tire's rim.

How do operators harvest the iron?

I know, because I watched one day.

Several hours after the skip cars pack the charge by unloading their contents into the furnace's throat, a tap drill appears via remote control to drill a 1¾-inch hole through the furnace's interior brick wall, and the instant that drill's rotary bit pulls back, molten iron spouts out of the furnace into a trough, like spring water flowing from a cloven rock. Twenty feet away, slag on the top of the molten iron runs into a "skimmer," which diverts it to a waste pile, but the iron itself flows on like a creek of lava toward open-hearth furnaces. The flow lasts 2½ hours. Given that the trough along which the iron travels is (thinking like a carpenter here) "let in" to the concrete floor on which the furnace sits, you can walk beside the moving iron, and when you do, it feels as though you were walking beside a bubbling brook. The brook runs at 4,000 degrees Fahrenheit; hence, nearby ground and the air overhead are always free of snow.

Amazing!

O brave new world that has such things in it!

The hitch is that there is a cost. I don't just mean that steel mills spew particulate matter, or that proximity to molten steel is dangerous, or that steelworker strikes have in the past been broken by Pinkerton guards with guns (1892, Edgar Thomson plant, Braddock). I mean that steel plant furnaces require a lot of coal.

Draglines

Around Pittsburgh, outcroppings were everywhere visible in 1875. That is why Carnegie sited his mills here. Indeed, the abundance of accessible coal in the tri-state area was the deciding factor in Carnegie's decision. The Appalachian coal basin wasn't just large (half the size of Europe); it also featured high-grade (if sulfurous) "Pittsburgh #8" coal *right near the surface*, and therefore the expense of procuring and shipping it was vastly reduced relative to other coal-rich areas.[112] In Pittsburgh the stuff was practically pre-delivered! All you had to do was build a mill, send out for ore, and light a fire! The problem was that once Carnegie did site his mills here, he practically guaranteed that coal in this area would be aggressively mined, and this meant that outlying western communities that could sell coal but not steel were at risk. In other words, there was a good possibility that as Pittsburgh went up (in terms of influence and power), coal-rich areas in the basin's center would go down, and seeing as how executives running Pittsburgh's fledgling industries all flocked east (toward Ligonier and Johnstown) when it came time to build a country retreat, the odds for betting against this inverse relationship weren't too good.

Cadiz, which lies about as far to the west relative to Pittsburgh as Ligonier and Johnstown lie to the east, was a wealthy place in 1875. After sloughing its outlaw status and becoming, by 1856, a capital for genuine agriculture (currant jelly, husking and quilting bees, herb beds with mint, thyme, sage and mustard, draft horses, sliding barn doors, county fairs, stewed peaches, the use of clover as a cover crop, sleighs, flour mills, chicken pot pie, shipping terminals for livestock, dried apples, McCormick reapers, tubs full of cucumber brine, fields sown to flax for linseed oil and linen), Cadiz became important enough to merit an entire branch line off the new, westward-tending railway.[113] In addition to gunsmiths, saddlers, blacksmiths, and wagon makers, there were druggists and attorneys in town. Hotel clerks. Milliners. Dry goods merchants, tailors, and newspaper editors. Even jewelers! Modest but real wealth had begun to accrue, and citizens began to be proud of their town. What was driving *this* growth? Unlike the Western Reserve east of Cleveland, which became known for dairies, vineyards, and nurseries, and the area around Carrollton, which became known for wheat, Cadiz farmers specialized in wool. After wool prices fell in the late 1820s, Vermont sheep farmers had thrown in the towel and shipped vast numbers of Spanish Merino sheep west, toward buyers who weren't burdened by high land prices or (owing to a more temperate climate) the need to provide shelter, and a lot of those sheep wound up in Ohio hill country. Then belated tariffs kicked in and the wool industry rebounded, thereby putting farmers west of Steubenville in an enviable position. They had almost no overhead, they already owned the inventory, and feed for keeping sheep alive grew wild on nearly every hillside. Hence farmers here began to realize annual returns—via sales of mutton, spring lambs, and wool—of nearly $4/sheep, and after the Civil War that profit margin began to have an effect on infrastructure.[114] Log cabins gave way to brick houses with 9-light sashes, multiple chimneys, and lightning rods. Barns got raised to shelter winnowing operations, carriages, and newly purchased dairy cattle. Split-rail fences became less ramshackle, orchards were established, and covered bridges were built where formerly there had been fords. Last but not least, artisanal concerns thrived in such a way as to reinforce an assortment of cultural microclimates ("Cassville," "Science Hill," "Georgetown") that were both independent from, yet tied to, the larger community of Cadiz.

Fortunately for those of us who live here today, there is a pictorial record of Cadiz countryside during this era. It's called "Caldwell's 1875 Atlas of Harrison County,"[115] and it comes to us courtesy of a Philadelphia company that was in the business of selling descriptive atlases that were part cartography ("derived from actual surveys by and under the direction of J. A. Caldwell") and part promotional brochure. Naturally, the pictures and words in this book are a bit wishful, but hopes do matter when it comes to conveying a region's character, and for this reason the resulting "atlas" functions as a kind of deep ("thick") land map. "Rural Home," reads the caption on page 89, under an engraving of a fenced vegetable garden with trellised vines, a drive leading toward a Federal-style two-storey brick home with a perpendicular wing, nearby barn, neat fence-work, and "free range" sheep. "Res. of Abraham Holmes, Short Creek Tp. A farm of 170 acres, being a part of sec.25, entered by my father Joseph Holmes in 1801, settled on in March the same year. (Fine wool grower.)" Then, on the next page, you see Mr. Holmes Sr.'s establishment on the far side of a pasture featuring cattle and spirited horses and, just beyond the buildings (this house was apparently added onto four times), an extensive orchard. "Wool grower," the caption reads. "200 thoroughbred sheep." The tour just goes on and on. "Stillwater Farm: J.M. Cramblett. Poultry Yards. Breeder and shipper of dark and light Brahmas, Buff partridge, white and black Cochins, white Leghorns, Sebright & yellow chick Wing game Bantams." Then: "Joseph L. Thompson, Cadiz: 334 acres well-watered and timbered." "Isaac Thomas, Short Creek Post Office: large fruit house, also a large wool grower." "W.E. Williams, on Pittsburgh, Cincinnati & St. Louis: Dealer in coal and fine brick clay." And: "Residence of John Stringer, Esq., Short Creek: 206 acres of limestone land well-watered and timbered with good coal and 400 fine wool sheep. Breeder of short horn Durham cattle." All of it is riveting, but the most fascinating section is the one at the back, where you find plat maps superimposed on section and range lines. Given that these maps show roads, schoolhouses, farm buildings, churches, orchards, drainages, cemeteries, and mineral deposits, they make three things abundantly clear: first, that there was genuine variety of land use in Harrison County, circa 1875; second, that the farms here were all roughly the same size; third, that the region was intensively farmed because it was completely and thoroughly *settled*. In other words, the maps don't just show prosperity. They also show fertility.

Bottom line: in 1875, Harrison County was comprised of townships that looked a lot like the ward republics Thomas Jefferson envisaged 90 years before, when he drew up plans for a Land Act.

Given that section-and-range logic undercut authentically landed society in important ways, the Cadiz area could never have really supported such republics, but townships here certainly called them to mind, and should an observer track their progress over the next fifty years, he or she might justly conclude that the patchwork quilt of fields and woods around Cadiz was about the best that America could produce in the way of an agrarian society. Responsibility for schooling, road maintenance, elderly care, and food production was widely distributed. People lived where they worked, thus encouraging good stewardship of resources, and they were their own bosses. Thanks to a branch line connecting them to the Pennsylvania Railroad, they also had good physical contact with the "outside" world (six trains per day in 1921), and the editors of their densely printed six-column newspaper, the *Cadiz Republican*, worked hard to brief its readership on whatever issues members of Congress were facing. What's more, Chautauqua Park (1914) featured whistling swans. Floral exhibits were on view inside nearby pavilions, and on summer evenings practically the entire county gathered to play or watch baseball. Cy "Farmer" Young and George Sisler both played here for visiting teams from neighboring counties before they became famous, and local residents like Cal Vasbinder and Ed Onslow went on to pitch for Cleveland and catch for Detroit. How could they not? This region practically glowed with confidence.[116] It was a place where home runs were possible, and the reason they were possible (here) was that streams ran clear, soils yielded an abundant harvest, and men gained authority on a fairly equal basis by tilling those soils. When the US Navy needed oak timber to rebuild the USS Constitution (the warship commissioned by Jefferson to fight Barbary Coast pirates), it made perfect sense that purchasing officers should turn (as they did) to Cadiz.

However, there was a storm on the horizon, and the clouds marking the coming storm (soon to be a wall of thunderheads) grew in direct proportion to a swiftly growing need for coal.

Eastern Ohio residents were, in the main, oblivious regarding the force of the winds that were soon to hit. "In addition to our splendid natural resources and our good farming community," opined one columnist in a September 1921 *Cadiz Republican* piece, "we are in the midst of one of the best coalfields in the entire country. . . . Real estate prices [are] soaring at unheard of prices, since it is certain that Cadiz for a hundred years will have prosperous conditions."[117] The columnist then concluded by speculating that "a large percentage of the people working in the coalfields within a radius of six miles" would make their homes in Cadiz, thus further driving up house prices. There were, of course, one or two people who were, shall we say, *thoughtful* about the character of the still distant cloud. After a 300-ton shoveling device materialized on a farm near Hopedale, ten miles to the east, in June 1915, *Cadiz Republican* editor Harry Burns McConnell noted that the machine lifted earth "up and away" from the underlying coal seam "with a rush of air" and deposited its load of rock and soil "upon a long, high pile behind it" in such a way as to build "a new topography called spoil banks," and though the tone of the piece was non-judgmental, you can tell that McConnell had taken note of destructive potential and carefully filed the aspect for further study. Nobody, however, really "got" it. If they had, they would have sold their holdings (except for mineral rights) while the market was high and then headed to Oregon with Cadiz native Clark Gable in 1922. But aside from Gable, who was poor and had acting on his mind, nobody did this. Even the smart money was fooled, and the reason it was fooled is that the impending destruction was literally unthinkable.

If Harrison County residents (and perhaps even coal company executives) had been told that in the space of just fifty years 50 percent of the farms in the four productive townships north and west of Cadiz, and 100 percent of the farms in the especially rich townships south and east of Cadiz, would be obliterated—just ripped apart and, in effect, erased—they would have laughed. Yet that is precisely what happened.[118] Whereas the 1934 plat map for this area showed an intricate patchwork of working farms with names like Holliday, Dickerson, Mitchell, Dunlop, Thomas, and Cope, the plat map now reads like a low resolution overview of ill-defined regions with names like Jeffco Resources (mineral-rights holding company), Chambers Development (dump), Harrison Mining (local surface miner specializing in seconds), Conservation Fund (stripped land deeded over to the State of Ohio), and Skyline Farms (hay operation on reclaimed land). And that's a picture of recovery. In 1980, the plat map was even scarier, for it showed just *one* owner. That owner was Consolidated Coal—the multinational corporation based in Pittsburgh now doing business as Consol—and when you get out a magnifying glass and comb that 1980 map for evidence of the riches on view in 1875, you find nothing. Farms, artisan hamlets, woodlots, one-room schoolhouses, viewpoints, orchards, small drainage courses dating from the Ice Age, celebrated picnic spots, drift mines—that stuff is gone. In most sections it's as if these things had never even existed.

Coal is rock that burns. It burns because it consists mainly of plant matter that accumulated in tropical marshes 300 million years ago during the Pennsylvanian Age at the end of the Paleozoic era. Owing to repeated flooding (and lack of exposure to air), a lot of those plants never decomposed. Instead, they were submerged and then buried in mud, thereby becoming peat. Eventually—owing to the weight of succeeding sedimentary layers and, too, horizontal compression resulting from collisions between continental plates—the atomic structure of that peat changed, but the plant aspect remained, and, indeed, to the folks who mine it, coal's biological origins are instantly recognizable. In deep mines just north and west of Steubenville, roof-bolting crews have to keep an eye out for bases to bell-shaped, once-hollow tree stumps, which (owing to an ultra-slick interface between bark-that-became-coal and mud-infilling-that-became-shale) can drop at any time. Called "kettledrums," these rocky stumps are the remains of lycopsid trees, which were leaf-covered poles with cone-bearing crowns. Other plants frequently on view in the coal here include seed ferns, sphenophyllum shrubs, scouring rushes, and ancestors of current-day conifers like sigillaria and lepidodendron trees. Coal, in other words, is simply old sunlight, concentrated. Thanks to plants growing in tropical marshes, energy in the form of light was captured again and again and again over the course of millions of years, converted into leaves (or stems), and then, thanks to the submersion and compression of that same plant tissue, concentrated and, in effect, preserved underground as a kind of hidden sun. Given that the earth's crust regularly gets "rumpled" during mountain building events, it is of course inevitable that much of the strata containing coal will be lost due to erosion. When sedimentary rock gets pushed up, it is exposed to wind and rain and eventually washes away. By the same token, however, it is also inevitable that depressed sedimentary rock featuring coal-bearing layers will wind up with an extra layer of protection, and when that happens—as it did after the second collision between the American and European plates when the Dunkard, Pocahontas, and Black Warrior structural basins were formed—coal can last all the way to the point where someone comes along and decides to burn it.[119]

At first, the Waynesburg, Uniontown, Miegs Creek, and Pittsburgh #8 coals in Ohio's Harrison, Jefferson, and Belmont counties were mined by bringing a wagon alongside an outcropping and filling it. Then, once that coal was exhausted and it became necessary to follow a seam into the earth, slope and shaft mines appeared. Slope mines followed a seam into the side of a hill, and shaft mines tapped seams that were 100, 200, even 500 feet below. In Steubenville, during the late nineteenth and early twentieth centuries, leather-capped miners with carbide lamps used to show up at the corner of 7th and Washington, ride an elevator ("Rolling Mill Shaft #1") straight down to a slightly darker, definitely more pillared city, and then walk to work, round dinner pail in hand, under the Ohio River. And around Cadiz, starting in about 1917, coal camps appeared with names like Robeyville and Duncanwood. In addition to tarpapered houses on a hillside with laundry drying on every other porch, these company-owned towns featured a schoolhouse, a footbridge over a creek, a post office, a tipple with a check-house, a recreation hall, a couple mule barns, and a company store where you paid with scrip. They were inhabited by Hungarians, Serbs, Poles, Belgians, Greeks, Italians, and Slavs, and the towns' sole purpose was to cut, rake, drill, shoot, and then ship coal from an infinitely retreating face 400 feet down. Duncanwood's owner was Akron-based Goodyear Corporation. Those operations eventually closed down in the early 1940s, for camps were costly, but deep mining in eastern Ohio continued, and, indeed, thanks to the installation of long-wall methods and continuous mining machines, underground mining remains a powerful local force today. Nevertheless, given that between Steubenville and Cadiz huge amounts of #8 coal were tantalizingly close to the surface, the idea of simply removing "overburden" to get at that coal had always been a temptation. Hence when technology finally arrived in the 1920s to make the pondered removal possible, most coal companies in the area quickly adopted it.

The technology had been under development for some time. The Ohio Central Railroad ordered a Bucyrus steam shovel as far back as 1882, and in 1913 the United Electric Coal Company used two electric shovels to mine #8 coal near Rush Run in Jefferson County. That event proved the worth of the new technology, and by 1915 the Marion model 271 electric shovel that had caught the attention of Cadiz newsman Harry McConnell was in use between Bloomingdale and Hopedale. But the operators of these shovels were still just trying to figure out what worked. When strip-mining companies positioned themselves so that they were looking toward Cadiz from Hopedale, on the other hand, operators knew what they were doing. The date was 1934. Coal companies with names like Tasa, Massilon, and Witch Hazel had been bulking up on the eastern horizon for years, and now—thanks to a big assist from Wheeling and Lake Erie Railroad, which had been founded to ship the coal that lay under every Harrison County farm—they were well-equipped to move with dispatch toward Cadiz. This they did, and within a year of their advance nearly every hill southwest of Hopedale featured a new, usually serpentine "bench" that was 50 feet wide, level as a playing field, and, well, endless.

Welcome to "contour mining."[120]

The system worked okay for the miners, but the approach was haphazard, and (as described in chapter 1) it quickly transformed the country between Cadiz and Bloomingdale into a maze of topographically incorrect mesas, stagnant lakes, smoldering fires, acidic streams, and jumbled banks of discarded slate.[121] Consequently there were calls for reclamation laws. Milt Ronsheim, McConnell's successor at the helm of the *Cadiz Republican*, pushed hard for laws that would require coal companies not only to smooth out and reseed land they had stripped, but, as well, to post bonds before beginning work, and though these calls were at first resisted, in the end (1947) coal companies acquiesced. Therefore, in a certain sense Cadiz won a reprieve through these efforts. In the long run, though, Ronsheim's efforts simply facilitated the next phase of the strip-mine juggernaut, for in order to post bonds, fight citizen groups with propaganda, lobby state legislatures, and beautify work sites, coal companies needed to be large, and that meant consolidation.

During World War II, hard push came to serious shove in eastern Ohio coalfields, and after dust settled, there was just one major player doing business here. Its name was Hanna Coal, and thanks to enhanced capitalization and new pressures exerted by a market that had been created by the war effort, this company probably did more to refine the art of strip mining than any other company. Ever. Its laboratory was central Harrison County, and shortly after committing its fortunes to those of Consolidated Coal (which originated as a consolidation of small companies mining Georges Creek coal near Cumberland in Maryland), Hanna Coal pioneered: (1) a series of extra-powerful shovels in order to minimize the costs of digging deeper into a hill; (2) a "Dr. No" processing plant (biggest in the world, in 1951) served by "unit trains" to sort, grade, and wash the bounty made available by those shovels; (3) a slurry pipeline to deliver that bounty to a power plant in Cleveland in addition to mills along the river; (4) new machines called "draglines" which were capable of completely removing overburden rather than simply chipping away at it; and (5) methods for systematically stripping an entire region rather than just a site.

The extra powerful shovels appeared in 1948. During the war Hanna had used shovels with 8-yard buckets, but starting in 1948, when "The

Green Hornet" started work at the Georgetown #12 "surface" mine, that bucket capacity jumped to 56 cubic yards. In other words, the Green Hornet took out two large-size dumpster loads of earth per bite, thereby enabling it to remove efficiently as much as 90 feet of overburden, and when it worked alongside the only slightly smaller "sister" shovels 46A and B, coal began to be harvested from under Cadiz and Short Creek Township farms faster than it could be processed. Hence the development of the preparation plant, a rail yard big enough to handle 840 cars, and an accompanying lake for "black water" on the north side of Dickerson Church, site of the first Cadiz camp meeting. What about the coal that lay under more than 90 feet of overburden? High walls like the one on the north side of Dickerson Church were proliferating, and, as they started to become continuous, the coal on the other side of those walls became, as it were, highlighted. Well, starting in 1956 Hanna Coal moved to go after that coal too. They got at it by commissioning and then installing a new machine that used steel cables to manipulate a bucket rather than a fixed secondary boom. The idea was to manipulate earth rather than an increasingly cumbersome arm, and it paid off, this idea, for after this first dragline was put into service, operators found themselves able to reach both higher and further. Executives proudly christened their new machine "Mountaineer," presumably to honor the machine's ability to cope in rugged terrain while also honoring the character of the Appalachian people, but the name also had ominous implications for the mountains on whose slopes Appalachian people lived, and starting in 1965, when Mountaineer's offspring appeared, those implications began to be realized.

After I first got settled in Harrison County, my smaller children learned to ask that we drive home after excursions via a little-used road that passes through a contour mine. They liked to be scared by abandoned equipment there, and, indeed, there were sights on that route that could frighten, particularly at night. One minute you are in a leafy surround listening to owls, and the next minute, while the car's tires randomly kick up a few stray pebbles, you find yourself dwarfed by a hulking shovel with a 50-foot boom, a bucket the size of your car, and not a few resident ghosts. The graffiti on one of them even says: *got milk?* But that is nothing compared to what I saw five years later while exploring the land Captain John Hunt Morgan rode through in 1863. I was about ten miles southwest of Cadiz, swinging east on a kind of arc, traveling along a ridge after climbing 200 feet out of a valley floor. I say "ridge" and "valley," but in fact these terms refer here simply to the tops of banks or benches left over from mining. The important thing is that I was for the moment on high ground, thinking about how raw the land looked—just rock, ice on the "valley" floors, and

Draglines

signs telling me that, if I heard a whistle, an explosion would follow. Then I came around a corner and saw what appeared to be the top of—what? A gantry beside a deep-water canal that had suddenly materialized in one of those floors? A Jurassic bird of prey from the land of nightmares? Whatever I was looking at, it was big, for though the riveted steel-plate trusses holding rigging aloft were clearly end points and therefore small relative to their base, those trusses were also massive. If that was the top, then the machine's footing had to be roughly 200 feet below! Following a newly bulldozed track that swung left to get around the promontory that was blocking my view, I quickly found myself confirming my original guess and looking up at a dragline that was as big as the derricks that unload container ships. The only difference was that this device had an engine house as big as a three-storey barn and a 150-yard bucket at the end of is slings rather than a railcar-sized container. The machine was an "earth-mover." Its owner was Consolidated Coal. Its name was "The Silver Spade," and its sole purpose was systematically to plow up rugged topography south of Cadiz and then (neatly) turn the whole region over, furrow by furrow by furrow.

There used to be two of these devices working south of Cadiz. While the Silver Spade worked Mahoning Valley mine "No.36" during the 1970s and 1980s, a sister dragline called "The Gem of Egypt" worked mine "No.33" near Barnesville, site of the first Quaker meeting house west of the Alleghenies, and though the Gem had a slightly smaller bucket (130 cubic yards rather than 150) and stood a little less tall (200 feet as opposed to 220), it accomplished similar feats. If either of these machines showed up today on the Conotton Creek flood plain below my house, and then lumbered south on its "crawlers," it would take out my ridge-nestled home and nearby trees with a single scoop of a bucket swinging from the end of a 200-foot boom, and we would be looking up at the machine's masthead when it happened. The Silver Spade and the Gem weighed 7,000 tons each, and they were powered by 12-cylinder Cummins engines. Once overburden was loosened by Air-Mite charges in regularly drilled 8-inch holes, the machines could pick up a 250-ton load of earth like it was a matchstick and, with a single swing, carry it the length of a football field before depositing it and going back for more. Bulldozer crews kept the working pad wide and level as a runway, and as long as equipment stayed oiled, the digging operation went on (via a battery of constantly moving klieg lights) night and day. Once they were dialed in, these machines implacably exposed and kept on exposing a flat, 200-foot-wide ribbon of coal. Everything on top—trees, drainage systems, boulders, human settlements, topsoil, ridge logic—all that just got wiped off like clay shapes on an artist's table, or like a conglomeration of driftwood, seaweed, and foam on a hard and very flat beach. Hence the appearance of land south of Cadiz today: some of it smoothed out and fitted with oddly placed but picturesque lakes, some of it jumbled and grey, and all of it void of trees, farmsteads, rain-carved outcroppings, and meanders.[122]

Clearly, something went wrong in Cadiz.[123]

It's not just that Harrison County now features silted creek beds, poisoned ("yellow boy") run-off, a fractured water table, and poor soils. Bad as that ecological toll is—and the cumulative damage here makes the establishment of business parks difficult, let alone farms—I am not referring simply to the degradation of soil and water. Nor am I referring, at this moment, to the loss of tax base and the consequent lack of funding for schools, law enforcement, libraries, historical preservation projects, and civic amenities like parks. Indeed, I am not even referring to the despoliation of de-facto town commons that preserve the memory of the dead and hope for the young people to come. In Cadiz that "common" was the 289-acre Morgan-Liggett farm on the south edge of town, and when that land got stripped, people here knew that a violation of trust had occurred. Owing to its proximity to courthouse, Custer Hotel, corner grill, bank, and post office, that farm had been known for years as the "town" farm, and when everybody woke up one morning in 1968 to discover that the dairy's pasture had been "relocated" (temporarily!) to harvest black gold 20 feet down, it was not unreasonable to conclude that the town had died. Newspaper reports were quick to assure readers that topsoil had been carefully replaced and that the farm's original appearance was restored, but people knew better. In fact, a collective moral compromise had been struck, and the very tone of the article proved it.[124] What, then, am I referring to if, when I say something went seriously awry in Cadiz, I am not referring even to that kind of wrong? It is this: in the mid-Sixties *topography itself became the target*. Until 1965, Harrison County was, by definition, a patchwork quilt of varied uses. It supported mining, dairy, wool, ceramic, and timber interests. Naturally, some of these uses were harder on the fabric than others. Therefore, the fabric weakened as certain sections got "mined out" or went up in smoke. But the fabric remained recognizable as fabric. Between 1965 and 1985, however, the mixed-use quilt itself, rather than the various patches constituting it, came under principled attack. The Gem and the Silver Spade began to remove not mere hillsides but terrain, and to that very extent Harrison County started to look, from the air, like one big moonscape.

How do you explain the acceptance of these kinds of machines in settled Ohio hill country? How did it happen that the inhabitants of the original Seven Ranges allowed their land to be stripped so aggressively?

One possible answer to this question is that residents here were blindsided by a ruthless coal company that got the upper hand and used that advantage to build itself up at everyone else's maximum possible expense. Hanna Coal, after all, was founded by shipping magnate Mark Hanna, the "Lord of the Great Lakes" from Sister Etter's hometown of Lisbon who became nationally famous for securing disproportionately large amounts of campaign funds for McKinley in 1896, thereby deep-sixing William Jennings Bryan's populist aspirations.[125] "No man in public life owes the public anything," Hanna once explained refreshingly to an attorney general.[126] (In addition to expounding on the ethical dimension to public life, Hanna also offered maxims: "There are two things that are important in politics," one of them went. "The first is money, and I don't remember what the second one is.")[127] Hence it is relatively easy to cast Hanna Coal as a villainous force that happily, even gleefully, used blatantly false propaganda to convince Harrison County residents to overlook the environmental and cultural costs being passed on to them and, indeed, to support enthusiastically the very same people who were busy robbing them.

"Reclaiming Ohio's Hills" ran the banner-like heading on one 1940s-era Hanna Coal publicity poster, and that tiding was obviously joyous, for supporting pictures and captions everywhere communicated most people's idea of a very good life.[128] One picture depicted canoeists paddling across a lake that looks rather like the one the Allagash River pours out of in Maine, and another picture depicted two men enjoying the rigors of outdoor life by harvesting a stout-looking tree. ("Timber operations will outlast the coal," the caption proudly proclaimed.) Other pictures showed frisky rabbits, fishermen, woodchucks, legumes, and (a different caption aiding me here) "Boy Scouts and high school athletes" in the process of planting seedlings. But that was nothing next to a 1972 Silver-Spade-era article about Hanna Coal restoration efforts in *Coal News*.[129] There, beneath pictures of peach orchards, children riding on bikes, and clear ponds with canoes floating on them, readers learned that an Oklahoma-trained manager had arrived in Cadiz to set up (at company expense) a 6,000-acre beef ranch on land the company planned to give away. Apparently Hanna Coal was following through on a 1946 assertion that "cattle gain weight faster on reclaimed fields than on adjoining, unaffected ones," but follow-up articles on the fate of the first "pioneer" herd (175 head) could not, unfortunately, be found.

All told, this particular company's willingness to traffic in falsehood was impressive. Therefore, it is not out of bounds to argue that Harrison County residents consented to stripping on a massive scale because they were tricked. But it is also possible to argue that landowners here understood propaganda for the lie it was and *welcomed* it as a means of hoodwinking legislators in Columbus who might otherwise be swayed by Rachel Carson types who would push for restrictions and thereby cause Harrison County residents to lose jobs. People here had been mining coal long before Hanna Coal became the dominant player. They liked working above ground where it was relatively safe; they took pride in their ability to shoot and load coal expeditiously, and they were comfortable with spoil banks. More to the point, they valued the 100% recovery rate offered by surface mining every bit as much as Hanna Coal did, for a lot of the residents here had stakes— either in Hanna Coal (owing to buy-outs) or in local companies (R&F Coal, the Hopedale-based Puskarich brothers, Valley Mining) that continued to do business alongside Hanna. This was not West Virginia, where mountain people inadvertently lost their mineral rights when they sold timber to companies that were interested in making turpentine, lumber, and ship masts.[130] Thanks in large part to section-and-range technology, Ohioans had full conscious possession of those rights, and they sold or leased those rights deliberately because they wanted their property to be mined. Hence many Harrison County residents probably would have peddled stories about reclamation efforts themselves, if Hanna Coal hadn't already done it for them.

Another reason people here accepted draglines is that they were participants in a generally extractive economy that predisposed players to de-value the obvious long-term benefits of activities like sustainable farming. Thanks to railroads and the accompanying steel industry there was an accelerated need for coal (railroads were invented as a means for transporting large amounts of coal), and then, thanks to the intensified mining of this fuel, an opportunity arose to sell "under-clay" (the lake bed that coal formed on). At that point—1933, the year Lew Reese founded Scio Pottery six miles north of Cadiz—a new eastern Ohio ceramics industry appeared that buttressed and to some extent fanned the growth of surface mining. And then, right as the steel industry turned away from local coals toward imported (West Virginia) ones that "coked" better, electrical generating plants came on line, and they needed even more coal than the steel industry had. ("Cardinal," the American Electric Power-owned plant that the Ocie Clark is currently moored beside, goes through 100 railroad cars of coal per day to create flames that are 100 feet high and 45 feet across, and the FirstEnergy-owned "Sammis" plant, just upriver from Steubenville, goes through 130 cars per day.) Hence the upper Ohio valley was locked into a positive feedback loop that continually reinforced extractive logic. People here thought more and more in terms of taking resources (using them up) rather than generating them. Therefore, it makes sense that eastern Ohio residents would value fertile soil less and less. Nevertheless even this relatively strong explanation for the acceptance of draglines in Harrison County has a serious limitation, for it doesn't explain the almost complete absence of a counter-movement.

Given that the county was at one time an agricultural capital, ought there not to have been at least a *few* local people who objected to the presence of draglines? As I've already indicated, *Cadiz Republican* editor L. Milton Ronsheim did mount a campaign to rouse objectors and curtail stripping operations in Harrison County. Starting in 1941, just a few years before Hanna Coal started tempting Columbus lawmakers with offers of expense-paid plane trips to Florida in the company of apparently unattached female escorts, Ronsheim ran an aggressive series of editorials (and cartoons) in which he carefully itemized costs, proposed moratoriums, angrily called bluffs, invited discussion, and in general lobbied for reclamation laws that had teeth. Yet, outside of one schoolteacher and two farmers who helped debate Hanna Coal representatives during public hearings at American Legion Post 34, Ronsheim was almost uniformly dismissed (locally) as a "romantic agriculturalist" who was doomed to fail. How do we explain that lack of support? Why did Ronsheim's arguments not get the respect they deserved?

I submit that it was because landowners here (like the rest of us) had no word for what they were losing.

I have said that six miles south of Cadiz there is a building called Dickerson Church (Methodist) on the south side of impounded slurry.[131] What I haven't said is that the presence of this building is a remarkable sight. The building itself is modest, featuring a small wooden steeple with bird nests, a lawn with a picnic bench, and a cypress windbreak. Its prospect, though, is stunning, for this edifice stands all by itself on a hill that offers a 360-degree view. No doubt the view was impressive when the church was first built in 1888, but it is especially impressive now owing to the complete absence of trees on surrounding land. Though the land directly under this particular church never got stripped, land belonging to neighboring properties most certainly did.[132] Hence when you look out from Dickerson Church windows today you see nothing but desert in every direction for about as far as the eye can see. (The vista covers approximately 100 square miles.) Six miles to the north you see the county courthouse, of course, for that building stands on its own prominent hill, but at all other points of the compass you see only rock, poverty grass, black water, and—this being winter—snow. In other words, the building functions now as a tombstone. Owing to the fact that nobody holds services there any more, the church itself is lifeless, and the setting, needless to say, is a graveyard. Yet the church also (by its very existence) commemorates the community life it once embodied. Consequently, when you visit the site it is doubly appropriate to discover, on the east side of its grounds, a plaque commemorating camp meetings that used to occur at the site before the present church was built—in particular the meeting that resulted in the 1828 conversion of Cadiz native Matthew Simpson, who went on to become a Methodist Episcopal bishop.

This is the same Simpson who was asked to deliver the eulogy at Lincoln's burial in Springfield, and the plaque quotes from the text of Simpson's Illinois remarks. "Hushed is thy voice," the brass letters read, "but its echoes of liberty are ringing throughout the world and the sons of bondage listen with joy." Obviously, the people who made and installed this plaque didn't intend for a reader to look up, after absorbing Simpson's thought, and see a desert. Rather, they expected that a reader would look up and see what Joseph Holmes' grandson saw in 1888 upon dedicating the church—namely, "many streams which shall make glad the city of our God." Well, those streams are gone, and therefore the commemorative power of the plaque is in one respect severely compromised. In another respect, though, that commemorative aspect is heightened, for thanks to the wasteland that now exists on all four sides of the church, the plaque on its lawn now signs for future generations the inadequacy of bipolar rhetoric as a means of protecting land fabric and the kind of freedom it underwrites.

By the end of the nineteenth century the south Cadiz Methodist circuit, like most other institutions in Harrison County, had strong roots in abolitionist sentiment. It had stood, during the war years, at the exact center of a triangle defined by "Radical Republican" John Bingham's alma mater Franklin College to the southwest, *Genius of Universal Emancipation* editor Benjamin Lundy's Mt. Pleasant offices to the southeast, and conductor-producing Underground Railway terminal Cadiz to the north. In addition, the families who had comprised this circuit sent relatively high numbers of men (38 from Dickerson Church alone) to fight for the Union in the Civil War. Hence freedom-versus-slavery rhetoric was strong here. In fact, the area was so friendly to abolitionist sentiment that future Secretary of War Edwin Stanton actually made a conscious effort to *not* go to school here, lest he be infected with "extremist" thinking. Down in Athens, on the Franklin College roof-top bell, an inscription said *proclaim liberty throughout the land and to all the inhabitants thereof*, and when that bell rang, everyone understood it to mean *self-rule*. Notions of freedom that involved mutual interdependence as well as self-rule didn't even get a hearing, and with that particular "middle" excluded it became difficult, if not impossible, not to exclude other middles as well, not the least of which were any and all definitions of worth whereby land could come into view as something that could rightfully be mined but not rightfully destroyed. When it came to assessing the worth of land about to be devoured by draglines, you were either a utilitarian or a romantic. There was—as surmised in chapters 3 and 5—no middle way, and as a result the idea that land might be a condition of both existential and political freedom was completely lost to view.

What *is* land, if it is not "res extensa" or "virgin wilderness" or a form of capital whose main significance is to cause bubbles in the larger economy?[133] This is a tough question to answer under any circumstances, but it is especially tough now, given that land in the biggest sense has almost everywhere been destroyed. Wendell Berry says that in order to know what land is, you have to leave society and head for the woods,[134] but of course (as Berry well knows) it isn't that simple—first because "the woods" have been managed approximately forever, second because one needs to see that managed dimension clearly. Not easily done! Luckily, though, we have a guide in our midst who can help us in our search for a clear picture. His name is Aldo Leopold.

Seventy-five years ago, before Leopold became famous as a conservationist, Leopold was an analyst working for the US Department of Agriculture in New Mexico, and—excited though he was to be entrusted with the job of helping to manage a National Forest—he found himself in a difficult position, because yields of fish and timber were steadily declining, and he had no baseline for picturing those resources in a state of health. Hence Leopold set about building a picture from scratch via forensic research. He called his new practice "land pathology," and it entailed visualizing a formerly rich but now vanished ecological whole by observing current-day streams, vegetation, and wildlife and then trying to understand how these latter features came to be.[135] Most of the time Leopold looked at insect epidemics, the absence of mega-fauna, and distorted bird populations. But he also looked at landscape. In 1933, for example (as recounted by Leopold in his essay, "The Virgin Southwest"), he waited for a little while on the seemingly lush vista of cottonwoods along the Rio Grande River, and then, after reflecting on how cottonwoods both favor and collect silt, found his way back to an erosion-causing disappearance of commercial-grade (wildlife-supporting) timber in nearby mountain foothills, the former presence of grassy riverbanks, and the former impossibility of irrigation (owing to the depth of the riverbed, in comparison with adjoining bottomlands). In short, Leopold recognized that in many instances snapshots of current conditions were de-facto *negatives*, and his legacy—if we can call it that—is that such negatives can be developed so as to bring into view that which has been lost.

What comes into view when we develop negatives recorded in Harrison County?

First, we see terrain—which is to say, the set of climatic and topographical givens that determine what is ecologically and culturally possible—and in this case terrain turns out to mean un-glaciated plateau. Unlike northern and western Ohio, the surface of southeastern Ohio was never rearranged or added to by a moving, 1,000-foot-thick pack of ice. Given that southeast Ohio comprised the foothills of a formerly high Allegheny mountain range, ice flowed around this area rather than over it. Therefore the sedimentary logic readable in Harrison County fluvial sandstone has been (until recent years) intact. Yet, by the same token, this area has also been steadily eroded by rain. That's why it is hilly—unfit for agribusiness but rich in microclimates.

This brings us to the second thing we see, which is flora and fauna. Whereas land in, say, the Western Reserve tends to support sugar maple and wolves, land in southeast Ohio favors oak and turkeys. Those are our so-called "indicator" species. Up close on our developed negative, however, we can see a bit more than oak and turkeys, for in the hollows, and along the creek bottoms next to turtles and catfish and teal ducks and bullfrogs in reedy sloughs, you can see black willow, box elder, hackberry, and—rather spectacularly—sycamores. The first European settlers called these latter giants "water beech" (on account of their preference for riparian climes) and they often built homes under them, on the assumption that ground that could support a tree of that size had to be fertile. In fact, though, ridges and hillsides were equally productive. That is where a lot of the older oaks are, and in their midst you can spot tulip trees, twelve different varieties of hickory, black cherry, and (in hollows where temperatures stay lower) stands of hemlock fir that date from the last glacial advance. In the understory, where warblers and vireos nest, you can see dogwood, sassafras, American hornbeam, and striped maple, and at the very base, amongst fallen and now mossy trees and decaying leaves, you can find flowers like violets, wintergreen, trilliums, wild ginger, and jack-in-the-pulpit. And that is before even beginning to tabulate the cougar, fox, black bear, and elk who have also made their home here.

Say, though, that we were to supplement an understanding of terrain with a complete botanical/zoological inventory and a grasp of the energy circuit (to use Leopold's terminology) that ensures stability in any given biotic community. Would we then have grasped the full meaning of "land"? No, for there is a cultural dimension to "land" as well as a geological and a biological dimension. I don't just mean that land is a resource and therefore figures in human activity as, say, a "burial ground" or a "timber tract" or an "ore bed." I refer, rather, to the kind of inseparable cultural dimension that is on view when we call to mind a "foreign" equivalent to the land we were born and raised in. Wheat and apples, for example, define the Middle East. Rice and silk define China, while corn, tomatoes, and peppers define the Americas. Or sharpen that gaze a little. Focus on products that are made from several uniquely available natural ingredients rather than from just one widely but not universally available ingredient, and suddenly specific areas within each continent come clearly into view. Navajo rugs (thanks to juniper root, sagebrush, prickly pear cactus, and ochre dyes) define Aldo Leopold's New Mexico, and "Tennessee Trouble" quilts (thanks to pokeberry, black walnut, peach leaf, and alum dyes) define Harrison County. How does it happen that things made by humans from the raw natural materials comprising land do more to sharpen our understanding of a given terrain's character than anything else? I think it's because distinctive natural features don't really become recognizable until they have been "raised" into a cultural dimension as well as a natural one. When the North American tectonic plate was south of the equator during the Devonian era, it supported a coral reef whose fossilized remains are now exposed in a ledge on the Kentucky/Indiana state line, but those fossilized remains and the rock in which the remains are embedded didn't become "land" until they created a two-mile stretch of falls on the Ohio River and obstructed river traffic significantly enough to force the creation of a town called Louisville.

Another important detail that we learn from looking at negatives is that land changes. In addition to showing four different seasonal "faces," thanks to shifts in the availability of sunlight, land evolves depending on micro-geological and historical developments. For example, land meant one thing when it was managed and to that extent created by Europeans who used draft animals to plant rye, and it meant quite a different thing when it was managed and to that extent created by eastern Woodland tribes who cultivated corn and beans by hand in an effort to supplement fish, hickory nuts, and wild grapes. Or look at Harrison County "land" as it appeared during the Hopewell era, which closed about the same time that St. Benedict founded his first monastery. At that point the land that we now call Harrison County was best on view courtesy of clay pipes and bowls, the use of meteoric iron, large-scale earthen mounds, carved flint, salamander effigies, and an accumulation of sheet mica from North Carolina, copper from Minnesota, shells from the Gulf coast, and also obsidian from Wyoming. How did these objects get here? Archaeologists believe they were tributes.[136] Precious metals and rare stones came into this area at a far greater rate than they left it, during the Hopewell era; hence researchers now believe that western upper Ohio tributaries were rich enough to function as pilgrimage sites between 200BC and 500AD—i.e., as places where the alignment of constructed mounds (or perhaps just arresting natural features like waterfalls cascading over lips of eroded Black Hand sandstone into pools bordered by fir) enabled visitors to "see" into the cosmos in uniquely effective ways.

But I am getting off-track.

The important point here is that land has a temporal dimension as well as a spatial one. Think of it, let us say, as a kind of geologically-determined glow whose intensity increases or fades in accordance with the amount of energy harvested from the sun by localized plants, and, too, the capacity of localized animals and particularly humans to convert that energy into diverse forms of biological and cultural capital. In some instances—here I think of an island in the Pacific that has just formed thanks to volcanic activity—that glow can be rather "young." But in other instances—and here I think first and foremost of the relatively undisturbed Cross Creek watershed southwest of Cadiz before it was stripped—that glow might already have lasted for a long time. How long? Given that earlier archaeological records are easily lost, we will probably never know for sure. But, by the same token, we can be sure that land lasts at least as long as it demonstrably already has, and in the upper Ohio valley, and specifically along Cross Creek, that carbon-dated "mark" currently reads 16,000 years.

This means that recently destroyed land southwest of Cadiz had been certifiably aglow longer than any other piece of land, anywhere, on the entire continent of North America.

The exact spot where you can observe an unbroken archaeological record stretching across 16,000 years is a naturally dry, overhang-protected dust shelf called "Meadow Croft Rock Shelter" that is situated 50 feet above an oxbow in West Virginia's west-running "Cross Creek." Luckily, that watershed was never stripped. Nevertheless you can be certain that Meadow Croft residents at least frequented the similarly sized, apposite, and now thoroughly stripped valley belonging to Ohio's east-running "Cross Creek,"[137] for, as the dual name implies, these two valleys comprised the eastern and western segments of a natural trade route marked by consistently gentle (if serpentine) grades and perfect alignment at the point where the two creeks pour their waters into the Ohio and form sandbars. In other words, the very same land that Joseph Holmes made engravings of to illustrate Caldwell's 1875 atlas was in all likelihood hunted, camped on, and in effect managed by men and women who worked on the sunny side of an ice wall that loomed over their heads to the north.

Sixteen thousand years ago the ridges, streams, and hillsides on view outside my kitchen window looked like Beringia! Instead of hickories, oaks, and soft maple there were dwarf birches, spruce, and cedar trees. Northeast of Cleveland, where Atlantic coast beach grass was established thanks to the unprecedented nearness of the Champlain Sea, a Laurentide ice sheet was still moving on churning, melted underparts, but here in Harrison County land was grassy and free of moraines. Toward New Philadelphia, Conotton Creek was a lake, thanks to till deposits left by retreating ice, but here below my house the creek ran across its flood plain exactly as it does today.[138] It ran at a temperature that was just a little above freezing, and animals grazing or hunting on its saxifrage-friendly banks would have included saiga antelope, extra-large lions, caribou, Dall sheep, and mastodons, which were the American equivalent of African elephants. There was no highway, and at night there were no lights except the ones emanating from fires. Sometimes that firelight came from a tree hit by lightning, and at other times it came from a smoldering coal bank. Most of the time, though, it came from cook fires. Those fires would have been tended by men and women who wore leather and carried "atlatls" for throwing flint-pointed spears, and they would have arrived, these fires, by being carried over the same Flushing escarpment "pass" that the CSX railroad follows today—to wit, the saddle between Hopedale and Cadiz at the headwaters of east-running Cross Creek.

Which gives me an idea.

Given that there is no consensus, yet, regarding the value and even the substance of what has been lost by aggressive surface mining here, ought we not to abstain temporarily from using the grand but perhaps overly used word "land" and go instead with a different label? That way we could at least remember that we have a big gap in our knowledge. Assuming, then, that this maneuver makes sense, and assuming, too, that "Word" and "Creation" no longer qualify as appropriate labels in a post-Christian age, I hereby nominate "place" as a provisional label, for when we say (for example) "Cross Creek" out loud we are instantly linked to: (1) topographical logic that makes a crossing feasible; (2) several different eco-tones that have at different points in time given the region smell and taste; (3) Presbyterian minister James McGready's first revivals;[139] (4) Hopewell trading patterns; (5) Pennsylvania and Norfolk Western Railroad grades that confirmed the rightness of Mingo and "Whiskey Rebel" path-finding instinct; (6) camp sites belonging to both Logan (the Mingo chief who precipitated the 1774 Lord Dunmore War) and George Washington (who stashed a canoe here in 1770 and then traveled overland before the snows); (7) coal seams exposed by two creeks as they wind their way through 600 vertical feet of sandstone; (8) related drift mines and the tarpaper-shack culture they gave rise to; (9)

steel mills at the mouth of east-running Cross Creek; and (10) bands of prehistoric nomadic hunters who drank from hillside seeps at each creek's source. That's a long list, yet every single "picture" figures crucially and irreplaceably in the overall meaning of "Cross Creek" and therefore also in the accounting of what vanishes from view once one loses "Cross Creek." In other words, by opting for a provisional label like "place"—rather than "overburden" or "pastoral landscape"—we would at least stand a chance of recognizing the erasure of Harrison County's geologically inflected biocultural light for the breathtakingly bold step that it was.

7

Organized Crime

Putting notebooks aside, I stand up and walk through a door leading out of the wheelhouse to a small deck festooned with bright red life rings and similarly cheerful axes. The sun is behind us now, but on all other accounts our situation is unchanged. The Ocie Clark is still laid up beside Cardinal mooring cells, the barges comprising our former tow are still fully loaded, and the river level is still a couple feet above ideal pool elevation. Bradley and Jim are repairing a broken winch on the foredeck, while the Captain works at a computer terminal. You would think that if a boat is moored, its pilot would get a breather. But Merchant Marine towing vessel licensee John Joseph Lynch has not stopped working. He has entered fuel and lubrication information, filled out a discharge report, fielded emails from South Point about how he wants his next tow built, completed a traffic log, and installed new management software that allows a pilot to make "event" entries relating to crew changes, arrivals and departures, unforeseen channel obstructions, and alterations in engine speed owing to rising water or changes in the weather. Trained though he may have been as a deckhand, engineer, and Black Warrior/Tombigbee steersman, this pilot is now for all intents and purposes an office worker. Well, I suppose that is how it always has been and always will be. No doubt Captain James Kirk did his share of paperwork, and I furthermore suspect he enjoyed it.

  For a while I study the generating station next to which we are moored with binoculars, and then, looking north/northeast toward the two Cross Creeks five miles upriver on the other side of Ohioan hills, I see a new, thickly-churning plume of exhaust climbing rapidly from what can only be Mingo Furnace #5. Knowing as I do that we may not get there on this trip, I try not to think about the fire in that furnace. Instead I duck back inside to read through my notes and organize my thoughts. Almost instantly, though, the fax machine comes to life. Jack reaches over, pulls a newly arrived document from a tray, and squints. Then he turns and looks out at me over the tops of reading glasses. "We're headed back to Shoemaker," he says. "They have twelve coal loaded, and we're supposed to take them north." So, I think. Here it comes. First Mingo, then Steubenville. I've been looking forward to seeing Steubenville from the water from the moment I got on board, but now that I hear we will actually come up on the place, 'round about midnight, I feel uneasy. There's a lot to puzzle over in Steubenville, given its peculiar mix of post-Reagan Republican orthodoxy and apparition-based gnosis, and before unpacking all of that we've still got to think through the second kind of strip-mining technology developed out in Cadiz—the one that had relatively little to do with draglines proper.

Quick recap.

The main thing we learned in the last chapter is that, thanks to the institution of bipolar logic and a turn away from medieval conceptions of land, we at some point lost the ability to understand the destruction of land as an egregious, perhaps even suicidal, act and became able, perhaps for the first time, to invent and deploy machines that were designed specifically to rip out an entire land fabric rather than mere pieces of a land fabric. Would it not also make sense that we might then invent and deploy a different kind of machine that could take out cultural capital like small towns in addition to land? In this chapter I propose to answer this latter question by scrutinizing ways in which Congressman John Bingham of Cadiz crafted the Fourteenth Amendment so that it could liberate the ancestors of modern-day multinational corporations at the same time that it shackled state power, which could have served to police and rein in those same corporations.

First, though, it will be wise to take a brief glance northward toward Steubenville, if only to discern what Bingham's kind of crime isn't.

❧

Like Cadiz, Steubenville was a lively, well-functioning place during and immediately after the Roosevelt/Taft years.[140] In addition to La Belle Iron Works and the High Shaft coal portal at the corner of Washington and 7th, the town's financial engine was powered by a glass company that made lamp chimneys, a stone quarry, a college for ladies on South 4th St, and a paper mill that employed two hundred people. There was daily train service to St. Louis, Pittsburgh, Cleveland, Wheeling, and New York. When long distance trains pulled in, they sometimes sported red Pullmans with gold letters spelling "Pocahontas," "Brandywine," or "Empress," and though most Steubenville residents probably dreamt about riding in those kinds of cars, they mostly rode on Tri-State Traction trolleys from downtown street corners to East Liverpool and Mingo Junction. The fare was 5¢—one jitney per pop. On the north side of town, at the site of the current US Rt. 22/State Rt. 7 interchange, there was Stanton Park, which featured a roller rink and a Merry-Go-Round livened by a Wurlitzer. (The amusement park was built by East Liverpool Traction Company to lure Tri-State riders.) To the south, on a plain below the Carnegie-funded public library that featured—of course—a Romanesque tower, circuses were sometimes encamped, and to the west, above a toll gate and a watering trough for horses pulling wagons up Market St. toward Cadiz, there was Moodey's Hill, which featured spectacular views of the river, hay meadows, and a new row of sizeable spec homes. An elaborate system of stone steps connected that new development to a workingman's Polish neighborhood that had sprung up at the hill's base, and (I know this because I bought and restored one of the original hilltop homes) along the way those steps passed a bandstand and an ice-cold, good-tasting, clear-flowing spring. Downtown, on sidewalks, people chewed "pepsin" gum (invented by Ohio physician Edward E. Beeman). They wore "dicers." They cut deals on cobbled streets in front of pushcarts and they read "funny papers." They heated homes with "house coal" (50¢ a bushel, delivered), they made their own ketchup and root beer, and they listened to "crystal sets" (radios). Even more wondrously, they dressed to the nines when it came time to shop downtown. They took their public lives seriously, and locally-owned businesses repaid the compliment. Sulzbacher's, a clothier with three floors of merchandise on the south side of Market between 4th and 5th, employed a staff of forty. Neighboring businesses included a steam laundry, a grocer, several billiard parlors, and a wallpaper shop. Tickets for trans-Atlantic crossings could be purchased at Morelli & Co., on 4th, and around the corner, at "The Hub" department store on North 5th, you could get a shave and then dine on chicken pot pie with gravy while waiting for a set of shoes to be repaired.

The air had soot in it, and acrid fumes from the paper mill confirmed the region's already sulfurous metabolism, but in terms of social and financial ecology Steubenville was healthy.

Starting around 1930, though, the character of this town began to change owing to the appearance of stripping operations that were, admittedly, a little like the ones that showed up out in Cadiz. In fact, though, there were strong differences, and foremost among them was Steubenville's fiercely-challenged (yet undeniably real) net gain in liveliness upon hosting its particular brand of extractive industry.

The type of stripping operation that transformed Steubenville was illegal gambling. Thanks to the passage of the Eighteenth Amendment in 1919 and the ensuing prohibition of alcohol sales, bootlegging became big business in the Twenties, and given that Steubenville was already well established as a way station for the shipment of iron ore from the Great Lakes to steel mills on the upper Ohio, it made sense that the new Canadian ore also known as bootlegged liquor would start to flow through town as well. At the same time, the Hanna-enabled, speakeasy-friendly "Ohio Gang" that had put Harding into office encouraged Cleveland and neighboring upper Ohio law-enforcement agencies to grow rich by looking the other way. Thus conditions were well-nigh perfect in eastern Ohio for the establishment of illegal gaming and prostitution, let alone smuggling, and in Steubenville, a town that boasted a large proportion of miners and steelworkers with weekly paychecks to burn, gambling establishments and related amusements proliferated to such an extent that they became transformative. In the mid-Thirties nearly every downtown street featured a cigar store where you could buy a newspaper from a tidily dressed merchant and then walk through a small door into a more commodious establishment where, under the watchful gaze of a man who had access to a sawed-off shotgun, you could shoot craps, wait for a steel marble to settle in a slot on a turning wheel, or lay down a bet on a horse or a number with one of eleven different town-based bookmaking ventures. In addition to Capital Cigar, Smokestack Cigar, Corner Cigar, and Penn Lounge Cigar, there was Olympic Cigar, Freddie's Cigar, Dixie Cigar, and Hy-Hat Cigar. Other venues included the Academy (which professed to be about billiards but in fact specialized in wire feeds from races all over the country), and the somewhat more candidly named "Turk Bertram's," which was across the street from the train station. But those were exceptions. Most of the action happened in joints that were fronted by ads for pipe tobacco and, to that degree, visually integrated with mom-and-pop businesses. Security personnel working at Cosmo Quattrone's Rex Cigar sat in an armored booth, yet on the outside that establishment blended almost seamlessly with next-door neighbors M&M Hardware and the still lively, heavily patronized "Hub" department store.

It wasn't so much that Steubenville had a secret "under-life." On the contrary, the prevalence of gambling was as plainly in view as the time-honored but now enhanced red light district on Water Street (twenty houses, two hundred "girls"). Sixth, seventh, and eighth grade boys ran numbers across town for bookies like Pooch Lloyd or Money O'Brien as naturally as they delivered papers, and if the errand boys were a couple years older they were more likely to learn what it was like to carry $5,000 in cash than to learn that in some towns gambling might be considered wrong. Kids who showed academic promise didn't so much think in terms of getting good grades as asking for a percentage rather than a tip. During the 1930s gambling didn't just occur in Steubenville. Rather, it was part of the air everybody breathed, thus cigar store "fronts" had everything to do with decorum and almost nothing to do with furtive attempts to hide. Just as it made sense to maintain a separate red-light district in order to not confuse homemakers with striptease artists (i.e., keep both vocations pure), so too it made sense to screen gambling establishments that were inseparably linked to the town's business district. The advantage was twofold. By putting actual gambling operations out of sight, gamblers could move and live and have their being in comfortable, even respectful, atmospheres at the same time that gambling critics could, in turn, live their life without the constant aggravation of seeing people gamble. As for right and wrong, that depended on where you were standing. To a lot of the Steubenville business establishment, life itself was one long hustle, and the best you could do, if you were running a gaming joint, was to provide an environment where, most of the time, customers could win a pre-figured amount fair and square. If the entire house suddenly became at risk owing to a weirdly lucky streak or an invader's ill will—well, at that point it made sense to call in a mechanic to fix the dice or the wheel that was the occasion of the house's loss. But if the house wasn't at risk, if its edge was constant, in that case managers had an almost religious obligation to ensure a level playing field.

Steubenville street corners were hopping places during the 1930s.[141] For a while in this town, it really did seem as though one could get something for nothing, and in order to celebrate this miraculous window of opportunity, night clubs and band stages sprouted up every bit as thickly as cigar stores had. Big acts—Glen Miller, Judy Garland—played at the 2,000-seat Capitol Theater on the corner of 4th and Adams. Other large-scale venues included the Grand (in the Griesinger Building on South 4th), the Paramount (on North 5th), the Strand (5th and Market), the Olympic (north side of Market, just west of the courthouse), and the Half Moon Club (site of the former roller rink at Stanton Park). But the serious music happened at small bars like the Venetian that were upstairs from, or next-door to, the gambling joints. Steubenville native Dean Martin learned to sing by sitting in with "The Starlighters" at Walker's on Washington Street during breaks from his job as a card dealer at Rex Cigar, and pianist Dorothy Sloop, who went on to lead female jazz bands in New Orleans, learned her trade at Tony Lamantia's Hy Hat Club on North 4th. Other musicians who apprenticed in Steubenville included pianist Dodo Marmarosa, who later did gigs with Gene Krupa, and drummer Mickey Scrima, who wound up keeping time for Harry James. It wasn't New York, but proportionally speaking Steubenville burned pretty bright—hotly enough, at any rate, to make it possible to nurse wounds or even refuel by ordering Chinese, come 3 AM, at the perpetually open "Imperial" just east of the train depot.

The hitch was that the establishment and eventual success of cigar stores necessitated financial tributes to whoever provided protection, and perhaps even more importantly to the Mayfield Road syndicate in Cleveland that controlled the Steubenville numbers racket. Organized crime had made Steubenville's boom possible, and now that it was reaping returns a pattern of graft became firmly established. Hence there were two governments in town—the elected one and the real one. This made the implementation of democratic ideals difficult, and that fact, in turn, led some citizens to start referring to Steubenville as "little Chicago."

Was the moniker accurate?

Given the extraordinary influence and indebtedness of Steubenville political bosses like Pinky Nolan and Hugo "Nunzie" Alexander, employing "little Chicago" in connection with Steubenville was certainly reasonable. In the end, though, it would be a mistake to rely on the "little Chicago" analogy as a *key*. For Steubenville's twin city wasn't Chicago. Rather, it was Vegas.

Several years ago I did a job on Lawson Avenue in Steubenville's once prestigious "Pleasant Heights" subdivision above the steel mill, and when I sat outside having lunch I got intrigued by the fact that one of the houses on the other side of the street had no place number. It turned out that the house had once belonged to a man named Cornelius Jones who had the misfortune of being publicly identified during the 1950 Kefauver hearings as a man who had durable ties to the Mob, and, naturally, this otherwise law-abiding Steubenville citizen took steps to restore his family's privacy. What did "ties to the Mob" mean? In Jones' case, it meant running a swanky East Cleveland nightclub called "The Mounds" for bootlegger kingpin Moe Dalitz, and—even more importantly—being one of the original owners of the Dalitz-directed Desert Inn out in Las Vegas. In other words, Steubenville resident Cornelius Jones owned a stake in a Vegas casino that: (1) predated Tony Accardo's Chicago-funded Stardust; (2) was the Cleveland syndicate's answer to Frank Costello's and Meyer Lansky's New-York-funded Flamingo;[142] and (3) was the site of Frank Sinatra's Las Vegas debut. (The Desert Inn opened in 1949 and the Stardust opened its doors in 1950, after Costello and Lansky cleared the way by taking over Bugsy Siegel's Flamingo in 1947; as for Sinatra, he went on to secure a stake in the Sands, which opened in 1952.) Moreover, three years after the Kefauver hearings, Jones upped his commitment by moving himself, his wife, and his two daughters to Vegas in order to *supervise* the western casino operation. And the story didn't stop there, for it turned out that Jones was not the only Steubenville gaming expert with an early Vegas link.

Steubenville native Tony Torcasio, for example, had been based in Nevada since 1946, so as to manage Desert Inn construction. And, after a stint in Havana, Bobby and Fred Ayoub (sons of a Steubenville clothing merchant) arrived in 1951 to help set up the Sands. (Bobby Ayoub later organized the casino at Monte Carlo.) In 1953, Rex Cigar roulette wheel operator Al Facinto emigrated to Vegas (alongside Jones) to work at the Dunes as a floorman. Later, Facinto helped found Caesar's Palace. Al's sons, Mokie and Al, Jr., were destined, respectively, to run the casino at Caesar's Palace and serve as president of MGM Mirage International, but before all that happened Al's childhood buddy Demetrios Georgios Synodinos, a.k.a. Jimmy the Greek, arrived in 1956 from Steubenville to parlay oddsmaker skills into a job promoting "betting propositions," and a few years after that fellow classmate James Marti arrived.[143] James, for his part, had been working as a croupier behind Steubenville cigar fronts since he was twelve. All told, at least twenty different Steubenville families migrated to Las Vegas in the early-to-mid 50s in order to either key or supervise new gaming operations. More families followed, and still other Steubenville families supported Nevada gambling by anchoring operations in *other* up-and-coming locales.[144]

Bob Sasso, who ran the Academy billiard parlor and co-owned the Mayflower lunchroom, went on to mentor Florida Beach Club owner Colonel William Riley Bradley in the art of horse-betting enterprises, and after that he ran the casino at Paradise Island, in the Bahamas. Joey Tamburo helped set up casinos in Reno. Steubenville High alumnus Joseph Nesline helped to establish the Amber Club in Washington DC before becoming famous for managing prostitution rings in Hamburg, and Rex Cigar ace mechanic Dino Cellini even won the top management job at the internationally renowned Tropicana in Havana on the basis of his Steubenville-honed bust-out and dice-cheat skills. After Fidel came to power and the Bay of Pigs invasion failed, Cellini by most accounts took a little time off to dissuade anybody and everybody who had a gripe against Kennedy from acting on that gripe, but after securing safe passage out of Cuba, Cellini reverted to form and helped set up new operations for Meyer Lansky in Atlantic City. And we haven't even gotten yet to the aforementioned Dino Crocetti, a.k.a. Dino Martini, who trained at Wells as a boxer, dealt cards alongside Cellini at Rex Cigar, and then went on to anchor just about every gambling operation the whole world over with deceptively simple crooner songs, off-color jokes, an ever-present martini prop, and high-voltage, Sinatra-balanced swing.

Can one even *imagine* Vegas in 1959 without the cannily drunk member of the Rat Pack, or New York City's 1947-vintage Copacabana without the "straight" man opposite Jerry Lewis? Without those particular Steubenville exports, gambling revenue in the United States would have been halved. But, as I say, we really don't need to factor in Dean Martin to assess the importance of Steubenville in the world of gambling. If we confine our gaze to cigar store expertise alone, Steubenville still figures as the secret enabler of the entire phenomenon.

Many Steubenville residents were of course proud of this distinction. However, just as many other residents weren't, and eventually this latter group of citizens put its foot down and called for the permanent closure of gambling establishments and brothels alike. After a man was killed in 1946 outside Slim Brewer's Silver Slipper at 200 Market Street, Presbyterian, Baptist, Lutheran, and Methodist pastors banded together and issued a challenge to the community at large. Calling the city "mortally ill" and "polluted with the vile salacious odor of immorality," they pledged to declare war on "pimps, punks, and prostitutes," even going so far as to ask the city council to "deputize" *ministers* so that presumably enlightened corrective measures might be adequately enforced.[145] At a subsequent meeting in an auditorium at Steubenville High, some 1,500 townspeople voiced their support by singing "Battle Hymn of the Republic." That was too much for Roman Catholic Bishop John King Mussio, to whom many of the Polish, Irish, and Italian miscreants were parishioners. In a pastoral letter published by Steubenville's *Herald Star*, the recently installed bishop stated that he would "not tolerate any attempt by anyone to legislate false morals for our people," and he backed that statement up with a pledge to resist vigorously "any attempt to put into law what is unreasonable, discriminatory, and based upon a puritanical attitude towards pleasurable occupations." Yes, prostitution was wrong. But—gambling? That was only a problem if it began to master a person. And so on. It was an aggressive letter that to some extent stole back moral high ground that had been claimed by the "clergy coalition," and as a result the idea of deputizing ministers was abandoned and gambling concerns revved back up to the point where Steubenville appeared, once again, to be a wide-open town.

In fact, though, Protestant ministers had delivered a lethal blow. The blow had landed in the exact same year that Franciscan Third-Order-Regular friars got it into their heads to found a new university in former Knights of Pythias offices above Walker's, the bar where Dean Martin learned to sing. Therefore, it was only a matter of time before calls for the protection of "our youth" trumped any and all calls for the legitimization of gambling, drinking, and whoring. By the late 1950s Steubenville auto salesmen were running for *mayor* on "anti-vice" tickets, and by 1966, thanks to increasingly generous FBI assistance and an open letter signed by Protestants, Jews, *and Catholics*, newly elected mayor Sam Pollock Miller pronounced the city "closed to crime."[146] Rex Cigar and Slim's Merry-Go-Round were gone.

Who, really, had had the upper hand in those 1946 debates? Which side had been wronged? Given that Steubenville is now an empty shell whose most distinctive markings are channels established by a long history of graft, it would appear that the clergy coalition's assessment was correct and that full-scale gambling did take a serious toll. Now that gambling has been exterminated, one of the coalition ministers might say, "look for yourself and see the size of the hole those gambling practices dug!" Courthouse scalped, rail service terminated, parish lines erased, downtown boarded up, four-lane highway and a jail where a park ought to be. Instead of working for a living in the 1930s, Steubenville citizens had been encouraged to *steal* from future generations, and now the rest of us have to live on a vacant lot featuring glass shards, spilled anti-freeze, and spiky mullein instead of in a functioning town! Yet if Rex Cigar's Cosmo Quattrone or Imperial Hotel proprietor William Becker were listening, they might interrupt at this point to assert loudly that vacant lots are the direct result of the clergy coalition's *attack* on gambling enterprises. Look at Vegas, they would say. If it hadn't been for the clergy coalition, Steubenville might have *held on* to the brave citizens who were busy building paradise and thereby become a tourist destination itself! That remark would of course bring out smiles, but the sentiment that would have driven it still has currency, and, curiously, it still enlivens the faces of a surprisingly large percentage of Steubenville natives.

Take Marty Sammon, the stockbroker and boxing referee who first explained to me how Prohibition-era Steubenville worked.[147] Marty learned how to box in Steubenville while running numbers for Pooch Lloyd, and after learning the referee trade by deciding fights in San Quentin Prison he went on to referee 58 world title fights. I first met Marty in the late 1990s when he approached me on a Steubenville sidewalk to ask what a guy with Californian tastes was doing in the smog-rich upper Ohio Valley. Given that my interlocutor also looked out of place—he stood about 6-foot-two, had a well-broken nose, and was wearing a spotless, extremely well preserved 101st Airborne flight jacket—I invited him over for breakfast, and after getting the lowdown on the jacket—Marty had served as a paratrooper and he wore the 101st Airborne jacket to commemorate a 1957 deployment to Little Rock Arkansas for the purpose of protecting (without live ammunition) nine black children who, thanks to the 1954 Supreme Court decision in *Brown v. the Board of Education*, had decided to brave hecklers and exercise their right to attend Little Rock High—I asked him about Cosmo Quattrone's read on Steubenville's demise. Marty concurred, and as he started to declaim on the beauty of a wide-open town, I learned some things about Depression-era Steubenville that I hadn't known before.

I learned, for example, that running numbers from one part of town to another (the guys young Sammon worked for called him "Fish") meant, well, running. I learned that Irish kids went to St. Pete's parochial school, Italian kids went to St. Anthony's, Poles went to St. Stan's, black kids went to Ulysses S. Grant public, and the rest—the ones who "weren't sure"—went to Holy Names (diocesan seat). Boxing clubs? Completely integrated. I learned, too, that grit in the air tasted differently, depending on which chimney it spewed from, and that Steubenville Pottery surged in 1938 owing to a new color called "sea-foam blue." I learned that there was a cop with a whistle in his mouth at 4th and Market all day long, that the 98¢ roast beef sandwich at the Palace lunch counter couldn't be beat, and that the river end of Dock Street was oddly quiet when "cruise" ship revelers disembarked on icy evenings for a night on the town. In short, I learned that on a fundamental level Steubenville was every bit as bright, during Prohibition years, as it had been during the Taft/Roosevelt years.

So, who was right: the ministers? Or Cosmo?

Luckily, we don't have to answer this question because to a certain degree they were both wrong. Downtown Steubenville wasn't destroyed by small-time thievery or crusades against vice. Rather, it was destroyed by a junket of federally funded urban-renewal projects that razed neighborhoods in favor of housing projects, a new "super" highway (1963) that foreclosed the possibility of a working waterfront, and a new form of seriously organized crime that ate away at the economic and societal essentials that small time thievery and moral crusades and indeed all town-based life forms depend on—namely, a constellation of locally-owned businesses, and a vigorously involved faith-based citizenry. (Gamblers too have a set of guiding hunches.) What, the reader might fairly wonder, is "seriously organized" crime? Jimmy the Greek once observed that "crime has always struck me as notoriously disorganized," adding that "if it were not, if there really was such a thing as organized crime, it would run the country,"[148] and though Jimmy may not himself have been respectably credentialed in these matters, it does turn out that he was surprisingly close in his assessment to the view of prestigious scholars like Karl Polanyi, who have speculated rather more systematically about the collusion between government and so-called big business during the creation and enforcement of so-called free markets.

That having been established, let us lift our eyes from Steubenville for a spell so we can focus attention, as our instincts first prodded us, on societal strip-mining technology that was developed in 1866 by Congressman John A. Bingham thirty miles to the west in the (bone-dry) town of Cadiz.

Bingham's list of accomplishments is long. His father was a carpenter like me, but after apprenticing with a Cadiz-based printer, Bingham got smart and attended Franklin College in New Athens (ten miles south) so he could pass the Ohio bar and get chosen, by popular vote, to represent Ohio's 21st and 16th districts in Congress. Except for one two-year interval in 1863 and 1864, when he failed to get re-elected, Bingham served in Washington from 1855 to 1873, and during all of those years, 1863 and 1864 included, Bingham proved himself to be a fierce supporter of Union war efforts. In addition to advocating for Cadiz wool growers, Bingham: (1) delivered a rousing call to arms outside the Cadiz courthouse in response to Lincoln's 1861 call for 75,000 troops;[149] (2) forcefully challenged Clement Vallandigham when the Peace Democrat questioned Lincoln's wartime suspension of constitutional rights;[150] (3) nominated both Custer and Stanton to the posts that made them famous; (4) helped to drive and orchestrate the aforementioned 37th Congress, which pushed through industry-friendly legislation that had previously been blocked by southern states; and (5) served as judge-advocate in the court where four of the seven people charged with conspiring to assassinate Lincoln were found guilty and subsequently hanged. Later, Bingham also served as prosecutor during 1868 impeachment proceedings against Democratic President Andrew Johnson. (Johnson had tried to fire Bingham associate and former War Secretary Edwin Stanton, and, in general, put a brake on reconstruction policies that had been designed to remake the South in the North's image.)

It's an impressive resume, and, indeed, on these counts alone Bingham certainly deserves the bronze statue erected in his honor outside the well-proportioned Second-Empire-themed courthouse in Cadiz. As it happens, though, Bingham also burnished his reputation with one other seemingly modest accomplishment, and that was to author, in his capacity as a member of the Reconstruction-directing Joint Committee of Fifteen, the first (quite brief but absolutely key) section of the Fourteenth Amendment to the Constitution of the United States.

We have already talked, in chapter 4, about the enormous significance of the Fourteenth Amendment. We noted there that though the ostensible purpose and (as Marty Sammons' deployment to Little Rock High reminds us) one eventual import of the amendment was to guarantee access by freed slaves to the same set of legal protections that white citizens enjoyed, the amendment also functioned in such a way as to redistribute power between the states and the federal government drastically enough to cause the United States of America to be re-founded as a centralized state rather than a republic. Should I also have pointed out that later generations of jurists were destined to discover, in Fourteenth Amendment language, a zone of privacy that enabled the passage of constructive decisions like Roe vs. Wade? I think not, for that particular detail might have taken us too far afield. Here though, as promised, we do have to analyze at least one other aspect to the Fourteenth Amendment's apparently limitless significance, and that is the way in which the legislation strengthened corporations as well freed slaves, the federal government, and progressively minded jurists.

Prior to 1868, which was the year the Fourteenth Amendment became law, state governments held corporations on a pretty tight leash. Perhaps because the memory of British East India Tea Company predation was still fresh, states granted corporations customized charters that could be revoked, should a corporation act in a way that proved injurious to a given community's ability to govern itself. Yes, there was Union Pacific. And, yes, the liberation of modern corporations was already underway thanks to the hotly contested arrival of "limited liability" concepts, Pennsylvania Railroad president Thomas Scott's invention of the holding company, and (a little further back) the Marshall Court's 1819 decision in *Dartmouth v. Woodward*, which implicitly created a zone where private corporate charters were to some extent immune to the threat of revocation in a way that public charters weren't. But the Union Pacific, created as it was almost by national behest, was clearly an exception, and even though after the Civil War regular corporations were becoming noticeably less accountable to the communities they operated in, they still had to apply to states for the "privilege" of doing business within any given state's borders. Additionally (assuming that they did business in more than one state), corporations faced wildly varying degrees of taxation and regulation. Well, the Fourteenth Amendment changed all that, and it did so by means of two clauses that prohibited states from discriminating between classes of "persons" when imposing fees or taking property.

Let us recite, once again, the entire text of Bingham's Section One: "No state shall make or enforce any law which shall abridge the privileges and immunities of citizens of the United States; nor shall any state deprive any person of life, liberty, or property without due process of law; nor deny to any person within its jurisdiction the equal protection of the law."

To the lawmakers who first read Bingham's draft, that phrasing was familiar, for text refering to "privileges and immunity" was lifted from the U.S. Constitution's comity clause in Article IV, Section II, which guaranteed the rights of citizens living in one state to conduct business in a different state, and text stipulating that persons shall not be "deprived of life, liberty, or property without due process of law" was lifted from the Fifth Amendment. Yet in another sense the phrasing was new—firstly because privileges and immunities are presumed by Bingham to have been granted by the United States rather than the several states; secondly because the forces that threaten to deprive persons of life, liberty, and property without due process are presumed by Bingham to be state governments rather than the federal one; and, thirdly, because the passages lifted from the comity clause and the Fifth Amendment have been linked by Bingham to a third and entirely new person-oriented "equal protection" clause. Given that in a juristic sense corporations had long been thought of as "persons," the insertion of that clause into the text of the Fourteenth Amendment had special import for empowering corporations as well as overcoming racism. It meant (implicitly) that the individual states comprising the United States would no longer be able to regulate corporations differently from how they regulated people or, indeed, assume that corporations were subservient to people. Should the proposed amendment become law, it would be within reach to assume that corporations, despite inbuilt avariciousness and potential immortality, had the *same rights as people*, and starting almost from the day the Fourteenth Amendment was enacted, corporate lawyers began pressing hard for that previously farfetched advantage.

Think of the turning point, if you will, as a grimly ironic coda to the nation-wide attempt to overturn the 1857 Dred Scott decision. Had not the Taney court previously defined a person as property? Good. Let the Civil War's chief and lasting fruit be a Fourteenth Amendment that turns the Dred Scott decision upside down and defines property as a person.

Bingham's professed intent, while drafting the Fourteenth Amendment's first section in the way he did, was to ensure the emancipation of black citizens by explicitly stating (Madison himself had worried that such a statement might be needed) that the Constitutional Bill of Rights (the first ten amendments) applied to incursions by state power as well as federal power. In letters to friends crafted during the time he was working on amendment language, Bingham added that because "each person" was "created in the image of the Lord," he considered it a solemn duty to protect their "inborn rights."[151] And there is no reason to doubt the veracity of these statements any more than we should doubt the veracity of his no-less-vigorous 1858 assertion that the "bastilles and dungeons of tyrants, those graves of human liberty, are giving up their dead. . . [and] the mighty heart of the world stands still, awaiting the resurrection of the nations and that final triumph of right, foretold in prophecy and invoked in song." Nevertheless, we would be remiss if we did not, at the same time, take note of the extent to which Bingham was tied to the railroad industry.

When he was a lawyer in Cadiz, Bingham worked across the street from the Kilgore Building at Market and Main, where Daniel Kilgore (soon to serve as proxy for Thomas Scott, president of the Pennsylvania Railroad) directed affairs for the Steubenville and Indiana Railroad. Hence Bingham was familiar with the railroad business, and when he set up shop in DC he regularly advocated for railroad companies, sometimes by sponsoring bills that extended iron duty credits to railroads, other times by helping to secure routes. The Camden & Amboy, Lake Superior & Mississippi, and Alabama & Florida railroads all gave him passes that allowed the congressman to ride for free. In 1857 Bingham bought land in Missouri in the hope that it would triple in value once the transcontinental route under discussion in Congress was set, and during the Civil War proper Bingham voted for the 1862 Pacific Railway Act while opposing the formation of a special committee designed to investigate rumored links between railroad companies and government officials.[152] After the war Bingham gave a speech urging quick passage of the Northern Pacific Railway bill,[153] and then, after accepting soon-to-be-valuable Credit Mobilier stock from former roommate Oakes Ames[154] (who wanted congressmen to have personal stakes in the Union Pacific railroad company he was trying to grow), Bingham argued aggressively and consistently for the *limitation of control by state governments over railroad companies*. During an April speech on the house floor in 1869, Bingham reminded his audience that Congress had "$25,000,000 invested in these roads," and then warned that "before next September" that money would be "substantially sacrificed by reason of the intervention of state tribunals which, if they had any decent regard for the rights of the American people, would not have interfered as they have."[155] The American people! Well, we shouldn't be surprised. After all, it had only been a year since, with Credit Mobilier stock certificates satisfactorily banked and already generating handsome returns, Bingham had stood on the same floor and delivered similarly grandiose remarks at the end of the Andrew Johnson hearings. "None are above the law," he at that point intoned. "Position, however high, patronage, however powerful, cannot be permitted to shelter crime to the peril of the Republic."[156]

But the best reason to question Bingham's explanation for the rationale behind his draft of the Fourteenth Amendment's first section is simply that, for those in the know, the word "person" had a definite pro-corporate charge at the exact same time that Bingham inserted it into the clause about "equal protection." Moreover he inserted the word, "person," after first disentangling it from obviously human qualifiers like race, color, and birthplace.[157]

Railroad people *knew* there were advantages to be gained if "person" could get associated with the concept of equal protection before the law. Lincoln himself had used an argument based on the idea of corporate personhood as early as 1854 in an effort to secure protection for a railroad client against a trigger-happy county in the state of Illinois that had presumed to dictate taxation terms to that client, and though Lincoln lost his case, the impetus for defining railroads as juristic "persons" in order to gain protection against non-uniform taxation only grew. By 1866, the year Bingham composed his draft for the Fourteenth Amendment, that impetus had the force of an oncoming locomotive. Hence it would have been surprising if someone had *not* tried to use the opportunity to lock in support for the personhood argument at the national level while hiding behind an altruistic cover. Was Bingham, a railroad insider, that man?[158] Or was Bingham, instead, a brave soul who risked public ridicule in order to insert "person," rather than just "citizen," and thereby protect illegal aliens as well as former slaves? All we know for sure is that Bingham (a) argued persistently (in Committee of Fifteen discussions about a proposed Fourteenth Amendment) for the inclusion of a clause that would have positively prevented state governments from "taking private property without just compensation,"[159] and (b) vehemently and consistently denied that his use of the word "person" in the finalized Fourteenth Amendment was intended to refer to corporations—those two things and the fact that, after the Credit Mobilier scandal broke in December 1872, Bingham lost his job in Congress and got tapped by President Ulysses S. Grant to serve as the United States' ambassador to far away Japan.

How did corporations secure the use of the equal protection clause once it was inserted?

Legal precedent allowing state control over corporations was not negligible, and for this reason convincing a court to accept a new argument that corporations should be granted protection as "persons" under wondrously powerful Fourteenth Amendment language loomed as a challenge despite the obvious elegance of that new argument. Moreover, the climate of public opinion on such matters was not favorable. The only reason Bingham's Section One passed muster in the first place was that the troublesome issues it raised were overshadowed by the seemingly more pressing issue of whether Section Three, which barred ex-Confederate soldiers from the right to vote, was too punitive. Had members of Congress actually zeroed in on the implications of Bingham's wording, Section One might have been scrapped, and had members done so in 1872 rather than 1866, it would certainly have been scrapped, for the news about Credit Mobilier scandalized most Americans and doubly convinced them that corporations should be kept on a tight leash. Moreover, the Supreme Court at that point *agreed*.

When slaughterhouses in New Orleans cited the Fourteenth Amendment's "privileges and immunities" clause in their 1873 suit against the state of Louisiana (after that state required the businesses to move their operations downstream from heavily populated areas), the Chase Court held that the Fourteenth Amendment was designed to protect actual citizens, not corporations, and Justice Samuel F. Miller, who wrote the majority opinion, went *out of his way* to acknowledge the importance of the decision. Was it because he was the son a yeoman farmer? Whatever the reason, Miller virtually eliminated the possibility of ignoring or downplaying the problematic aspect to a "wide" interpretation of the Fourteenth Amendment's import:

> No questions so far reaching and pervading in their consequences, so profoundly interesting to the people of this country, and so important in their bearing upon the relations of the United States and the several states to each other ... have been before this court during the official life of any of its members.[160]

And then, in 1877, the Waite Court essentially followed suit in *Munn v. Illinois* by ruling that grain elevator companies and associated railroad companies could not, as "persons," invoke the Fourteenth Amendment's "due process" clause in order to avoid having their rates fixed by state governments. "Down to the time of the Fourteenth Amendment," Waite wrote in his majority decision, "it was not supposed that statutes regulating the use, or even the price of use, of private property necessarily 'deprived' a man of his property without due process of law."[161]

Thus it was becoming increasingly clear that corporate lawyers faced an uphill battle in their efforts to make use of Bingham's slickly crafted first section.

However, it was also becoming increasingly clear that the ability of state governments and even counties to dictate terms to corporations was, from the point of view of corporate directors, intolerable. Thanks to Thomas Scott's invention of the holding company, corporations like the Pennsylvania Railroad were now national in scope, and not surprisingly such corporations found it difficult to streamline operations when different communities exacted different demands. Additionally, the appearance of vertically integrated companies like Carnegie Steel meant that capital was being generated at exponential rates, thereby making possible yet more nationally oriented corporations with budgets dwarfing those of most state governments. Hence pressure was building to take advantage of Bingham's gift despite the wall erected to block that move.

The break came in early 1886, when a lawyer named Bancroft Davis pressed against a weak point in the now populist-branded defense. Davis was President of the Newburgh and New York Railway. In 1871 he had achieved some fame (the library I read in at Berkeley was named after him) by successfully arguing in Geneva that Britain should pay the United States $15,000,000 for damages inflicted by British-built Confederate warships, but now (1886) he was serving out a rather obscure appointment as Reporter for the United States Supreme Court. Hence it is natural to conclude that Davis knew what he was doing, when he inserted into case history head-notes a line suggesting that the court knew corporations were persons. But, as with Bingham, we don't know for sure. All we know is that the deed was done—that and the fact that the man who was serving as Chief Justice at the time, Morrison Waite, had been Davis' boss during the 1871 Geneva negotiations.

The occasion for the insertion was a twist in a suit that had been filed by the Californian county of Santa Clara against Southern Pacific Railroad.[162] When lawyers for the South San Francisco Bay county stood up in the Supreme Court on January 27th to argue that Southern Pacific had no right to plead for the invalidation of target-specific county rules by invoking the now familiar personhood argument, they were cut off. "The court does not wish to have argument on the question whether the provision in the Fourteenth Amendment to the Constitution, which forbids a state to deny to any person within its jurisdiction the equal protection of the laws, applies to these corporations," Chief Justice Waite explained. "We are all of the opinion that it does." The Santa Clara team was caught off guard by this maneuver and to some extent frustrated, for they had built their case on a rebuttal of the personhood argument, but, knowing as they did that Waite's remark carried no legal weight, they went home assuming that even if they lost the case, the fight about the legitimacy of a wide Fourteenth Amendment interpretation was far from over.

Well, Santa Clara County did lose that case—on a technicality regarding an improper assessment of fencing costs. When it came time to type up the synopsis in US Reports Volume 118, though, Court Reporter Davis didn't mention the reason for the Santa Clara decision up front. Rather, he placed there a summary that highlighted Waite's remark about the personhood argument. Right at the top, where cases are typically summed up in the briefest possible form, Davis wrote: "The defendant corporations are persons within the intent of the clause in Section One of the Fourteenth Amendment to the Constitution of the United States, which"—here he was simply quoting Waite—"forbids a state to deny to any person within its jurisdiction the equal protection of the laws." The reader isn't told until the third paragraph that this assertion had nothing whatsoever to do with the decision proper, but by that point it is too late, for the second paragraph invites yawns, and prospective readers are likely to turn the page and move on to the next case synopsis so that they can stay awake.

Now along comes Stephen Johnson Field, who grew up in a Congregationalist household in Stockbridge Massachusetts, the same town Jonathan Edwards fled to after inciting the first Great Awakening. Though renowned for approving a whipping post in a Gold Rush municipality, inserting racist remarks about Chinese immigrants into U.S. Supreme Court opinions, and even carrying on a feud with a California Supreme Court justice that ended when a bodyguard employed by Field eventually shot and killed the California Supreme Court justice, Field's real achievement had nothing to do with obviously provocative acts like these. Rather, it had to do with his willingness—indeed, his drive—to follow through on the work that had been so neatly and perhaps courageously begun by Bingham and then Davis.

Back in 1869, while penning the majority opinion in *Paul v. the State of Virginia*,[163] a case in which an insurance company claimed protection under the Fourteenth Amendment in a dispute about fees, Justice Field looked hard at the recently enacted amendment's compatibility with the project of freeing corporations from control by the several states and, like Miller, was scared by what he saw. "A grant of corporate existence," he said, "is a grant of special privileges to the corporators, enabling them to act for certain designated purposes." He added that "corporations, being mere creations of local law, can have no legal existence beyond the limits of sovereignty where they were created," and then he even expanded on this latter point, arguing that recognition of a corporation's existence by other states "depends purely on the comity of those states—a comity which is never extended where the existence of the corporation or the exercise of its powers are prejudicial to their interests or repugnant to their policy."

Sometime in the late 1870s, though, Field changed his tune. Was he alarmed by the sentiments driving the 1877 railroad strike in Pittsburgh? Perhaps he was just worn down (there is evidence for this) by the sheer volume of requests for Fourteenth Amendment protection. Whatever the reason, Field recalculated his position on corporate use of the personhood argument. By 1885 he was implicitly affirming that the Fourteenth Amendment applied to *all* classes of persons, and in 1888, after the Supreme Court had signaled a willingness to start deciding that states cannot regulate interstate commerce, Field referenced Marshall court nomenclature regarding personhood in a majority opinion and flatly declared, in *Pembina Mining v. the State of Pennsylvania*,[164] that the Fourteenth Amendment applied to corporations as well as human beings.

There: the stage was set.

Would someone now be willing to follow through and "anchor" this opinion in precedent that did not really exist?

Ten months later, on January 7, 1889, Field himself obliged, this time while explaining the court's decision in *Minneapolis & St. Louis Railroad v. Beckwith*, in which the court upheld Iowa's right to collect "double the value of stock killed" after a railroad company failed to install fencing. On the surface this was simply another pro-state decision, but this time when Field explained the decision he took a moment to stop and recognize legitimate portions of the railroad attorney's argument. "It is contended by counsel, and we admit the soundness of his position, that corporations are persons within the meaning of the [Fourteenth Amendment] clause in question," Field wrote.[165] "It was so held in Santa Clara Co. v. Railroad Co, 118 US 394 ... and the doctrine was re-asserted in [Pembina] Mining Co v. Pennsylvania, 125 US 181."

To the angels in the wings this must have been a freighted moment, and as for the rest of us—well, let us just say that the completion of Field's clearly duplicitous last sentence (where Field says "It was so held in Santa Clara") still occasions a quick intake of breath.

Like Bingham, Davis and Field did neat work! Thanks to their perhaps unwitting but nevertheless textbook-grade sleights of hand, one hundred years of precedent affirming the public's right to oversee and if necessary shut down corporations was negated almost overnight. Rather than functioning as a country of competing *people*, we were from here on out to function as a country of competing *corporations*, and, needless to say, corporations jumped at the chance to seize the laurel that had been handed them. Between 1890 and 1910, 94 percent of all cases involving Fourteenth Amendment protection heard by the United States Supreme Court involved the consolidation, by corporations, of newfound gains,[166] and once that flurry of legal activity was over and the only choice vis-a-vis the maintenance of early nineteenth century wealth patterns was either "progressive" redistribution or the facilitation of philanthropy, an entirely new front emerged whereby corporations slowly won access to Bill-of-Rights freedoms, on the basis of Fourteenth Amendment access. Overall, the increase in corporate power resulting from Field's 1889 decision was enormous, and, even more amazingly, it occurred *without any public discussion whatsoever*. Indeed, the operation went so smoothly that, had they known about it, even graduates of Bobby Ayoub's Steubenville-derived School of Dealing would have been impressed.[167]

What about the new world that corporate power makes possible? Ought we not to be grateful to Bingham, Davis, and Field for recognizing the beneficial aspects to this new world and taking the steps necessary to ensure that it came our way? After all, modern day corporations provide jobs, material goods, and dividend checks. Thanks to corporations, the American middle class is now comfortable in ways that past ages couldn't even imagine, and as if all that isn't enough corporations have also (in an effort to get us hooked on a growth economy) secured for us unparalleled freedom of movement. In fact, the list of benefits is so extensive that we probably ought to be building statues of Davis and Field, in addition to Bingham. We've already inscribed "equal protection under the law" over the entrance to the Supreme Court. Why not also install busts in its entrance hall to celebrate the three men who made it possible for that phrase to, well, *ring*? The problem, as everyone knows but nobody wants to admit, is that the empowerment of corporations has come at a great cost, for the resulting concentrations of capital have warped the playing field that most us still call "the free market" to such a great extent that local economies like the one in Steubenville during the 1920s have collapsed, thereby inclining the entire nation and indeed the world at large toward prosthetic, top-driven, standardized "Main Streets" that are frequented by deracinated "consumers" rather than deal-making, therefore sovereign, humans.

Thanks in part to the aforementioned vigilance concerning the possibility of exploitation by companies like the British East India Tea Company, Adam Smith's 1776 theory that a society grows richer and more diverse in direct proportion to the removal of mercantilist policies and the encouragement of spontaneous, individually conceived profit-making initiatives was superbly relevant during the American constitutional era.[168] And, thanks to wise decisions where Chief Justice John Marshall defined the danger of monopolies, the nature of contracts, and the importance of then novel "private" corporations, Adam Smith's model continued to describe accurately (and guide) American economic life in the first half of the nineteenth century. Competition was robust, and it tended, most of the time, to strengthen the positions of small businessmen who had a vested interest in building up whatever town or region happened to be enriching them. However, when booster rockets like Carnegie's steel mills, Scott's railroad, Frick's coal ovens, and Mellon's banking instruments fired all at once, the quickly lifting "free market" economy became somewhat detached from the Adam Smith ideal it was meant to serve, and once railroad companies and their prodigy gained Fourteenth Amendment protection in addition to the advantages inherent in holding-company tactics, that detachment became more pronounced. More and more manufacturing concerns began to be held by fewer and fewer people, and in the 1880s and 1890s an entirely new fault line appeared that was defined by black, white, rural, urban, farm-based and union-led "populists" on the one side and something called "big business"

Organized Crime 171

on the other. Clearly, the market that had inspired Adam Smith was at that point broken, as the playing field was no longer level.

Yet even then all was not lost.

Though condemned by classical liberals (who dislike governmental regulation only slightly less than they dislike inflationary policies), Marxist economists (who tend to see reform as an effort to defuse revolutionary energy), and populist critics (who distrust legislation crafted by congressmen who make their home in Washington, DC), regulatory measures instituted during the Roosevelt, Taft, and Wilson eras did act to a significant degree as a counterweight, and the relative health of Steubenville, in the early part of the twentieth century, proves it. In addition to building National Parks, Theodore Roosevelt: (1) intervened on behalf of striking anthracite miners; (2) enforced a formerly decorative Sherman Anti-Trust Act; (3) strengthened the Interstate Commerce Commission's ability to regulate railroads; and (4) in general spearheaded efforts to shelter small businesses and rein in large ones "as the public welfare requires." Taft and Wilson then followed suit by regulating communications and at least trying to regulate the notoriously murky area called "banking" in an effort to ensure that small private initiatives would "not be hindered." Thus a kind of balance was achieved, and it held, this balance, right up to and even through the Second World War. Regardless of whether one believes FDR took interventionist energies too far by presuming to take money out of rich persons' pockets in an effort to protect most American people from hunger, accidents, low wages, unemployment, ignorance, closed hospital doors, and "fear itself," one can't get around the fact that during the first half of the twentieth century town life on the whole remained vital while corporations prospered.

Starting in the early 1950s, however, there began (right after Nisbet completed his book!) to be fresh concerns about scale. Worries appeared even among Austrian economists who had famously continued to believe that Adam Smith's model adequately described the twentieth century marketplace. Perhaps because Ludwig Von Mises et. al. focused excessively on the admittedly powerful, economy-directing nature of decentralized purchasing decisions, Austrian economists had steadfastly opposed efforts by governments to construct artificially a level playing field, but in the boom years after World War II Austrian-trained thinkers like Wilhelm Röpke grew thoughtful as purchasing decisions began to be made by fewer and fewer merchants.[169] Weren't Keynesian tune-ups and welfare states the enemy? What were these new things that were starting to become known as "multi-national" corporations? Was it possible that, say, the Seven Sisters could enslave a citizenry, in their seemingly innocuous way, every bit as thoroughly as Soviet collectivist movements? Standard Oil and IBM were nothing, though, compared to what was shortly to come, for starting in the middle 1970s the entire game changed and concerns about scale gave way to worldwide astonishment as second-stage rockets ignited and corporate power really took off. That happened for five reasons: the abandonment of the gold standard, the liberalization of world trade agreements that had been engineered in 1946 at the Bretton Woods resort in the mountains of New Hampshire, the arrival of widespread computerization, the fetishization of individual "choice" via increasingly sophisticated visual advertising, and, last but not at all least, the procurement of First Amendment constitutional rights in addition to Fourteenth Amendment ones.

First Amendment rights were won in 1978 when, in three separate cases, the Burger court awarded corporations both the ability to "speak" in an uncensored fashion through advertising and campaign contributions, and to not speak, i.e., remain silent when accosted by citizen's groups seeking information. As for the liberalization of trade agreements, that had happened a few years earlier in 1973, when talks in Tokyo constituting Round Six of the negotiations begun at Bretton Woods resulted in the removal not just of tariffs worth ten or five or even forty billion dollars, as had occurred in former years, but, instead, tariffs worth three-hundred-billion dollars, and then again eight years later, during the 1986 round of talks in Uruguay that produced the World Trade Organization, at which time tariffs were cut world-wide by another forty percent. The other thing that happened in 1986, of course, was that gates were completely opened for the importation of textiles, and this fact, in turn, led to the infamous rise of Walmart and (close behind, in its jet stream as it were) Bill Clinton, who repaid the debt by signing the 1994 North American Free Trade Agreement and, not incidentally, helping to facilitate an internet revolution that enabled corporations to take advantage of high speed trading and efficiently mine an entire globe for societal and natural resources at the same time that purchase orders were fanned by an increasingly sophisticated refreshment of corporately managed desires.

Have we grasped yet what has happened in the last thirty years?[170]

Thanks to the institution of "disintermediation" (a most pregnant phrase) and the subsequent replacement of genuine assets like locally-owned businesses with new kinds of "securities" that are bought and sold by insiders at lightning speed in dark pools that only computers can see, regional distinction is on the wane, the middle class is shrinking, and Ohioan downtowns are boarded up. Entrepreneurial spirit still exists, but there is less of it in hinterlands where the devaluation of labor relative to capital is intensifying. Most eastern-Ohio citizens like me now *depend* on standardized businesses with cartoonish signs in faux "shopping villages," which are about as existentially anchored as Disneyland's Main St USA. In place of Sulzbacher's, the Corner Grill, and the Ft. Steuben Hotel, we now have Macy's, Applebee's, and the Hampton Inn. If you want to stack lumber or select it you go to Lowe's; if you want to provide or secure medical attention you go to Highmark; and if Arlo Guthrie should decide now to dispose of something at a dump or perhaps drive a bulldozer there while working for Alice he would first have to pass through a portal called Waste Management International. Profit? That goes elsewhere. But this is okay. Returns come back to us in the form of yet more shopping venues that are increasingly baubled and smart. Why, if we're lucky, our little corner of the world might one day merit a more authentic looking village with park benches, variously sloping steel roofs, and an Anthropologie outlet. And, if that rationale seems too selfish, and you would rather see profit going to charity, in that case we're still covered, because corporations are happy to donate money to causes that are favored by customers and employees. Thank you United Parcel Service Kenya! Thank you Chipotle! Thank you Alcoa! Really, it's enough to make you throw in the towel and head to a Vegas poker game where you can at least lose with dignity. But, as it happens, even that option is closed, for the Desert Inn is long gone. Vegas now belongs to MGM and the Hard Rock Café.

Who arranged this? How did it happen that fake towns got substituted for real ones? Were we not looking? It's almost as if we have been the victims of an elaborate hustle, and, indeed, given that real towns can be mined for accrued wealth—given, too, that such a mining operation, should it exist, would be consistent with other criminal activities noted earlier in this chapter, like rigging markets, subverting democratic processes, and employing violence to settle disputes—given all that, it does seem within bounds at least to note the richness of a parallel between grand scams on the one hand and the substitution of prosthetic devices for real towns on the other. Say, though, that the parallel turns out to be unnervingly complete. Would it not be wise to handle such news discretely? At the very least, potential publicists should be aware of one small, seemingly insignificant detail, in addition to the nature of the hustle proper. It's that, like Bingham, we are (many of us) holding shares of the very same companies that are undermining our towns. Maybe it is through a retirement account. Maybe it is through an investment vehicle opened after coal yielded unexpected returns. Maybe it is through a hedge fund that uses a computer program to approximate casino skimming. No matter how the relationship got established, many of us have become partners in the very same destructive enterprise that we would be proposing to identify and possibly resist.

8

Disturbed Area

Pike Pool. 2,300 hours. Mile 82. The hour is late, and after a stint outside in the cold with my collar up and watch-cap pulled low I have returned to my lookout post in the wheelhouse to ask whether American exceptionalism underpinning post-Democratic Steubenville's neo-conservatism might provide clues that could help us to explain conclusively the size and character of the explosion that appears to have taken place in this region. Captain Lynch, for his part, has his hand on the control for the starboard searchlight so as to guide its powerful beam back and forth between the river's east bank and, of course, the far-away head of the tow. The man is looking for a wolf he thinks he once saw at the mouth of the creek whose sandbar is directly to port, but after picking up only grape vines, dark wavelets lapping onto a muddy bank, and the startled eyes of a deer, Jack turns the light off, and our eyes start to readjust to enveloping darkness.

Given that the wheelhouse itself has been lit all this time solely by the glow of brown, green, and purple instrument-panel displays, the process doesn't take long, and soon the captain resumes the story he had been telling.

It's about a mountain he visited as a boy. Being from Alabama, he'd never seen the Rockies, and when his high school science teacher proposed to take a group of students to Wyoming on a field trip to study rocks, the future captain jumped at the chance and felt badly for a classmate who fell sick at the last moment and couldn't be part of the trip. Hearing the story, I instantly understand why the captain was sorry, for, as it happens, I know this mountain. It's the first mountain you see after you climb up out of the Great Plains via the snaking power cable known as Interstate 80 and descend toward Laramie. The peak is called "Medicine Bow Mountain," and if you see it in the morning, the mountain as a whole appears to hover above a steadily-watered, perpetually-greening plain like a visitation. You can see lodge-pole pines, then firs with pockets of aspen. Above that there is an alpine zone with fast-moving streams and columbines, and higher still, on a not-too-sharp crest, there is snow. Even when the temperature is 92 down on the tarmac, you can see avalanche chutes and cornices, and when the sky is as blue as the meadows at tree line are green, the resulting contrasts flip a kind of interior switch that causes a beholder to consider abandoning closely held plans and heading straight for the mountain's summit. I myself have never obeyed that impulse while traveling west. I have always been in a hurry to meet some obligation or chase some other, ultimately less important goal. Hence (unlike Owen Wister, who stopped there long enough in 1885 to conceive *The Virginian*) I have merely given interior thanks for the vision and sped on by. Captain Jack, though, was lucky enough actually to walk in that far country for twenty-one days.

Why does he think about the mountain now, on this stretch of the river? "To get away," he says. "Above Wheeling," he explains, "the land changes. Fatigued bridges, half-sunken wrecks, abandoned oil tanks, slag dumps. What can I say. It's a disturbed area." When I hear these remarks I raise my head and look around, ready to agree, but right now the Ohio valley is eerily beautiful. The river's surface is smooth as glass, the boat itself and its tow appear to be regally *gliding*, and perched on hills crowding the river there are houses that look like keeps. At this point the captain breaks his Wyoming reverie and takes hold of mid-mast sticks, for we have passed Short Creek now, and the head of our tow has reached a bend in the river. Backing RPMs down a notch and swinging sticks hard to port, the captain waits a beat, and then, as the water current releases its hold on the tow proper and the blue light above the mailbox starts to move laterally against a far bank, Jack guns the Ocie Clark engines and commits to the turn. Soon a W&LE railroad track comes into view off the port bow, and after that we see a brush-infested sidetrack with a long line of rusted empties.

"Seven miles to Skull Run," the captain says. Turning away, he reaches for a phone to learn the results of his daughter's softball game. But I barely hear him. I am three bars back, thinking about stories we tell, and by the time Jack starts commiserating with his daughter about a loss, I am thumbing in my head through well-worn copies of *The Frontier Thesis*, *Land of the Free*, and—most engaging of all—*City on a Hill*.

Most of us are aware of the idea behind Frederick Jackson Turner's 1893 thesis, if not the academic paper in which the idea was presented, and that fact all by itself suggests that Turner (like Wister) was onto something important when he crafted his story line. He called his paper "The Significance of the Frontier in American History," and it was written so that he could read it with a sense of importance and a feeling of ease and a modicum of ceremony before the American Historical Association, but the arguments in that paper are invigorating, and it is just as exciting to follow Turner's reasoning today as it was in 1893.

Turner's hypothesis, bluntly stated, was that "a return to primitive conditions on a continually advancing frontier line" gave to the American people a unique blend of vitality and ingenuity. Unlike European cities that were founded on the ruins of older cities, American cities were in every instance the outgrowth of frontier towns that had been platted by colonists, trappers, homesteaders, and entrepreneurs who had grown strong by direct contact with wilderness so-called, and this fact, in turn, ensured that the governmental institutions they assented to would be both limited in their powers and democratic. Indeed, Turner traced almost every distinctive American trait to enlivening aspects of frontier life. "As successive moraines result from successive glaciations," he observed, "so each frontier leaves its traces behind it," and in addition to a preference for democratic institutions, those traces included directness, impatience with manners, courage in the face of mortal danger, self-sufficiency, capitalist biases, and a truly prolific talent for technological invention. Never mind that Turner's picture of westward expansion relied perhaps overly much on the idea of taming presumably "uncivilized" nature.[171] As a myth that grew out of the undeniably real courage of original settlers, the story had genuine power, and, not surprisingly, it won a large and varied hearing. Historians delighted in its key-like aspect. Successful Anglo-Saxon males on the street delighted in how the theory accorded well with their self-conception, and, as for the rest of us, we tended to delight in it also, for who among us does not on some level believe that Hester Prynne in *The Scarlet Letter* really did become stronger through time spent in the woods? It was true. America (the Old Northwest included!) amounted to the light of frontier vigor, shining.

As for the story, *Land of the Free*, that comes to us courtesy of attorney Francis Scott Key, who witnessed the 1812 bombardment (by British war ships) of Ft. McHenry in Chesapeake Bay, and then looked up, like a watchman for morning, to see stars and stripes still flying after "rockets" and "bombs bursting in air" had done their work. Thanks to the recent addition of Tennessee and Ohio to the original thirteen states, the American flag featured fifteen stars in 1812, and when Key saw that flag's "broad stripes and bright stars" still shining forth across "the mists of the deep," he was moved to imagine the United States of America as a "land of the free." Needless to say, that phrase caught on, and over time it began to function as a kind of shorthand for a political story of light shining.

The story has two versions—one long, one short.

The long version, already referenced throughout chapters 2, 5, and 7, articulates the ways in which Americans are still to this day invited to act as citizens rather than subjects, and when you read (or tell) this version, you find yourself picturing individuals who maintain essentially sovereign powers thanks to widespread property rights, equality before the law, and a system of self-government deriving from contracts struck with an allegedly federalist state. This is the story that the founding fathers oriented themselves by, and it is also the story that Lincoln claimed to be oriented by. Indeed, it is the story that all of us claim to be politically oriented by, whether we are of a conservative persuasion, in which case we worry about the decline of federalism and associated restraint, or a more progressive persuasion, in which case we mine the Constitution for pre-destined "rights" that the founding fathers did not yet know about. Which means: this long version is very powerful.

And the short version of the story too is powerful, for that version lends itself well to cinematic representation and imprints our very dreams. Think John Wayne in Stagecoach, or Gary Cooper in High Noon. People say the Western is over, but so far as I can tell the arrival of barbed wire and then cities has just changed the setting for the standard Western plot in which ordinary people discover themselves able or not so able to act rightly in a situation where the option of outsourcing enforcement is not available. So. Two versions. Is one truer than the other? I suppose the cinematic version answers more questions and satisfies more desires, but for our purposes it doesn't much matter which version you adopt. Either way, you find yourself reasonably and perhaps even justly picturing America as the *Land of the Free* and to that extent a beacon of hope.

Now: *City on a Hill*. This is the most powerful of the three myths. Indeed, this story has the power to knock you silly, therefore you need to make sure you are standing on firm ground should you ever call it into view. For it isn't just that the story serves as a kind of foundation for *The Frontier Thesis* and *Land of the Free*. (Sturdy Massachusetts Bay Puritans pioneered "contact with wilderness," and the covenant-based "compact" they signed their names to while sailing to Plymouth was a kind of prototype for the "contract" that the original thirteen colonies signed when they ratified the Constitution of the United States.[172] Also, Lincoln interpreted Civil War casualties as redemptive sacrifices through which our nation was enabled really and truly to cast light.) Rather, it's that *City on a Hill* has a strangely riveting power owing to its capacity to flatter beholders.

The "city on a hill" phrase is scriptural in origin. Jesus used it to describe the light-casting role of his followers ("You are the light of the world; a city on a hill cannot be hidden; neither do people light a lamp and put it under a bowl"), and it has long been understood to refer, also, to Zion, the twelve-gated heavenly Jerusalem from which clear waters flow and toward which (according to Scripture) we are all of us supposed to be traveling. American use of the phrase dates from 1630. John Winthrop, future governor of Massachusetts Bay Colony, incorporated "city upon a hill" into a sermon while sailing on the *Arabella* (flagship for a convoy of fifteen) toward what would become Boston, and Winthrop's purpose in using the phrase was to encourage his shipmates in their calling, which was to take advantage of the clean slate offered by American wilderness and actually build a heavenly city so that other, less pure and more benighted souls back in Europe would have a template for what they, also, ought to be building. At the time Winthrop used the phrase, of course, it functioned mainly as an exhortation. "The eies of all people are upon us," he explained. "If wee deale falsely with our god in this worke wee have undertaken and soe cause him to withdrawe his present help from us, we shall be made a story."[173] Over time, though, "city on a hill" began to be used less and less as an exhortation that appealed to a fear of falling short, and (in direct proportion to the growing affluence of the thirteen colonies and then the United States) more and more as a reminder of ancestral accomplishments. The Civil War was the turning point. After 1865 we started talking confidently in terms of a "resplendent Union" (see Bingham) and even using assumed city-on-a-hill status as justification for continued assertiveness (see Wilson's democratic universalism, let alone William Tecumseh Sherman). Thus we eventually became, in the popular mind, a flawed but fundamentally "just" society. In the second half of the 19th century we *merged* with "the city upon a hill," and if we face an obligation, now, it is solely that we defend that city so that it can continue to function as the beacon we believe it to be.

Well, I concur. To a certain if qualified extent I buy these stories, and not just because anti-Americanism is a repugnant default position. Rather, I allow these fictions to organize my thinking because they make sense to me. I believe them.

Given the huge numbers of immigrants who have risked their lives to emigrate to America's shores, our status as a beacon is historically verifiable, and given too that we are a nation that is formally dedicated to the proposition that all men and women are of equal worth, the life-saving aspect to the message we cast is genuine. Moreover, other aspects to American identity cast light simply by virtue of obvious goodness, beauty, and truth. Witness literary achievements like "Big Two Hearted River," *Huck Finn,* and *The Great Gatsby.* Witness the game of baseball, where action strangely balances contemplation. Witness jazz—Pittsburgh's Gene Kelly or Pittsburgh's Earl "Fatha" Hines, it makes no difference. Witness, finally, the sheer diversity of cultural climates that even today remain on view when you drive the old Lincoln Highway (Rt. 30) from the intersection of 42nd St and Broadway in Manhattan, past Pittsburgh, Rock Island, and Medicine Bow Mountain to the pier in Berkeley where Santayana boarded a ferry to San Francisco on his way to Rome. *America,* at such times I earnestly think. *May God thy gold refine.*

Simultaneously, though, I wonder whether it is right for those of us who live in The Seven Ranges to tell stories like *The Frontier Thesis, Land of the Free,* and (particularly) *City on a Hill.* Given what we've learned over the course of these investigations about our perfection of land commodification, our establishment of bipolar energy flow, our hostility toward tradition-based culture, and, last but not least, our willingness to destroy land and empower corporations at the expense of communities in which we were born—given all this, ought we not to temper or at least qualify claims that we cast salvific light?

By way of answering this question, let us create a short précis of American history as it might be told should we find merit in the conclusions reached so far. Sometime after the first Spaniards or far-wandering Gallic fishermen make landfall on the North American coast, disease kills off vast numbers of native Americans—nobody knows how many, but it is safe to assume that the toll is roughly as large as the toll taken on the European continent by the bubonic plague in the fourteenth century. This event leads English colonists (and, later, John Locke) to think of American land as pristine "wilderness" ready for imprinting, and that idea, in turn, facilitates the wholesale destruction of the North American hardwood forest and the displacement (by violence) of remaining indigenous tribes. European colonies prosper and eventually unite under contractual terms that favor human flourishing, but the imported traditions that sustain the colonists' ability to protect the common good, already weakened by the romantic exaltation of "nature" at the expense of "civilization," are drastically undermined by the substitution of section-and-range technology for medieval ways of measuring land, and the rise of a religious kind of "enthusiasm" in which conversion serves as an end in itself rather than a means of successfully contemplating that which is beautiful or good. Next a long simmering Civil War erupts in such a way as to cause: (1) the loss of constitutionally embedded counterweights to political centralization; (2) the conversion of

Jeffersonian agrarianism into a merely reactionary force; (3) the outright (i.e., forced) elimination of still extant tradition-based cultures, be they Native American (as in the case of the Lakota Sioux) or Appalachian (as in the case of small Southern and Northern upland farmers); and (4) the commitment to strife in social, political, and economic contexts, in addition to religious ones. With subsistence agriculture and small-scale artisanship now sidelined, a rural proletariat appears, and not "the territory" but *cities* begin to function as the chief American magnet. This creates a labor pool at the exact same moment that technological advances in the manufacture of steel make it possible to turbo-charge the growth of railroads and increase the demand for steel. Widespread industrialization results, and owing to the wholesale externalization of costs made possible by the political conversion from tradition (which used to speak for the dead and unborn) to universal suffrage, the quality of soil, air, and water begins to be compromised. By the middle of the twentieth century, huge swaths of farm country fall prey to draglines that take out even topography itself. Meanwhile, American-style corporations become more and more "enfranchised" as a result of Fourteenth Amendment protection, and soon, thanks to computerization, they gain the ability to mine natural and societal resources on a global scale. At the same time, trade agreements prohibiting corporate freedom of movement are relaxed, and from that point forward multinational corporations begin to undercut small town retailers, jobbers, and middlemen to such an extent that local economies are irreparably weakened and in some cases actually replaced by faux versions of communitarian life so as to maximize better short-term corporate profit.

Given that the above summation is at the very least plausible, can it really be argued that America casts light to a degree that other nations do not? In important, not negligible ways, America resembles a kill-floor rather than a city on a hill, and lest any have doubts in that regard I invite them to visit Harrison County, the place where westward migration officially began. Go ahead, I will say. Catalog your impressions. For this Fifth Range is no mountain of inheritance. Rather, it's a sink. It's a structural depression, an economically depressed area, a gravity-field dimple into which Native American refugees, coal miners, and back-to-the-land types fall, never to return. It's a potter's field, a pit, a sandy concavity where, owing to sulfurous content, few living things grow and even rivers burn. If it can be said that this region gives off light, in other words, it's because the good things in it have gone up, and still are going up, in flames. When immigrants bound for the newly formed state of Ohio arrived in 1803 to swell the ranks of Whiskey Rebels, trees were already charred pillars, coal banks were already smoldering, and the minds of farmers themselves were in the process of being incinerated by premature rapture. And then the new immigrants went and lit a fire themselves! What, was the road they had traveled out of Philadelphia a kind of fuse? And were they themselves the fizzing, eagerly moving spark? I submit that, as suspected in chapter 1, the answer is affirmative.

When Herman Melville spotted this fire in 1850 he concluded that our country was "a pitch and sulfur freighted brig" bearing down on history's end from a "midnight harbor."[174] He said we were inclined to institute heaven by force, that we used "broad sheets of flame for sails," and that the means for achieving these ends involved removing "masks" and going, like Ahab, right for the mirage-like thing-in-itself. Would the Yankee artist phrase things any differently if he could see, now, what we can see? Given the current-day triumph of visual media, the resulting devaluation of words, and the growing irrelevance of traditional conceptions of truth, I suspect that Melville's original picture would only be sharpened. For when you look around today, in an effort to get a read on the potentially destructive power of cultural tendencies, you see, on almost every front, the heat of immediacy—the "rush," if you will, of direct access to consumer goods, political power, and even to being itself owing to "dis-intermediation," or the removal of nearly every mediatory agent that has served in the past to both guarantee the freedom of the individual, and, at the same time, ensure a wide distribution of biological and societal wealth. That kind of rush amounts to massive energy release.

Up ahead, the dark, impossibly long mass of the Ocie Clark's three-wide tow stands out against the silvery water like the deck of a square-bowed tanker afloat on a deep void. There is no wind, and therefore starlight shines from the liquid, mirror-like surfaces on either side with enough exactitude to make it appear as if space beneath is equivalent to space above, and given that Captain Lynch is tuned to a Bach cantata at this point in his watch rather than to NASCAR, given too that the ship's screws right now are free of logs, the towboat's forward motion appears to be an effect of perfectly-achieved and hauntingly-deep choral harmony. A few minutes go by. Then I notice that there is a glow emanating from the far side of steep hills crowding the river. Looking now toward the green/brown electronic display indicating the Ocie Clark's real-time position on Army Corps of Engineers navigation charts, I realize that we are at last coming up on Cross Creek, the former ford that served Meadow-Croft hunters, Whiskey Rebels, Shawnee warriors, and VIPs like George Washington. According to the nautical charts, there is a wide flood plain at that juncture with a steel mill on it—the aforementioned Wheeling-Pitt plant at "Steubenville South," or Mingo—and, sure enough, the captain soon puts down his notepad to monitor tow behavior relative to oncoming current. Checking progress against a swing meter, Jack adjusts throttles and rudders over the course of twenty long minutes, and by the time he's through, the sight-blocking bend is behind us and the entire, heavily rusted plant is fully in view.

Directly off the port bow I can see twelve acres of railroad siding, 3,000 feet of river terminal, and a fifteen-ton stiff leg derrick with a grab bucket and a magnet and a barge shifter. And beyond, on the other side of a hot mill whose bays look like teeth in a jack-o-lantern, I can see down-comer pipes and a skip car climbing slowly toward a bell.

Let us change our focus slightly so that we are looking at the persistence with which Americans maintain the city-on-a-hill conceit. Why do we cling to it despite mounting evidence that our legacy could be something more complicated?

One explanation may simply be that we have an increasing need for cover, given the extent to which we have all signed off on this originally Puritan myth. Poet laureates like Ralph Waldo Emerson believed in it, and Walt Whitman even went so far as to peddle the Manifest Destiny variant, let alone the more highbrow version.[175] Therefore it follows that disowning this myth would involve giving up heroes as well as a foundational story. A daunting prospect! But that is nothing compared to the possibility that our own integrity might be found wanting. Might neighbors or future generations think that our comfort was achieved by building ourselves up at the expense of the dead and the unborn at the same time that we claimed to be due-paying members of a just society? That is a charge most of us probably would prefer to avoid, and certainly it could reasonably be argued that doubling our commitment to the very same story that is giving us trouble would be a likely line of defense. Nevertheless there is a problem even with this explanation, for it does not address the extraordinarily consistent intricacy of our claim that we are the new "city on a hill."

We have already talked about how John Winthrop, while sailing to Massachusetts Bay, explicitly linked his covenanted project to Abraham's journey out of Mesopotamia to a "promised land" on the west bank of the Jordan River. Additionally, we have talked about how Abraham Lincoln used baptismal logic and the idea of redemptive sacrifice to strengthen and even lock in the idea of America as a new Israel. But there are also other ways in which America functions as a kind of modern-day alternative to the Jerusalem that was envisioned by Israelite prophets. First, we are a nation to which peoples "stream" from every corner of the earth. At Ellis Island, infants ("the wealth of nations") used to arrive in the arms of mothers almost exactly as Isaiah and then John foretold it. Second, Lincoln himself was a Christ figure who died on Good Friday after leading us out of slavery. Third, we appear to be hard-wired for expansion and evangelization to the same degree that the early Christian church proved to be, after the alleged descent of a Holy Spirit. Just as we exploded westward and began showering the world with American inventions after Lincoln's death, so too did formerly cowardly apostles spread Christianity to China, Africa, northern Europe, the Near East, and even the Far East in record time after Jesus' death. All three of these angles provide a convincing glimpse into the way in which America "stands in" for Israel. And if one assents also to the admittedly provocative but historically valid premise that medieval Christendom was nothing other than the Judaic temple rebuilt, then the various aspects to the resemblance between America and the Jerusalem on view in Scripture become even richer. Our towns were built on land that had formerly been wilderness just as medieval towns were, and thanks to the popularity of Henry Hobson Richardson's reproductions of monasteries in Germany and southern France, our towns even began (during the second half of the nineteenth century) to look like the ones in medieval Europe.

Much is made of Alexis de Tocqueville's concern that Americans, while professing to promote and embody freedom, hurry instead toward servitude. And it makes sense that we should make much of this concern, for Tocqueville was a careful observer, and his prediction that we would one day defer to "an immense and tutelary power" (or beneficent State) that presumes to secure "gratifications" and "watch over our fate" has turned out to be scintillatingly correct.[176] Valid as this perspective is, however—nay, sobering and tonic and instructive as this perspective is—I begin to wonder if Tocqueville didn't miss the biggest danger of all. Might it not be the case that our real calling is not so much the centralization of power as the replacement of real things with relatively lifeless replicas of those same real things?

☙

The Ocie Clark, still gliding forward as if on voices, is now even with Mingo Furnace #5, and for a few moments Jack and I can see straight through an open bay to where liquid iron is transferred to a bottle car for transport. Our timing, it turns out, is perfect. Not three hundred feet away, on the other side of dead-calm, ice-coated water and a maze of railroad tracks, a rivulet of yellow fire pours from a cleft in the rock of a ladle's refractory concrete lining, and as that rivulet falls into a similarly molten pool in the torpedo-shaped car below, splashed metal liquid rises up to illuminate the surrounding darkness and then fall like snow. I look, then I look again, and this time I have a momentary glimpse of American promise as pretense. I see a place where every game is fixed and greenery itself is a precinct for a large, very intelligent bird of prey. I see spurious local economies (outdoor Main St USA malls featuring multinational tenants), spurious land (re-contoured strip mines south of Cadiz), and spurious freedom ("lighting out for the territory"). And behind all that, in a kind of cueing or sponsoring role, I see fake city-on-a-hill status being studiously maintained despite an ingrained, even defining bias for bipolar logic and against the very same sacramental biases and incarnational anthropologies that serve as the cornerstone for the city-on-a-hill idea.

Once again: might it not be the case that our real legacy is the substitution of prosthetic devices for real things?

I would describe our predicament more cautiously.

I would say that we are good actors who loyally play a part that has been assigned to us in order to contribute to a master and nominally Judeo-Christian story that tells all of us who we are. Is not the exceptionalist creed an important part of that story? Somebody has to give it life. Therefore we Americans step up and speak our lines boldly, knowing that if we don't, we will be lost—adrift at sea on a starless night and completely without bearings.

There are of course other master stories, and, indeed, one of the salient features of our time is that we as a people appear to be switching our allegiance from the Judaeo-Christian one to another more palatable, relativistic, and egalitarian one. Nevertheless, that switch has not yet been fully executed. We are still, even if only dialectically, under the sway of the Hebraic and Greek traditions that formed us, and therefore it makes sense that when push comes to shove we gravitate (like prophets!) toward roles in a story that goes beyond merely associative logic and involves a decisive battle between the Christian/Greek idea of Logos on the one hand and forces conspired against that Logos on the other. Whether we like it or not, we are tuned to the notion of "ultimate reality," and to that very extent we are equipped to construct and maintain prosthetic versions of what used to be called Christ-light.

※

Say, though, that we eventually succeed in our efforts to abandon Judeo-Christian roots and steer by a different narrative. Would we then be able to step outside destructive roles and start casting a genuinely salvific light?

Here we run into something odd, which is that so-called "rival" stories feature similar plots.

Take the narrative currently being told by ecological historians in general and Melbourne curator Tim Flannery in particular as they capitalize on gains made possible by technological advances in the detection and dating of pollen samples from long-dead plants. When these guys look at America, they see important differences from the Asian, African, and Eurasian continents, and one of those differences is that America features a kind of *immigration bias* that in a certain sense underwrites the scripturally-based notion of America as a land to which peoples stream.[177] Given the relative abundance of bones and fossilized remains indicating a once strong diversity of life forms here, paleo-botanists and paleontologists have long believed that America functioned as a kind of font that produced many of the life forms that created the biological and zoological world we know today. Now, however, it is becoming clear that America has in the long run been a net *recipient* of plants, animals, and prehistoric humans owing to the periodic flooding of the Beringia land bridge and thus the periodic closing of the very same door through which biological "colonists" entered. According to Carnegie Museum's Christopher Beard, our only successful prehistoric "exports" have been camels, horses, and dogs; less hardy species stayed here.

Another provocative observation made by ecological historians is that America's geography greatly favors the production of tornadoes, which for obvious reasons epitomize polarity-driven storms. Thanks to the north/south orientation of the Rockies in the west and the Appalachians in the east, America's mountain ranges systematically "buckle" prevailing atmospheric flow, thereby creating a low-pressure area east of the continental divide. At the same time, the Great Plains act both as a wide conduit for cold, dry, high pressure arctic air flowing southward, and, too, as a funnel for the injection (so to speak) of warm, moist, north-tending air that was only hours before directly over the tropical Caribbean Sea. Consequently the chance of hot air coming into contact with cold air is dramatically heightened over this continent, and during the spring, when the Great Plains heat up, it is statistically certain that a large number of tornadoes—90 percent of the world's total—will result. In other words we are *by nature* a land of climatic extremes.[178] During the interval of a year on the Great Plains we go from sub-zero weather to 92 in the shade. During the geologic interval of 10,000 years at that same location we go from a one-mile-thick ice sheet (more ice than is currently in all of Antarctica) to (one blink later) the largest reservoir of fresh water in the world (the Great Lakes). And during the space of just a few minutes, our tropical air mixes with down-coming arctic air in such a way as to generate (in association with neighboring warm air) vortex-driven winds that approach 300 miles per hour. We are, literally, a land of fire and ice.

Note, too, that in addition to documenting an immigration bias and pointing out how the North American continent regularly produces the world's most violent natural storm, ecological historians also observe that the North American continent underwrites life "bursts" that look like fertility but in fact constitute outright expenditures of capital.[179]

Flannery, for his part, argues that the chronically exploitative American pioneer who "mined" agricultural capital and then "broke for the timber" in a kind of leapfrog act with section-and-range survey teams was only the most recent player in a continental dynamic that has been unfolding for millions of years as plants, animals, and eventually human invaders wiped out keystone species again and again and again in a kind of sustained frenzy of ecological "release." Unlike adaptation, which occurs when species are forced by a paucity of resources to live in such a way as not to upset the availability of resources, release is a consequence of plenitude, or at least an absence of predators or deadly bacteria, and it is marked by a kind of flare, or burst of light, that signals an absence of constraints. Furthermore, such "flares" occur at the expense of species that would otherwise be available to widen the gene pool, ensure the feasibility of adaptation, and curtail ecological release. That, at any rate, is what the first Amerindians put in play when they ventured south between the Cordilleran and Laurentide ice sheets, discovered a kind of promised land, and then exploded across what is now the "lower 48" in a mere two hundred years. How were they able to spread out so quickly? Simple. They developed a fluted spear point that was equivalent to a Kentucky long rifle. Just as Whiskey Rebels achieved deadly marksmanship at long range owing to the way their bullets rifled (drilled) their way through the air, so too (starting about 15,000 years ago) the fluted design of the spear points used by Clovis people enabled spears to fly true over relatively long distances, and in consequence 73 percent of America's mega-fauna disappeared almost overnight.[180]

But we need not focus just on stories told by evolutionary biologists about the Paleo-Indian period when assessing the extent to which Greek and Judeo-Christian narratives agree with other, potentially rival, narratives. We could also focus profitably on stories that archaeologists tell about Ohio's Late Pre-historic period—and here I think especially of the ones prompted by the giant earthwork known as Serpent Mound, which is 100 miles west of Marietta.

Serpent Mound is a Native American earthwork, constructed around AD 1070 on Permian rock that geologists now think of as "disturbed," owing to the fact that it was ground zero for a five-mile-wide meteoric hit that occurred 258 million years ago.[181] The earthwork was built by the "Ft. Ancient" culture that rose up in conjunction with eastern Ohio's Monongahelan culture to replace the relatively peaceful, trade-oriented Hopewell cultures that were descended from the attali-throwing hunters discussed in chapter 6, and if you see the monument from the air, ideally in winter, you see what appears to be a large, 1,330-foot-long snake stretched out in the sun along the flattened portion of a ridge above a creek. It has its mouth open, this snake, and it appears to be devouring a large, raptorial egg. The body of the snake, which is now covered by well-tended grass, is at no point higher than four feet above the plane of the bluff proper, but the serpent's girth is five times that distance and in consequence readily visible to people standing on the ground, let alone people looking down from the air. If you stand right next to the effigy and look across its languid, 100-foot-wide, S-shaped curves, you half expect the serpent's tightly coiled tail suddenly to unwind and, like an earthquake-generated wave running through the ground, topple you into the stream sixty feet below. Then you remember that you're in Ohio, that the age of the dinosaurs is long gone, that you are walking along a path on a "fairway" that leads eventually to an "interpretive center" maintained by a "historical society" that will put the monument in "context": *central uplift area, ring graben, largest serpent effigy in the world*. At that point you take a deep breath, for now you know that all is well.

What does this effigy mean? Why is it here?

It turns out that the upper Ohio Ft. Ancient culture and its eastern Ohio Monongahelan twin were two of about seven regionally distinct, contemporaneous cultures that appeared after the late Woodland period and together comprised what archaeologists now call the Mississippian "ideological interaction sphere." In addition to the Ft. Ancient and Monongahelan cultures centered on the upper Ohio River, there were the Oneota, Caddoan, Plaquemine, South Appalachian, and Middle Mississippian cultures centered, respectively, on the upper Mississippi, the Arkansas, the Mississippi delta, and the combined Cumberland, Tennessee, and Black

Warrior watersheds. These cultures featured pottery flourishes that indicate separate historical roots, but starting around AD 1000, which is the date Aztecs use to start the timeline recounting their journey south toward Mexico City, resemblances became stronger than differences, and the seven Eastern Woodland cultures started to grow (and later decline) as a clearly identifiable whole[182] that became progressively more focused on the seeming integration of dualistic aspects that in fact remain unchanged[183] and then—assuming of course that clay and copper images depicting business-like executions of prisoners in fetal positions are as typical in this ceremonial "complex" as anthropologists say they are[184]—progressively more oriented toward extinguishing life rather than building it up.

Serpent Mound is itself a definitive dualistic statement thanks to the positioning of an egg in the earthwork in addition to a serpent. By incorporating the egg, builders ensured that viewers would see sky-based raptorial spirit brought close to the earth-based serpentine kind, and, indeed, the monument now stands as the archaeological record's strongest rendition of the Mississippian sky/earth "unit" so-called. Thunderer/reptile, overworld/underworld, fire/water, eagle/snake[185]—each of the polarities (all of them roughly synonymous with modern notion of spirit/flesh) is there, and owing to the fact that polarity (thanks to the emphasis on linkage rather than incarnation) is heightened rather than reduced, the overall effect is not dissimilar to that produced by images of Quetzalcoatl, the "feathered serpent" who famously told the Azteca people to settle where they saw the inverse of the scenario depicted at Serpent Mound—to wit, an eagle with a writhing snake in its beak.

In other words, if you step outside an explicitly Judeo-Christian-Greek viewpoint and do your best to see solely by the light of biological and archaeological evidence, you wind up seeing the same anti-incarnational bias that you see when you look from within the Judeo-Christian-Greek viewpoint. When you train your eye to see like an evolutionary biologist, you see immigration bias and drawdowns masquerading as fertility, and when you train your eye to see like an archaeologist, you see intensifying dualism and a growing abandonment to the storms that tend to occur as allegedly polar opposites get close to one another.

※

Can it be possible, then, that seventeenth century Transylvanian immigrant Johannes Kelpius was right? I used to think Johannes was crazy. Kelpius was a Pietist nut who thought the world was going to end in 1694.[186] He thought that when the End came, one ought to be standing near "the woman with twelve stars" who (according to Genesis) was destined to "crush the serpent with her heel," and after calculating that this woman probably fled into woods west of Philadelphia, Kelpius promptly booked a passage on a ship and took up residence in a cave west of Germantown. He stayed there too. He stayed there until he died. Can it be possible that Kelpius knew something the rest of us didn't? After all, Aztecs did claim, back in 1631, that they saw a pregnant woman with twelve stars treading on a serpent. The woman appeared to them to be "clothed with the sun," which to them indicated God-like status, and this fact induced those same Aztecs to become Christian, thereby forming modern-day Mexico. But these are just stories. All we know for sure is that eastern Ohio functions for beholders like a dragon's lair. To one person the land will appear as a smoking brazier; to another it will appear as a seven-ranged assortment of badlands from which Garryowen-whistling horsemen ride forth, and to still another it will appear as a "wilderness" into which a serpent-crushing woman flees. In all these cases the immediate trans-Allegheny West functions, ultimately, as a kind of end zone where referees stand with two hands raised. Storylines converge here. They reach their terminus in this spot and mean.

9

Forty Acres and a Mule

Five years later. Rumley Township, Section 23. My neighbor is here, mowing off a field south of the chicken-house, and though the day is hot—high eighties—his horses are sprightly and light on their feet. I use a Sixties-vintage Massey Ferguson 50 that runs on Ohio crude, which will soon be flowing from shale formations 5,000 feet deep in the Earth's crust, but my neighbor favors horse-drawn equipment, and today, as I look out from a rarely taken but gratefully accepted vantage point under our land's sole pie-producing cherry tree, I see why. With a tractor there are wide, heavy wheel prints that either compress ground you are about to till or matt down and crush the stems and seed heads of newly felled grass. But when you use a sickle-bar mower pulled by a team, compaction occurs only under hooves, and even then the pawing motion of those same hooves tends to loosen and stir crust, thereby improving tilth. Plus, the draft animals scatter highly valuable, sweet-smelling manure as they go. "Gee," Elmer says, while riding on a floating, slightly springing steel seat. Then: "haw." When he needs to turn a corner, Elmer stops the team for a beat, gets it to walk the tongue on the mower backward and forward until the mower is aimed in a perpendicular direction, and then—"step!"—off the unit smartly goes, up the same hill my tractor loses power on.

These horses are Percherons—one is a gelding, the other a mare—and they stand about fifteen hands high. I am (or once was) 6'1," but when I stand next to the pair and look into their eyes I am looking up. Hence they have tremendous leverage, and when they lean into their harnesses, flare their nostrils, and really "step," things happen. Thick oak roots pop out of the ground, cars return out of ditches, and two-gang plows slice open long-fallowed ground. Yet the animals (not being stallions) are also docile and content to stand still for long periods of time. Therefore Elmer is free to drive and stop the team pretty much at will, and when the man's straw hat disappears over the brow of my hill, along with the clackety sound made by the mower's well-oiled scissoring parts, I stare off into space for a minute and marvel both at the financial efficiency of Elmer's operation and, too, at the peace and quiet from which that operation seems to derive. Ought my family to be switching to horses?

The thought is daunting, for keeping a horse alive is harder than fueling a tractor, and we barely even know what oat plants look like when they are growing in the ground, let alone how to winnow their chaff and feed them to a horse. Hence I file the possibility of farming with horses for future, definitely not present, consideration, and then, delighting now in the smell of newly mown grass and the thought of quality hay soon to come our way (we get one third of the bales produced), I make my way back to a barn to install new rubber belts on a still viable, PTO-driven, Allis Chalmers baler.

Who knows?

Perhaps our experiment here will succeed after all.

When I first got off the river, I had a little trouble seeing straight, and I guess I shouldn't have been surprised. Who would not be blinded upon catching sight of The Seven Ranges as a staging ground for Armageddon? There is a stigma attached to sightings of Lastness that a lot of us, for reasons of propriety and social standing, want to avoid. Hence, upon being asked what I'd learned on the river, I decided to be selective about what I divulged, until one day it struck me that people who think in terms of an End are rather good company compared to people who believe history is a clock—and also that the important question is not so much whether or not to adopt an eschatological view. Rather, it is which eschatological position should be allowed to inform our thinking.

People like to think that eschatology is over "there," where religious people sit, and enlightened thought is over "here," where policy makers ought to sit, but in fact everybody (and every profession) needs an eschatology of some kind or other, and the problem we face now is that our current eschatological "choices" are merely two different variants of millennialism, which is the scripturally-based belief in a thousand-year period of righteousness that will either precede or follow Christ's second coming.[187] In the latter case, which has been best articulated by Sister Etter and, more recently, Johnny Cash in his sharply etched, dark-yet-jubilant song "When the Man Comes Around," the Second Coming will be a violent, crisis-driven event in which fire-bound chaff will be separated from wheat, and in the former case, which has been best articulated by, well, "progressives" of all stripes, from Congressman John Bingham to present-day advocates for inclusion and tolerance, the Second Coming will be a gradually-achieved, post-religious accomplishment whose surest marker will be respect for all living creatures and enduring peace. At first glance, these two perspectives appear different enough to occasion—nay, even demand—commitment to one side or the other. And, lest there be any doubt on this score, one need only reflect for a while on the not insubstantial difference between Polk's belief in manifest destiny and John Quincy Adam's belief in a call to set democratic *examples*.[188] In fact, though, the similarities between the two persevtives outweigh the differences, for both alternatives incline us toward interpreting and (with the help of the United States military) *tweaking* current events so that these same events fit and to some extent legitimate messianic narratives that were intended by their authors to be interpreted allegorically rather than practically. The alternatives comprise a false choice, and *that*, dear reader, is both the measure of our current-day predicament, and, too, the clue that will deliver us.

Let us back up for a minute to refresh our memory of the dichotomies noticed in chapters 3 through 6, where we discussed the nature/grace polarity empowering Cane Ridge revivalism, the simultaneous appearance of atomized individuals and a centralized state, the false Lincoln-era choice between tyranny on the one hand and no constraints on the other, and the wilderness/civilization polarity empowering the expansion of the United States. In each instance it became clear that polarities under scrutiny comprised false alternatives—which is to say, alternatives that appeared to be mutually exclusive when in fact the "opposites" under discussion were simply two different versions of the same phenomenon. Well, it is the same with fundamentalist pre-millennialism and progressive post-millennialism, and if it weren't for the fact that, at this point in our journey, we are equipped to see how and why we tend to oscillate back and forth between spurious "opposites" that cannot in a million years support dialectical reasoning, our chances of orienting ourselves to what's real and true would appear to be, well, nil. What is it, then, that we can see at this point in our journey? Put succinctly, it's that absolutized contraries derive at each and every instance from the removal of an integrative center. Dare we call this center the real "I AM" as opposed to the ("I think, therefore. . .") Cartesian substitute? The safest course is probably just to call it Christian belief in the Incarnate Word, which reached a high-water mark during the Middle Ages. Whatever we call the center, though, oscillation evidently occurs upon its removal, and Exhibit A in defense of this proposition is the fact that this book's very Table of Contents reads like a flowchart that describes both the removal itself, and, next, the effects of that removal.

In chapters 2 and 3, which served as keys for the chart that followed, we became familiar with incarnational logic as it was on view in medieval ways of thinking about land, and bipolar logic as it came into view at Cane Ridge during the Second Great Awakening. In chapters 4 and 5 we charted the arrival of the Civil War and the de-facto decision by both Northerners and Southerners to destroy our medieval inheritance and commit, instead, to universal suffrage as a means of steering the American ship of state and, by extension, our individual lives. And then, in chapters 6, 7, and 8 we detailed the results of that collective decision, foremost among them being the arrival of oscillatory dynamics that entrapped us in romantic/utilitarian alternatives for thinking about land, free-market/socialist alternatives for thinking about economics, and premillenial/postmillenial alternatives for thinking about eschatology.

That's the bad part.

The good part is that, owing to a need to hide or disguise or at least lessen the cost of the medieval integrative center's removal, modern false-opposite sets frequently mimic the genuinely thought-enabling medieval sets that they replace. They are imitative, in other words, and that fact, in turn, means that they can function to an important extent as, well, shadowgraphs of the more thought-enabling oppositions they replace. Take the modern distinction between "body" and "mind." That looks a lot like the ancient dichotomy between "letter" and "spirit," but in fact these two pairings are different as night and day, for "body" and "mind" are what you wind up with when you remove "pneuma" ("spirit") and try (in vain) to picture the world simply as "letter." Similarly, the modern distinction between gritty realism and romanticism looks very much like the medieval distinction between nominalism and realism, but in fact these sets too have radically different meanings, because gritty "realism" and romanticism are simply what's left over after you remove a Logos-based ideational center. And there are others, not least among them the modern divide between manual labor and desk work, which looks like the difference between technical and discursive arts but is in fact what you are left with after removing praise and the leisure embedded in that praise. All of these shadowgraphs are potentially revelatory, and when you combine them with our latest example—namely, the modern-day "choice" between premillennialism and postmillennialism—scales can rather conclusively fall from your eyes. Of *course*, you're apt to say. The either/or of a Fundamentalist Christian's interest in the return of Jews to Israel, and a Wilsonian Democrat's wariness regarding that same focus, are what's left over after you remove St. Augustine's genuinely eschatological explanation of how time-based moments, thanks to the Incarnation, are informed by an End that gives them meaning and worth.[189]

The bottom line is that though we live in a dark age, an age where illumination occurs solely by virtue of flare-like drawdowns on medieval capital, we can with effort "see." Just as one can get a read on topography by looking (with Aldo Leopold's help) at its absence—i.e. a strip mine—so too you can get a "fix" on truths that have demonstrably underwritten human flourishing.

Mountains, in other words, are in view!

We may only be able to see prosthetic devices at this point in our journey, but thanks to the imitative aspect of false-opposite sets we can also see a country whence—as Plato would say—*shadows* fall, and for this reason philosophical traction is still assured.

Assuming, of course, that someone is looking.

People who understand that we live in a bombed-out landscape have widely divergent ideas about what needs to be done if we are to recover footing. There are the citizen-initiated conservation easements and trusts for historic preservation that have sprung up in multiple locations to protect cultural and biological capital like families, locally-owned businesses, tidal estuaries, and historical neighborhoods from the ravages of enhanced, often turbo-charged market forces. There are the slightly less-widespread but soon-to-be common attempts to shore up America's vaunted middle class by refusing to accept governmental regulation and "the free market" as either/or propositions and deciding instead to identify how rules that currently govern contracts, new forms of property, and monopoly prevention can be improved so that the accelerated separation of labor from capital can be slowed. Additionally, there are the phenomenological attempts to overcome (through "bracketing") the Kantian epistemological traps bequeathed to us by the Enlightenment, the widespread attempts by environmentalists to heed Aldo Leopold's call for a de-facto re-fealtization of land ownership,[190] and—last but not by any means least—the remedial efforts that chemists and biologists have been patiently making to render brown-fields, gaseous exhaust, and acid-laced streams less toxic. (One proposal on that front rather spectacularly involves seeding formerly industrial sites with deep-rooted plants that "harvest" heavy metals like mercury and then "package" those metals in plant tissue so as to make them ready for transport.)

Each of these projects, needless to say, is of worth. Indeed, I think it safe to say that securing conservation easements, re-imagining the free market, developing phenomenological tools like "bracketing," and cleaning up brown-fields are essential steps if we are to get serious about fixing what is broken and in that sense redeeming the ever-present and apparently unavoidable American "call" to build a "New Jerusalem." And the mere presence of a reclamation movement is heartening, for it means that the American "frontier" has in a certain sense closed, and that destructive versions of our expansive energy might, one day, diminish. Yet, I am convinced that unless such efforts are coupled with a recognition of the historical importance and continuing relevance of the societal, natural, and personal flourishing that derived from medieval deference to the "Word," on the one hand, and incarnational logic implicit in the way material vocables become invested with sense, on the other, all advances will be lost.

Given that this deference is an explicitly Christian habit, some readers might at this point object that I am advocating a return to theocratic principles, and, of course, if that charge were correct my advice would be problematic. But it's not correct. Far from advocating theocracy, I am trying to shore up the hard-won medieval *separation* of church and state that our founding fathers took for granted and protect that arrangement from brazenly theocratic, even totalitarian postmillennialists who are convinced that the preservation of democracy requires the exclusion of overtly Christian discourse from the public square. Sure, I do think it would be a good thing if everyone were to become fluent in the theological underpinnings and liturgical practices of the one faith that has demonstrably ensured human flourishing. But such fluency certainly shouldn't be compelled, and let us mention too that it isn't even necessary for our survival, as a nation. The necessary things are simply: (1) glimpses of the integrative center that has been lost; (2) honesty regarding our indebtedness to that center; and (3) steadfastness in our effort to keep the center in view long enough to effectively disable polarity-driven storms.

What we need now isn't so much a political, cultural, economic, or even scientific revolution, as—well—firetowers. Remember Gary Snyder on lookout duty at Sourdough Mountain in the North Cascades? That man spent 1952 in a room with a fire-finder, a cot, a bag of rice, and saucers of glass to stand on in the event of a lightning storm. When he needed water he went outside and melted snow. Result? Glimpses of a "burning bush"— which is to say, a universe positively blazing with meaning and order beyond comprehension. We need more of that, and the way to increase the number of times it occurs is to recommit to the idea of watchtowers. Call them "hojokis" or call them "hermitages." Call them "Walden Pond." Call them, simply, "places where contemplation is possible." Whatever we call them, *build them*, for every kind of watchtower can become a vantage point where things get re-presented and to some degree re-cognized through words, and glimpses are thereby won of land, personhood, community, and the common good.

To some extent, of course, progress has already been made on this front, and here I think particularly of Wendell Berry's 1963 decision to reside (and think) in Henry County, Kentucky, rather than in Palo Alto or New York, where he had earned professional degrees. In addition to writing novels, essays, and poems about the importance of place, Berry has shown alertness to oscillatory dynamics, and unlike his friend Gary Snyder, Berry has consistently referenced the Johannine conception of the Incarnate Word as a model for societal, ecological, and personal health. However, Berry's project has also been in important ways compromised—first, by a typically modern imprecision regarding crucial terms like "spirit," "flesh," "soul," and "mind,"[191] and, second, by a decision to define "incarnation" in opposition to, say, the Council of Nicea rather than in the light of that same Council. Given Berry's Baptist upbringing and a resulting wariness toward "organized religion," these lapses make a kind of sense, but Berry claims also to have been strongly influenced by Shakespeare, and that fact, in turn, only makes Berry's lapses more prominent, for who was Shakespeare if not a man in whom the medieval idea of Incarnation is prominently in view? The Shakespeare who wrote *King Lear* and *As You Like It* learned to think in a text-based vineyard that had been cultivated and preserved by Black Friars at Oxford before King Henry VIII expelled them.[192] Therefore, Berry's sort of watchtower project might have cast a brighter light than it already has if he had recognized and perhaps even wrestled with the texts that comprise the world in which Black Friars, by definition, think.

Can there even be such a thing, though, as a Scholastic-based American realist? Santayana hoped that there could, but by the end of his life he had pretty much given up that hope. After all, this is the land of Emerson. More to the point, this is the land where romanticism, the modern prosthetic substitute for medieval realism, thrives—not least by idealizing the Middle Ages! How, then, can one ever hope to hold romanticism at bay long enough to cultivate twenty-first-century ways of seeing that are rooted in pre-modern ways of seeing? My answer to this latter question is that by grasping the dangers of romanticism—i.e. by understanding that, if it is brought close to founding Enlightenment principles, romanticism can generate a massively destructive tornado—you have already to some extent passed through romanticism to some other place. You are a survivor. Hence you stand at least a chance of maintaining de-facto detachment and not returning to the perpetrating role you formerly had. Additionally, times are worsening even as we speak. More and more we are being forced to choose between "simulacra" and reality, let alone competing perspectives like romanticism and classical realism, and this darkening could work to our advantage. Though the two sets of choices are of course identical, the former difference between simulacra and reality is stark. Therefore, it is possible that we will be able to act now with a decisiveness that would formerly have eluded us. And that is before considering that, as Americans, we have one other significant advantage—to wit, our habit of immersing ourselves in road-less areas commonly labeled "wilderness."

Now, I understand that "wilderness" is a loaded term. As we discussed in chapter 2, positing a zone called "wilderness" can amount to defining trees and rivers as zones that are in some crucial sense separate from the human one, and thereby getting into a predicament where we are inclined either to worship nature or destroy it. Moreover, these two latter attitudes feed each other (as we have seen), and consequently the destructive process becomes hard to stop. Hence, in an ideal world it would make sense to avoid the term called "wilderness" altogether and go instead with "trees and rivers" or "greenery," so as to avoid the temptation of thinking that ecosystems and towns aren't two different aspects of a single entity called "nature." However, we do not live in an ideal world. On the contrary, we live in a profoundly disordered and even darkened world where "nature" in this classical sense is all but invisible. Hence, it makes sense now to hold on to the idea of wilderness, recognize it for the hugely important referent that it is, and try with all our might to *see* it. For what is a road-less area but a place where prosthetic devices are for the most part absent? Instead of simulacra, you see rocks, twigs, and salamander eggs there. You see viney specificity, lettered parts, astounding degrees of there-ness, and, in general, the consonants and vowels of God-speech. In short, you see that which Christians used to call "creation." None of it has been manufactured, and all of it tells of origins that we can't even begin to fathom. Normally, we would get frequent glimpses of this dimension simply by living in our built environment. We might pass a building that perfects the land into which a city is set, for example, or witness an act of self-sacrifice—even grasp for the first time the changing meaning of a word. Now, though, those glimpses of wildness are in short supply, and as they slowly disappear from view, the fund of glimpses still available in "wilderness" becomes more and more valuable.

Who could have guessed? The American habit of periodically heading for "the woods" has become an asset.

Consider, too, that in those few instances when an American has manned a watchtower for contemplative purposes, he has developed a kind of makeshift realism that, in its deference to common sense and pre-scientific thinking, is not unlike the kind developed by Plato. Here I of course think of self-proclaimed "dharma" (truth) bums like Philip Whalen, Jack

Kerouac, and Gary Snyder. In addition to dialing in on section lines etched onto Osborne fire-finder tables at the Sourdough, Desolation, and Crater Mountain look-outs with their pagoda-like, wind-secured, sun-shielding awnings above the Skagit River in the North Cascades, these guys also focused on "ice-black" lakes, tin buckets, slide-aspen, and hooves "clanging on riprap." Berkeley-based Whalen, who reported that serving as a look-out amounted to being "conscious even while sleeping," called the Sourdough watchtower a "glass house on a ridge encircled by chiming mountains," and Kerouac (to some extent) even let go of his romanticism (while working as a lookout) to focus on "stark naked rock." Mainly, though, I think of Robert Frost in the Green Mountains of Vermont, where he habitually stopped to "watch the water clear," and, too, of Henry David Thoreau, who thought of the mind as a kind of pond in which objects appear and then become solid after being "clarified and deepened with thought."[193] As noted in chapter 1, Thoreau was not a primitivist. Instead, he was a highly advanced thinker who had the good fortune to wake up one day to "an answered question" and then live just long enough to tell everybody what that experience was like. Look around, he says. See? There are "animalized nuclei" here, and rusty nails, and "twinkling icicles" amongst grass stems! Eh? What's that? You want me to quit wasting time and start doing "good"? "I would say, rather, *be* good." Be *here*, *now*, in the same way that my axe is *here*, for "it is reality we crave,"[194] and—well—if you actually sound this pond that we are all afloat on, you will find that "there is a solid bottom, everywhere."[195]

Another advantage enjoyed by Americans is an ecological tradition that is unreconstructed and therefore strong. Indeed, it is strong enough that even physicists are now drawing on this tradition to make sense of "emergent"—or what Platonists would call "formal"—properties that come into view in atomic "lattice registries" once crystalline structure gets sufficiently complex.[196] The tradition itself is an ecological school of thought that is descended from Frederic Clements' research on vegetation succession at the University of Minnesota between 1907 and 1917, and it has been out of favor since the late Fifties, which is when New York Botanical Garden staff ecologist Henry Gleason's theory that "ecosystems," "climax" vegetation patterns, and even "succession" itself were overly neat constructs that poorly reflected and even obscured a fundamentally random and constantly changing show of plant growth.[197] Prior to the late Fifties, in other words, ecologists in this country looked at a mountainside (or a desert) and saw a biotic "community" that, thanks to interdependent parts that could not be fully understood without reference to their status as community members, was clearly identifiable as a distinct whole. Moreover, a biotic community of primary producers, herbivores, and carnivores was, in the view of Clements, et. al., to some extent predictable, for it appeared to manifest whenever (and wherever) climatic conditions were "right" and disturbing forces were absent. Given that elevation, rainfall, and sun angles in the African savannah were roughly equivalent to the ones in the American savannah, for example, it made perfect sense (prior to the adoption of Gleason's theory) that each continent should produce an elephant. (The American mastodon mirrored the African elephant.) And it still does![198] True, most ecologists now see "continuums" of climate difference and therefore "individuals" rather than species or types. Also, they use statistics to predict floristic occurrence rather than extrapolation from an observed whole. But this doesn't mean the former bias is obsolete. Rather, it just means that early twentieth-century ecology has not yet found its "time." After all, it was known even in Clements' day as "naïve realism."[199] Perhaps after distinctly Platonic theories like "self-organization" and "emergence" get more firmly established, the "naïve" part will drop away or at least ring with an ironic sense that, indeed, is already here.

In sum, originally classical and medieval viewpoints can grow in American soil. Given our proximity to still road-less areas, the existence of a homegrown hermitic tradition, and the unlikely presence of Platonic emphases in forgotten corners of our universities, we have the makings here of an entirely new realism. Shall we call it hillbilly Augustinianism? Given St. Augustine's fondness for Plato and his implicit (vertically oriented) critique of Enlightenment positions, let alone his still trenchant critique of millenialism, I can think of no better appellation.[200] And if we combine this newly viable bias with the Jeffersonian idea of sections—in other words, if we start picturing "Walden-Pond" sites as pieces of land that are big enough to raise crops on and a family too, thus areas where manual labor can genuinely augment and perhaps even facilitate contemplation—well, in that case we might even have the beginnings of at least a few "ward republics." Let us then move forward. Let us start thinking of look-outs as quarter-quarter sections that actualize the promise in Lincoln's idea of "forty acres and a mule."

※

We have fifty acres, but that's only because the land has been sold and resold enough times for the county road, rather than a section line, to become the deciding border. If you look at our property from the air you see a quarter-quarter section, as northern and western property lines are contiguous with township ones. Hence we think of our place in exactly that spirit, and in the most important sense we are right to do so, for "forty acres and a mule" is what General Sherman awarded to freshly emancipated blacks after fighting in the Civil War, and—well—we too have righteously advanced one or the other of the false opposites fueling that conflict. Furthermore, we are also former slaves. We have never been owned by another person, but we have been subject to epistemological captivity. Therefore, it is in some sense right that we should claim our forty acres just two miles north and east of a valley where, starting in 1842, manumitted and run-away slaves found shelter. The descendants of those slaves have for the most part scattered, but the church they founded—it's called "Zion Church"—is still alive. I haven't been to services there, but I feel as though I could, for my neighbor attends regularly, and I can tell that the story of the ex-slaves' escape, encoded as it is in quilt signs that tell of bear paws, stars, drunkard "paths," and flying geese, closely mirrors my own. And of course, we as a family—I think I can speak for my wife and children here—take pleasure in the fact that our home is twenty miles north of New "Athens."

Harrison County is still a crater distinguished by rusting shovels, abandoned transformer stations, jumbled topography, orange streams, weed-like hybrid poplar, and collapsed farmsteads (where they exist). Nevertheless, Zambone's catfish pond is still stocked with bass, bluegill, and northern pike, in addition to flathead, channel, and bullhead catfish. The warbler part of the songbird population in southeast Ohio is precipitously declining, but the previously endangered Henslow's sparrow is making a comeback, thanks to the new presence of extensive grasslands in areas that have been stripped. Other birds thriving in former strip mines include northern harriers, upland sandpipers, short-eared owls, and vesper sparrows. And in urban centers there are similar signs of spring, for it turns out that onion grass, fuzzy lamb's ear, and goldenrod seeds sprout in soot that has collected in the cracks running through Steubenville's concrete, thereby raising soil pH. At the same time, new strains of bacteria are consuming a good portion of the heavy metals deposited by glass, paper, and coal-washing industries, and as for air, that zone too has improved, for Weirton Steel and Wheeling Pitt Steel are now owned, respectively, by Belgian and Russian steel conglomerates that have bought the plants to mothball them and thereby eliminate competition. "Rotten egg" steam from slag dumps is still a problem, and the flume at the Follansbee coke plant is still as mighty as the columns of exhaust that continue to rise from coal-fed fires heating boilers at the Cardinal and Sammis generating plants, but, as I've said, scrubbers are now in place at both facilities, and thanks to the closure of its kickback-prone Steubenville office, the EPA can now tell, with at least some degree of accuracy, the risk that residents here face, should they decide to go golfing or walk to work.

Best of all, some people in this wasteland have become rich, thanks to the new presence of oil and gas companies who are now consolidating "leaseholds" in eastern Ohio. This latter phenomenon heated up after Chesapeake's "Buell Well" and Gulfport Energy's "Boy Scout Well" became the most successful oil-producing wells in Ohio minutes after tapping a formerly inaccessible (very deep and very dense) shale formation known as the "Utica," but before those wells could be drilled and host shale formations hydraulically fractured, company landmen had to secure drilling rights, and though these salesmen offered only a fraction of what those rights turned out to be worth, most farmers (horse-and-buggy Amish included) readily bit on the carrot that was offered them. Needless to say, it would have been better if these Harrison County farmers had waited a beat or two, but seeing as how a lot of them (thanks to Mr. Thomas Jefferson) owned a whole section, Chesapeake and Gulfport not infrequently wrote lease-signing checks worth seven figures and sometimes (since "farms" on formerly stripped lands need, for obvious reasons, to be huge) even more. Well, let us hope that local beneficiaries steward their windfall prudently, for there is a steep production decline in wells that feature horizontal drilling, and, indeed, the only way companies can keep Baaken, Texas Eagle Ford, and Utica Shale numbers marvelous is to drill new wells approximately as fast as ones drilled two years ago go dry. There's a bust around the corner, and the only unknown is when it will arrive.

Though Scio's college is long gone and its pottery long defunct, this little town directly north of Cadiz does have a Main Street, and you can still to this day take out an insurance policy there, mail a package, or hoist a beer at Bob's Pub. On roads leading to and from Cadiz you can drive a turbo-charged car in a demolition derby, stop in for a burger at Bessie's truck stop on 250 (cup of coffee for a nickel), or watch topless karaoke at the Joy Spot, just north of the Nelms Mine portal. And in Cadiz proper you can negotiate a line of credit, take classes that certify you as a trained criminal justice "technician," and even sail golf balls over the bomb crater that yawns almost without limit to the south and west of the Country Club. True, architectural options for new home construction are somewhat limited. Should somebody decide actually to move here (not likely), they will either have to assemble a prefabricated home with vinyl siding or install a doublewide with a fiberboard deck. But that's okay. Other options (as I well know) are expensive, and doublewides have the added advantage of being traditional, for mobile homes are the modern variant of the building typology that was in use when Scots-Irish people first moved into the Seven Ranges and fashioned, out of logs, the same stone cottages their forefathers had built in the borderlands of northern Britain.[201]

The key fact is that civic spirit persists in this area. The Second Empire French courthouse with the statue of John A. Bingham out front is the pride of the town, and, even more wondrously, the editorial offices of the paper that did battle with Hanna Coal have been remodeled. Subscriptions at the *Cadiz Republican* (now the *Harrison News-Herald*) are up—and at the very moment when bigger, national dailies are either going bankrupt or switching to electronic formats! All told, things could be a lot worse in Harrison County, and when you factor in the strength of local volunteer fire departments, the ongoing if rote traditions of harvest-day parades, and the consistently strong turn-outs at hilltop cemeteries when American Legion Post 482 annually honors fallen veterans of foreign wars with an invocation, a congressman's remarks, and a 12-gun salute—if you factor all that in, you realize that in many ways this county is healthier than other, seemingly more affluent ones. And that is before even mentioning baseball, which continues to be played in real earnest on reclaimed land in Sally Buffalo Park above a "fjord" created by a shovel's last pass, as well as at small fields along Conotton Creek just north of the constantly passing unit trains with their loads of scrap metal, #8 coal, Utica Shale crude, and landfill-bound freight.

What is it about baseball? Is it that the game was devised in the pre-Civil War era? That umpires use individualized hand gestures rather than whistles or flags? That announcers don't so much provide "color" or "analysis" as *tell calming stories*? Whatever the reason, the game has a contemplative core that other sports lack. Baseball features plenty of "action"—indeed, at regular intervals, the game can be confrontational, violent, and dangerous—but owing to the absence of a ticking clock, players and spectators "wait" for action in a kind of chew-based, hat-fussing, signal-baiting leisure. The game is about standing still as much as it is about digging toward first. Moreover, this "quiet" appears to well up and carry over even into hitting, running, and fielding, for the crack of a bat is sweet, and it tells of spring. Well, that game is still played in Cadiz. The gridiron is of course overtaking baseball here, just as it is everywhere else, but so far baseball is still at least taught in Harrison County, and in this capacity it can therefore be said that our region casts a most genuine form of End-light. *Straighten it out, Tony.* (Spit and re-adjust chew in mouth bit by coal dust.) *Give it a ride.* (Touch ear, then cap.) *Now you're ready.*

Out here on "the ridge" we have our problems. A couple months after we moved in we nearly burned down our newly constructed house by mishandling deceptively cool ashes. Then locusts attacked our apple grafts, and after the scars from that invasion healed, leaf curl arrived to begin an off-and-on residence. Blight regularly takes our squash, and after a couple years of self-imposed ecological disturbance thanks to an initial, very large input of straw-based manure designed to soften clay soils, we now fight yearly battles with rhizomatic weeds that are difficult to shade out or uproot. Calves have arrived stillborn, and once I had to put down a cow that could not drop a calf. The learning curve is steep for West Coast expatriates, and we are not getting any younger. Moreover, I have on many occasions questioned the practicality of crucial parts to our overall plan.

As readers may or may not remember, one of our original goals was to subvert the hallowed distinction between "servile" labor and more "liberal" arts. Shouldn't it be possible to live on less and thereby find a contemplative zone *within* manual labor that would otherwise be lost, and perhaps even find time on the side to work a bit (as a card-carrying craftsman) in letters? Much as I would like to say that my experiment has been successful, the truth is that on this particular score I face an uphill battle that I will probably lose, for the more I have grown committed to letters, the less interested I have become in objecting to the use of the term "servile" to indicate manual labor. Yes, I like to swing an axe and pound a nail. But, this does not mean that I want *only* to do those things, and I have discovered that it is all but impossible to reduce a family's need for cash to the point where one doesn't have to, say, manage a high-end construction project "all the time." Five years after moving here I developed the habit of flying to wherever I could find a job for a total of six months straight in order to subsidize "rural" life, and though this stratagem worked as a means of paying bills, it was hardly a solution to either our original hopes or a sustainable personal life. Hence, when the oil/gas boom hit ten years later I made haste to capitalize, as it were, on the miracle of a Cadiz rental market that had suddenly become pressurized in the way rental markets in the Bay Area are pressurized. Without even blinking an eye I located a couple fixer-uppers in a neighborhood that would allow for the creation of a parking lot for flatbed trucks, sold enough oak trees from our woods to cover the purchase price for the fixer-uppers as well as the services of a logging crew comprised of Amish neighbors, and created a de-facto inn for oil/gas workers from east Texas and Louisiana—the very same place Ocie Clark crewmembers hailed from.

I guess a Distributist would say that I have joined the enemy, given that I have looked favorably on the idea of disassociating labor from capital, but thankfully I am not a Distributist, and now that there is an income stream flowing from a small chunk of capital that wouldn't even have been there if I'd only owned "three acres and a cow," I give thanks, every day, for the way income flowing from equity can protect and to a certain, if humble, extent *endow* a Walden 2.0 project.

Would we return to Berkeley, though, if we could?
No.

Views are spectacular on this ridge we live on, and, unless a thunderstorm is approaching from the west (in which case skies are black), skies tend to be blue. Every evening and sometimes during the night we hear the rumble of Norfolk Southern, Ohio Central, Rio Grande, or Wheeling & Lake Erie diesel engines on CSX tracks one mile to the north, and when these freight trains are past, the sound of their leaving is replaced with the steady gentle clank of a windmill drawing cold, not-yet-ruined water up 170 feet of shaft. Also, someone manually rings a huge brass bell over at the Methodist church once a week, and in the winter time, when smoke from a coal-based furnace stands in the air above fields of snow, that occasion becomes vaguely liturgical, thanks to the combined presence of what people used to call "smells and bells." And the woods! They don't burn like they used to when steam locomotives like the Spirit of St. Louis threw off sparks as they raced, all lit up with diners and sleeping cars, along contour-grade tracks toward Cincinnati or Pittsburgh. But the woods do shine with thereness, and this year they have actually begun to approximate a burning bush. In part this is simply because we have finally learned the names of the plants growing here and therefore know what to look for as Earth approaches that point in its orbit when the northern hemisphere tilts toward the sun rather than away from it. Mainly, though, it's because we ourselves have in some sense woken up. It's as though we are on a search for something, and, indeed, when I picture our life here I can't help but think of armed hunters, orange-clad, fanned out across a wooded slope that looms over our creek bottom. It is the first week of December, snow has just fallen, and it is cold enough to see your breath on the air. Nevertheless, these guys I have in mind are climbing swiftly and without any thought whatsoever of turning back, for they are trackers and they sense that their quarry is close.

Let me put it like this. If we had stayed in Berkeley, we wouldn't have stood a chance of even tasting such a hunt, let alone participating in one. Sure, we would have spent time in the Sierras or at Pt. Reyes National Seashore. And time spent at those places would have been (and was) a step in the right direction. Here, though, we are able to wake up as *Americans* who are at risk of losing our newfound country and the hope for which it stands. We play now for mortal stakes, and that (as Robert Frost puts it) has made all the difference.

Several weeks ago, while driving early one morning along a two-lane blacktop east of my home, I decided on a whim to visit "Harrison State Forest," which (according to an engraved wooden sign that looks exactly like the ones I used to read as a backpacker in U.S. Department of Agriculture "Wilderness Areas") lay only a mile and a half to my right. Following a well-graded gravel road that wound upwards through stands of white pine,

I quickly found myself at a trailhead that featured picnic sites, trailer slots, and a hitching post for horses. The trail itself was coded with yellow blazes that led to the north, and after parking my car I put on a baseball cap and started following. The trail crossed a muddy area supporting cat-tails, and then penetrated a tangle of alder. That thicket turned to briars, and next, after a quick rise over an artificial lip, I abruptly found myself walking out onto a huge and seemingly limitless expanse of meadow. There were copses on either side of me and far to the north, but the meadow itself appeared not so much to be confined by these boundaries as *defined*, for fields kept opening as my progress along the trail continued. What, I began to wonder, would things look like around that next bend? At this point I began to really stretch my legs, for the day was not yet hot, skies were fair, and the trail itself was purposeful and drained like crushed stone on a sprint track. It was a grand morning! True, I was walking in a former "surface" mine. I was following a changing suite of views that had been engineered forty years earlier by a bulldozer and shovel operators who had followed a four-foot-thick seam of coal. But, at this particular moment, I didn't really mind. Rather, I counted myself fortunate to be alive under a bright, not-too-hot sun and abroad, with two feet under me, in a world that was at least partially real and completely free of tweets.

Then it occurred to me that the world I was walking in was a lot like high country. Was not the soil thin here, and rocky? Were there not hollows nearby that, owing to recent "glaciation," had filled with water? Was the light not hard and direct? Very well then! In addition to being partially real, this ground over which I was walking was also a shadowgraph of an alpine landscape! I was on this day *advancing* toward the real rather than just keeping it in view, for by walking on this ground I was learning the lineaments of a new mountain that I hadn't even known existed when I moved east.

Picking up speed now, I pushed on, and after about thirty minutes of serious walking I came at length to a new vantage point from which I could see land that lay at a lower elevation to the north. Because the air was dry, I could see a long way. Indeed, it seemed like I was seeing all the way to the imaginary line that Thomas Hutchins hung his ranges from in 1785. The hilltop hamlet of Rumley, birthplace of Custer, was in view, and so too was the Methodist church steeple at Kilgore, the town to which Custer's parents fled after worshiping near me. I could even see a cell phone tower outside Carrollton on the road to Lisbon, the birthplace of Vallandigham, leader of the Copperhead movement, not to mention the Stone-Campbell movement's famous healer, Sister Etter. Were there also watchtowers on those hills, or at least farms where waiting and watching was practiced? Doubtful. On the other hand, it was statistically possible that there were one or two fire-towers out there. And that would be enough! After all, when Jack Kerouac put down his Diamond Sutra and stepped outside to look at the stars before going to sleep on burned-over Mt. Desolation in the summer of 1956, he saw just two kerosene-generated hut-glows on neighboring peaks, and between them those three watchtowers guarded 800,000 acres, or 34 whole "townships." Hence I began to grow hopeful as well as content, and, reaching up now to adjust a pack strap that turned out to be missing, I headed on down the trail.

Five minutes later I reached the western boundary of the park. There was another wooden sign there, this time indicating two choices. I could either return to my car quickly by retracing steps, or I could return via a longer and lower route that would skirt "cirques" that had been formed when shovels came to the end of contour-mining benches. Naturally, I took the low road. I mucked my way through three acre-sized bogs, saw an entire contingent of geese lift up from a lake all at once, and got back to "camp" about six. It turned out that there was potable water there, and it was cold. Hence, I drank, gratefully, and then—fortified like a man who had just gotten down on his knees to drink from an icy stream descending from a rocky crag—I climbed into my car, drove down the graveled road to the valley floor, and wended my way (through evening light!) toward home.

Endnotes

1. See Thomas More, *Utopia* (London: Penguin, 2003), 56–59, where More (writing in 1516) proposes a six-hour work day and the importance of "cultivating one's mind."

2. Scott Wiedensaul, *Living on the Wind: Across the Hemisphere with Migratory Birds* (New York: North Point, 2000), 63–65.

3. Harvard's landmark study on the health risks of airborne particulates appeared in *Environmental Health Perspectives* (http://ehp.niehs.nih.gov/1408133) on December 18, 1994. For further, corroborating evidence that we were headed someplace grim, see Sabrina Tavernise and Robert Gebeloff, "With Death Outpacing Birth, A County Slows to a Shuffle," *New York Times*, May 6, 2011, on how the normal national statistical ratio of 171 people born to 100 people dying is exactly reversed in Weirton.

4. Thomas Jefferson, *Notes on the State of Virginia* (Chapel Hill: University of North Carolina Press, 1982), 10. ("The Ohio is the most beautiful river on earth. Its current gentle, waters clear, and bosom smooth and unbroken by rocks and rapids, a single instance only excepted.")

5. Bernard Bailyn, *The Peopling of British North America: An Introduction* (New York: Vintage, 1986), 9. Bailyn states that almost all of these immigrants debarked in the port of Philadelphia before heading west. For an explanation of why the immigrants didn't settle near Philadelphia, see David Hackett Fischer, *Albion's Seed: Four British Folkways in America* (London: Oxford University Press, 1989), 633. ("The North Britons brought with them the ancient border habit of belligerence. . . .. Among Quakers there was talk of restricting immigration as early as 1718, by 'laying a duty of £5 a head on some sorts and double on others.' But this idea cut against the grain of William Penn's holy experiment and was not adopted. Instead, the Quakers decided to deal with the problem a different way, by encouraging the borderers to settle in the 'back parts' of the colony.")

6. See Sara Lee Johnson, *Fine Aires, Strathpeys, Reels and Jigs* (Cincinnati: Kitchen Musician, 1991). According to Johnson, tunes played on Ohio flatboats in the late eighteenth century included "Exile of Erin," "Money in Both Pockets," "Gilderoy," and "The Sprig of Shillelac."

7. For a first-hand account of torching settlers' homes on the west bank of the Ohio in 1785, see "The Report of Ensign John Armstrong" in Emily Foster's *The Ohio Frontier: An Anthology of Early Writings* (Lexington: University of Kentucky Press, 2005).

8. Fischer, *Albion's Seed*, 611–634.

9. The most famous instance of treasonous activity in this regard was exhibited by

Kentuckian Colonel James Wilkinson, who (a) visited New Orleans in 1787 to secure a promise of Spain's protection in the event that western settlers decided to secede, and (b) subsequently accepted payment from the Spanish viceroy to advocate for Spain's interests in the upper Ohio river valley. See Samuel Eliot Morison, *Oxford History of the American People* (New York: Oxford University Press, 1965), 287.

10. According to papers on the Local History shelf at Puskarich Public Library, the surnames of early Cadiz residents overwhelmingly trace to southwestern Pennsylvania and the Virginian piedmont. Additionally, other papers on that same shelf indicate that by 1787 one Joseph Huff was squatting on the Flushing escarpment at the site of current-day Cadiz.

11. For a detailed account of Washington's suppression of the revolt occasioned by the imposition of a federal tax on small-time whiskey distillers, see Thomas P. Slaughter, *The Whiskey Rebellion: Frontier Epilogue to the American Revolution* (New York: Oxford University Press, 1986), 104–105 (excise tax), 147–148 (small time distillers), 182–187 (rebellion proper), 118–120 (Washington's decision to suppress the revolt), 214–221 (invasion).

12. For more on Jefferson's fondness for the decimal system and squares, see Andro Linklater, *Measuring America: How the United States Was Shaped by the Greatest Land Sale in History* (New York: Penguin, 2002), 110–111.

13. See Slaughter, *The Whiskey Rebellion*, 40.

14. Slaughter, *The Whiskey Rebellion*, 82–85. Washington's holdings were on the east side of the river, and would appreciate in value if efficient trade routes could be established between the trans-Allegheny west and the Potomac river watershed. Hence his interest in the Potomac Company, incorporated January 5, 1785. For more on Washington's land speculation and the ways in which he disguised his purchases so that he would not run afoul of Pennsylvania Colony limitations on absentee ownership, see Linklater, *Measuring America*, 45–49.

15. Slaughter, *The Whiskey Rebellion*, 86.

16. Slaughter, *Whiskey Rebellion*, 87–88.

17. Linklater, *Measuring America*, 80–81.

18. Slaughter, *The Whiskey Rebellion*, 83.

19. For a sustained discussion of King Henry VIII's enclosure act and the way it foreshadowed its alleged American equivalent, see Linklater, *Measuring America*, 8–12.

20. Linklater, *Measuring America*, 10.

21. Slaughter, *The Whiskey Rebellion*, 216–217.

22. The best way to understand the section-and-range concept underpinning the Public Land Survey System in the United States is to look at a chart depicting the so-called "geographer's line" and the associated original Seven Ranges survey in eastern Ohio. See, for example, "Plat of Township 2, Range 7 in the Ohio Seven Ranges" in the "Public Land Survey Township Plats 1789–1946" series at the National Archives. Better yet, see Truslow Adams, *Atlas of American History* (New York: Scribner's, 1943), plates 86 and 87.

23. Another way to gauge the extent to which section-and-range logic is compatible with the commodification of land is to note that 640 acres is the basic unit of measurement for Fsquare.com, a crowd-funding platform for farmland investors.

24. Linklater, *Measuring America*, 168.

25. Linklater, *Measuring America*, 75–79.

26. *Journal of John Matthews in the Western Country, July 10, 1786 to April 1, 1787*, John Matthew Collection, Marietta College Library.

27. I learned about this tradition by watching my stepfather pull up stakes driven by road survey crews working near a cabin he owned, but there are also other ways of learning about it. See Fisher, *Albion's Seed*, 631.

28. For a depiction of the speed with which the grid of meridians and baselines exploded westward, see Linklater, *Measuring America*, 216–224.

29. Letter from John Adams to Benjamin Rush, 25 January 1806 (National Archives).

30. For a well-executed portrait of this period in Jefferson's life and the possible beginnings of an alleged affair with Sally Hemings see E.M. Halliday, *Understanding Thomas Jefferson* (New York: Perennial, 2002), 70–112.

31. Halliday, *Understanding Thomas Jefferson*, 102.

32. Jefferson, *Notes on the State of Virginia*, 146.

33. Letter from Thomas Jefferson to Joseph C. Cabell, 31 January 1814, National Archives. (After confiding that he had "long contemplated a division into hundreds, or wards" Jefferson signs off by saying: "There are two subjects indeed which I shall claim a right to further as long as I breathe, the public education and the subdivision of the counties into wards. I consider the continuance of republican government as absolutely hanging on these two hooks.")

34. Letter from Thomas Jefferson to Joseph C. Cabell, 2 February 1816, National Archives.

35. See Victor Davis Hanson, *The Other Greeks: The Family Farm and the Agrarian Roots of Western Civilization* (Berkeley: University of California Press, 1999), 140, 189–193, 237, 357.

36. See "Summary View of the Rights of British North America, 1794," *The Political Writings of Thomas Jefferson* (London: Cambridge University Press, 1999), 77–78 (where Jefferson marvels at how "Saxon laws of possession" proved strong enough to withstand the invasion of "William the Norman").

37. For a textbook lesson in the difference between medieval and modern means of measurement, see Linklater, *Measuring America*, 10, 22–26, 233.

38. For a richly detailed account of the etymological root to our Middle English word, "defy," see Marc Bloch, *Feudal Society Volume I: The Growth of Ties of Dependence*, L. A. Magnon, tr. (Chicago: Chicago University Press, 1961), 228. ("In Lotharingia and northern France, a ceremony of breach of homage took shape, in which perhaps was revived the memory of the Salian Frank, in times gone by, to renounce his kindred. The procedure was adopted occasionally by the lord, but more often by the vassal. Declaring his intention to cast away from him the felon partner, with a violent gesture he hurled to the ground a twig—sometimes breaking it beforehand—or a thread from his cloak. . . . This proceeding was not without its dangers. Consequently, in preference to the gesture of throwing down the 'straw' . . . the practice developed of making it a simple 'defiance' (défi)—in the etymological sense of the word, that is to say, a renunciation of faith—by letter or by herald.")

39. See Lewis' journal entry for 6 September 1803, as quoted in U.S. Army Corps of Engineers, *Ohio River Navigation Charts: Centennial Edition* (Pittsburgh District: 2003), Chart #204.

40. *Narrative of Richard Mason in the Pioneer West, 1819* (New York: Heartmans, 1895), University of Illinois Library. (Mason passed through Cadiz on his way to Illinois via the Mingo Trail, a.k.a. current-day Rt. 22.)

41. Fischer, *Albion's Seed*, 652–654.

42. After the Council of Nicea in 325, during which Athanasius, on the strength of training amongst desert-based monks, brokered an agreement whereby Christians everywhere recognized the crucial if scandalous importance of the Incarnation and the word-made-flesh conceit, occasions for lessening the scandalous aspect of that conceit continued to occur, as when arguments broke out about whether it was correct to call Mary the "mother of God." Antiochines, who were from the Greek city of Antioch (in current day Turkey), tended to see the importance of Jesus' human nature, while Alexandrians, who were from Alexandria (in Egypt), tended to see the importance of Jesus' divine nature. These arguments were not completely resolved until the Fourth Ecumenical Council at Chalcedon, in 451, whereupon it was agreed by all that in Christ there are "two natures in one person." For a most helpful introduction to these early Christological debates see Justo L. Gonzalez, *The Story of Christianity Vol. I: The Early Church to the Reformation* (New York: Harper Collins, 2010), 296–302.

43. For more on the difference between Cane Ridge revivalism and the standard Calvinist/Roman Catholic spectrum otherwise known as Christianity, see Paul K. Conkin, *Cane Ridge: America's Pentecost* (Madison: University of Wisconsin Press, 1990), 164–168 (where it is argued that ecstatic experience replaced sacramentalism as an organizing principle at Cane Ridge, and too that Cane Ridge revivalism is "misleadingly" called Calvinist); also Vinson Synan, *The Holiness-Pentecostal Tradition: Charismatic Movements in the Twentieth Century* (Grand Rapids: Eerdmans, 1997), xi (where it is argued that Pentecostalism should be considered a "rival tradition" to Catholic, Orthodox, and Reformed traditions). For more on David Hackett Fischer's and Eric Leigh Schmidt's contrasting position, see Fischer, *Albion's Seed*, 705–708 (where it is argued, somewhat peremptorily, that camp meetings were "transplanted" from the border country in Britain and not "invented" on the American frontier), and Leigh Eric Schmidt, *Holy Fairs: Scotland and the Making of American Revivalism* (Grand Rapids: Eerdmans, 2001), 64–65 (where, after a concession that revivalism in the new republic was becoming "ever more complicated and heterogenous," it is argued that Cane Ridge, like the earlier revivals on the Gaspar and Red Rivers, was intended to be a sacramentally-based "communion occasion").

44. Perry Miller, *Errand Into the Wilderness* (Cambridge: Harvard University Press, 1956), 172. (For more on Edwards' nominalist disposition and his apparently complete abandonment of incarnational logic, see pp. 176–178, where Miller quotes Edwards reflecting in his journal about "naked ideas.")

45. Miller, *Errand Into the Wilderness*, 155. (Miller says that Edwards looked at the rope fixedly enough to "look it in two.")

46. For an entertaining account of Whitefield's sermons and his tour of the American colonies with Wesley, see Walter McDougall, *Freedom Just Around the Corner: A New American History 1585–1828* (New York: Harper Collins, 2004), 130–131. For a more cautious account, see Justo L. Gonzalez, *The Story of Christianity Vol. II: The Reformation to the Present Day* (New York: Harper Collins, 2010), 264–273.

47. For an understanding of McGready's crucial role in the events leading up to the Cane Ridge revival see Conkin, *Cane Ridge*, 53–59, 62–63, 69; Richard Beard, *Early Ministers of the Cumberland Presbyterian Church* (Nashville: Southern Methodist, 1867), 7–17; and especially Schmidt, *Holy Fairs*, 61–68.

48. John Rogers, "The Biography of Elder Barton Warren Stone," in Frank M. Masters, *A History of Baptists in Kentucky* (baptisthistoryhomepage.com/ky.masters, chap9.revival.html), 31–34.

49. For a careful and discriminating summation of first-hand reports that confirm the multiple ways in which behavior at the revival "skirted the bounds of Presbyterian propriety," let alone Stone's loss of control, see Conkin, *Cane Ridge*, 92–114.

50. Methodist churches in Cadiz trace their origins to camp meetings fanned by an 1801 revival near Wheeling, which drew 10,000 people. See Conkin, *Cane Ridge*, 116–117, also 175.

51. The best introduction to Sister Etter's kind of charism is probably her autobiography. See Maria Woodworth-Etter, *A Diary of Signs and Wonders* (London: Harrison House, 1916).

52. For a description of glossolalia and the history of its appearance in Holiness churches, see Synon, *The Holiness-Pentecostal Tradition*, 109–111, also 31–34, 77, 84, 97.

53. Synon, as previously indicated, states that the Catholic Charismatic Renewal ought best to be considered a subcategory of American Pentecostalism. (See Synon, *The Holiness-Pentecostal Tradition*, xi, 219.) That established, it should also be said that Synon appears to qualify this claim by tracing the appearance of the Charismatic Renewal to: (a) ecumenism that surfaced inside the church after Vatican II; (b) Pope Leo XIII's 1897 call for a new devotion to the Holy Spirit; and (c) the 1949–50 Cursillo movement in Spain. (See Synon, *The Holiness-Pentecostal Tradition*, 236–237.)

54. See Elijah Wald, *Escaping the Delta: Robert Johnson and the Invention of the Blues* (New York, Harper Collins, 2004), 44, 48–50, 56, 58.

55. Wald, *Escaping the Delta*, 37–38.

56. My source for this fact and most other things people might want to know about Elvis' youth in Memphis is Peter Guralnick's amazingly well researched biography of the performer. See *Last Train to Memphis: The Rise of Elvis Presley* (Boston: Back Bay, 1994), 38–39 (high school years in downtown Memphis), 47 and 67 (All-Night Gospel Sings and Assemblies of God), 75 (tutorship at East Trigg Baptist Church and radio fare), 110 (first performance), 141 (breakthrough Hayride shows at Shreveport's Opry equivalent).

57. This can be discerned three ways: first by noting that there was a near riot among 9,000 jubilant ticket holders when Elvis showed up at a 1956 gala event for "colored" radio station WDIA on the other side of the river from Memphis; second by noting that Elvis quickly topped R&B charts as well as the pop variety; third by noting sincere salutes to Elvis by black performers like Little Richard, who was strongly influenced by shouter Sister Rosetta Sharp.

58. Guralnick, *Last Train to Memphis*, 151 (where Guralnick cites Gladewater, Texas promoter Pappy Covington saying: "When Elvis was performing, everyone had the same basic reaction. It was almost spontaneous. . . . It reminded me of the early days of where I was raised in east Texas and going to them Holy Roller Brush Arbor meetings:

seeing those people get religion").

59. Custer made the drinking song "Garryowen" the 7th Cavalry's official march tune in 1867. It's an Irish tune—a quick step—dating from the eighteenth century.

60. Evan S. Connell, *Son of the Morning Star* (San Francisco, North Point, 1984), 422.

61. Connell, *Son of the Morning Star*, 83.

62. Connell, *Son of the Morning Star*, 67, 71.

63. For more on this fact, as well as Custer's participation in local parades and his amorous attachments, see Stephen E. Ambrose, *Crazy Horse and Custer: The Parallel Lives of Two American Warriors* (New York: Anchor, 1996), 87–88, 93.

64. See Connell, *Son of the Morning Star*, 107; also Ambrose, *Crazy Horse and Custer*, 99, 102.

65. Ambrose, *Crazy Horse and Custer*, 103.

66. Walter McDougall, *Throes of Democracy: The American Civil War Era 1829–1877* (New York: Harper Collins, 2008), 470.

67. Connell, *Son of the Morning Star*, 167.

68. For more on this fact and others concerning special treatment awarded Libbie Custer, the requisitioning of company property for personal use, and nicknames, see Connell, *Son of the Morning Star*, 120–122, also 184.

69. The stroll aspect is well conveyed in Connell, *Son of the Morning Star*, 232–248. Dates, motivation, and events are corroborated in Ambrose, *Crazy Horse and Custer*, 374–380.

70. John J. Niebuhr, *Black Elk Speaks: The Complete Edition* (Lincoln: University of Nebraska Press, 2014), 17. (Black Elk's glimpses of "frightened swallows," "setting the smoke-flap poles," "twelve black horses," and "the sacred hoop of my people" are detailed on pp. 20–26.)

71. One could of course argue that Connell is himself a New Western Historian, given that he essentially revises Ambrose's more standard, rather valedictory account of Custer as a fallen warrior, but my use of the label, New Western History, is intended to refer to historians like Patricia Nelson Limerick who discount the importance of the frontier as a character-building environment so that they can focus all the better on the societal and ecological costs of conquest.

72. Barbara Freese, *Coal: A Human History* (New York: Penguin, 2003), 126.

73. These remarks are excerpted from Senator Hammond's "King Cotton" speech. See James Hammond, *Selections from the Letters and Speeches of the Honourable James H. Hammond of South Carolina* (New York: John F. Trow, 1866), 311–322.

74. These phrases are from a highly charged 1856 Muscogee Herald article about "Free Society" Northerners whom Lincoln apparently referenced during one of his debates with Douglas in Illinois. See *Illinois State Journal*, 1 November 1858.

75. For a relatively complete history of Treasury Secretary Salmon P. Chase's perpetual disgruntlement, see Doris Kearns Goodwin, *Team of Rivals: The Political Genius of Abraham Lincoln* (New York: Simon and Schuster, 2005), 518, 574–596, 631–637. For a satisfactorily complete account of Mary Todd's frosty relationship with Chase's beautiful daughter on the evening of November 11, 1863 see John Oller, *American Queen:*

Endnotes   213

The Rise and Fall of Kate Chase Sprague, Civil War Belle of the North (Boston: Da Capo, 2014), 82.

76. James M. McPherson, *Battle Cry of Freedom: The Civil War Era* (New York: Oxford University Press, 1988), 558; also Goodwin, *Team of Rivals*, 459, 463–68.

77. The Beards' project culminated in the publication of *A Basic History of the United States* (New York: Doubleday, 1944), which for better or worse was a kind of predecessor to Howard Zinn's *A People's History of the United States: 1492-Present* (New York: Harper Collins, 2005).

78. See David Herbert Donald, *Lincoln Reconsidered: Essays on the Civil War Era* (New York: Vintage, 2001), 106.

79. For an understanding of how railroad companies tried to lure prospective settlers to the arid west rather than fertile valleys in Oregon and California, see Linklater, *Measuring America*, 227–229.

80. See letter from Robert E. Lee to Lord Acton dated December 15, 1866 in Douglas Southall Freeman, *Robert E. Lee: A Biography, Vol. 4* (New York: Scribners, 1934), 515–517.

81. Laurence Tribe, *American Constitutional Law, 3rd ed* (St. Paul: West Academic, 2000), 1293–1303.

82. For a concise summary of this argument, see Mark Noll, "America's Two Foundings," *First Things*, December 2007. For a less concise, distinctly pro-egalitarian summary of the same concept, see Eric Foner, *The Second Founding: How the Civil War and Reconstruction Remade the Constitution* (New York: Norton, 2019).

83. John Stauffer and Benjamin Soskis, *The Battle Hymn of the Republic: A Biography of the Song That Marches On* (New York: Oxford University Press, 2013), 18.

84. Morison, *History of the American People*, 503.

85. See "Declaration by the People of the Cherokee Nation of the Causes Which Have Impelled Them to Unite their Fortunes with Those of the Confederate States of America," 28 October, 1861. http://www.unitednativeamerica.com/cherokee.html

86. Nisbet, who retired from teaching at UC Berkeley in 1978, one year almost to the day after I arrived in Berkeley, was a native Californian who grew up in the San Joaquin Valley where his father ran a lumber yard, and he is justly famous for demonstrating the importance of intermediary institutions and thereby helping to establish (in tandem with Russell Kirk) the American version of Burkean conservatism. The "picture" I am referring to here is his theory that the modern age, and the United States of America in particular, are best defined in contra-distinction to the medieval era. See Nisbet, *Quest for Community*, 73.

87. See the chapter entitled "The Virgin and the Dynamo" in Henry Adams, *The Education of Henry Adams* (Boston: Houghton Mifflin, 1918), 159–164.

88. Connell, *Son of the Morning Star*, 227. (Sitting Bull "spoke no French and very little English. He might have understood both languages better than anyone ever suspected, but all he ever said was 'hello,' 'you bet!,' 'Seeda Boo,' meaning his name, and 'How ma' tchi?'—which would mean either 'how much,' or 'how are you? can I borrow a match.'")

89. For a rudimentary yet reliable field guide to medieval aspection, see Will Durant, *The Age of Faith: A History of Medieval Civilization—Christian, Islamic and Judaic AD 325-1300* (New York: Simon and Schuster, 1950), 517–591 (rise of feudalism and

decline of slavery); also 615-649 (fairs, trade, agriculture, guilds, finance capital, and "com-panies"). For a deeper grasp of that aspection, an understanding of the tension that developed between rural and urban areas, and a sense of how dynamics resulting from that tension caused the High Middle Ages, so called, see Marc Bloch, *Feudal Society*, 59-71, 219-230 (where Bloch details mutual ties of dependence), and Henri Pirenne, *Medieval Cities: Their Origins and the Revival of Trade*, translated by Frank Halsey (Princeton NJ: Princeton University Press, 1962), 152-153, 207-209, 216-221, and 231 (where Pirenne details the appearance of burghers and the justice-oriented municipal law that enabled them to thrive).

90. Wagner signals modernity's end in two ways, first by demonstrating that exclusive reliance on Enlightenment-derived procedural democracy creates a longing for the very same gods it allegedly replaces, and second by idealizing the "strong" gods of Nordic myth rather than the Judaeo-Christian tradition in whose womb procedural democracy was born.

91. See James Gleick, *Isaac Newton* (New York: Vintage, 2004), 100-103 (alchemy), and 107-113 (Newton's interest in the Apocalypse).

92. For a quick reminder that the idea of majesty was created in direct proportion to the decline of medieval civilization, see John A. Garraty and Peter Gay, eds, *The Columbia History of the World* (Harper and Row, 1972), 405.

93. The first clear separation of church from state was achieved during the second half of the eleventh century after Pope Gregory III and Holy Roman Emperor Henry IV agreed to disagree about who had the right to nominate and invest bishops. See George Weigel, *The Cube and the Cathedral: Europe, America, and Politics Without God* (Boston: Basic, 2005), 100-101.

94. It is not an accident that Bartolomé de las Casas articulated his now famous indictment (of Spaniards who had enslaved Native Americans) at the exact same time (1515) that Henry VIII and Charles V were exploring the reaches of absolutist power. Tocqueville may have overstated the case when he claimed that "Christianity had destroyed servitude," and too that slavery had "contracted to a single point, attacked by Christianity as unjust," but his following assertion that "Christians of the sixteenth century reestablished it" was spot on. See Alexis de Tocqueville, *Democracy in America*, translated by Harvey C. Mansfield and Delba Winthrop (Chicago: University of Chicago Press, 2002), 326, 348.

95. Christopher Dawson, *The Judgment of the Nations*, Washington DC: CUA Press, 2011), 44.

96. For a more detailed account of Descartes' dream, the Rosicrucian circumstances of his presence at "winter quarters near Ulm," and the duplicity on view in *Meditations*, see Etienne Gilson, *The Dream of Descartes* (New York: Philosophical Library, 1944), 13-15 (dream proper), 20-25 (*scientia mirabilis*, import of), 41-45 (duplicitous tendencies). Gilson's approach is tactful yet unrelenting: "As Mr. Blondel puts it, he [Descartes] pushes his doctrine imperceptibly by 'tacking' as much as is necessary so as to always have at his disposal the means of disavowing what he has put forward.")

97. This is a remarkable book. Though chatty and loosely organized, it has comprehensive power owing to the elegance of Weaver's thesis, which is that "the defeat of logical realism in the great medieval debate was the crucial event in the history of Western culture." And: did anyone else speculate as sagely—before Warhol—about the nominalist pull toward "immediacy" or the substitution of sensation for reflection? I think not.

See Richard Weaver, *Ideas Have Consequences*, paperback edition (Chicago: University of Chicago Press, 1984), 24-25, 29-30.

98. My summary of Occam's thought is derived in large part from Frederick Copleston, SJ, *History of Philosophy Vol. III Ockham to Suarez* (Mahwah NJ: Paulist, 1953), 50-73, 101-118.

99. Copleston, *Ockham to Suarez*, 101.

100. Alasdair MacIntyre, *Three Rival Versions of Moral Inquiry: Encyclopedia, Genealogy and Tradition* (South Bend: University of Notre Dame Press, 1990), 163-164. Also Copleston, *Ockham to Suarez*, 114.

101. Copleston, *Ockham to Suarez*, 63.

102. This Italian humanist lived from 1463 to 1491, and he is significant chiefly because he redefined the Great Chain of Being. After Pico della Mirandola came along, we no longer occupied a central position in the cosmos owing to our status as incarnated creatures. Rather, it was because we had the ability to choose between angelic and bestial modes of being.

103. This concept was first articulated by Burke in his reflections on the French Revolution, but it was also effectively articulated by the late British philosopher Roger Scruton. See Edmund Burke, *Reflections on the Revolution in France* (Oxford: Oxford World's Classic, paperback edition 1999), 96; also Roger Scruton, *The Meaning of Conservatism*, 3rd ed (South Bend: St. Augustine, 2002) 47-48. Here is Burke talking: "Society is indeed a contract. Subordinate contracts for objects of mere occasional interest may be dissolved at pleasure—but the state ought not to be considered as nothing better than a partnership agreement in a trade of pepper or coffee. . . .. It is to be looked upon with other reverence; because it is not a partnership in things subservient only to the gross animal existence of a temporary and perishable nature. It is a partnership in all science; a partnership in all art; a partnership in every virtue, and in all perfection. As the ends of such a partnership cannot be obtained in many generations, it becomes a partnership not only between those who are living, but between those who are living, those who are dead, and those who are to be born."

104. See Eugene Genovese, *The Southern Tradition: The Achievement and Limitations of an American Conservatism* (Cambridge: Harvard University Press paperback edition, 1996), 27, 46-49. (Genovese describes the extent to which Burke's views accorded with the South in general, and John C. Calhoun in particular.)

105. See McPherson, *Battle Cry of Freedom*, 778; also MacDougall, *Throes of Democracy*, 487-489.

106. See Fischer, *Albion's Seed*, 207-225, 240-246, 264-280, 354-360, 374-382, 387-389, 411; also Morison, *History of the American People*, 213.

107. See Orestes A. Brownson, *The American Republic: Its Constitution, Tendencies and Destiny* (Wilmington: ISI, 2003), 251-253.

108. "That is the real issue. That is the issue that will continue in this country when these poor tongues of Judge Douglas and myself shall be silent. . . .. They are the two principles that have stood face to face from the beginning of time, and will ever continue to struggle. The one is the common right of humanity and the other the divine right of kings. It is the same principle in whatever shape it develops itself. It is the same spirit that says, 'You work and toil and earn bread, and I'll eat it.' No matter in what shape it comes, whether from the mouth of a king who seeks to bestride the people of

his own nation and live by the fruit of their labor, or from one race of men as an apology for enslaving another race, it is the same tyrannical principle." (Abraham Lincoln, 15 October 1858, during a debate in Alton, Illinois)

109. Steubenville's Wheeling-Pit operation closed in May 2005, and its South Plant subsidiary in Mingo Junction was idled in September 2006. Weirton Steel (now owned by Arcelor Mittal) was also closed in 2006.

110. James Parton, "Pittsburg," *Atlantic Monthly*, January 1868. (Parton visited the city on December 6, 1866, and as a way of orienting his readers he wrote that the town "lies low, as at the bottom of an excavation." Other articles in the January 1868 issue of *Atlantic Monthly* were penned by Charles Dickens, Nathaniel Hawthorne, Harriet Beecher Stowe, and Ralph Waldo Emerson.)

111. When the WPA Writers Project staff examined this area in the late Thirties, they found that Wheeling Steel, owner of Steubenville's La Belle Iron Works, "employed 6,500 men, covered 1.5 miles, produced coil, bars and steel pipe, had two blast furnaces, eleven open hearth mills, and a hot strip mill." See Works Project Administration, *West Virginia: A Guide to the Mountain State* (New York, Oxford University Press: 1962).

112. Freese, *Coal*, 105. For more on the extraordinary aspects to the coal possibilities in southwestern PA/eastern OH and the "stage" onto which Carnegie walked when he sited his mill at Braddock's Field, see Freese, *Coal*, 105–110.

113. See R. Carlyle Buley, *The Old Northwest: Pioneer Period 1815–1840* (Bloomington: Indiana University Press, 1962), 138–239 (tillage and husbandry), 315–394 (schools, spelling bees, quilting and wedding dinners).

114. Buley, *The Old Northwest*, 191.

115. According to credits on the title page, the atlas was derived "from actual surveys by and under the direction of J. A. Caldwell." See *Caldwell's Atlas of Harrison County* (Condit, OH: 1875), Puskarich Public Library.

116. For a telling snapshot of Cadiz on the eve of its destruction, see Writer's Program, Works Project Administration, *The Ohio Guide* (New York: Oxford University Press, 1962), 462, 478. ("Cadiz, designated 'the proudest town in America' in 1938 when a Hollywood publicity group sought the American town with a population under 5,000 having the most illustrious roster of famous sons, . . . lies on a large hill in the heart of a rich sheep-raising and coal-mining district. For decades it was considered to have the highest per capita wealth in Ohio. Cadiz is bone dry. Unlike many Midwest 'Main Streets,' the town subscribes to no booster campaigns. Citizens like to see their young people return after college and settle down, but when they seek broader fields the town sits back and waits for new Cadiz names to appear in *Who's Who in America*.")

117. *Cadiz Republican*, September 15, 1921.

118. My understanding of this fact was helped enormously by aerial photography projects undertaken by the United States Army (which deployed soldiers here in 1932 to keep the peace after violence erupted during a strike by coal miners at Duncanwood, the company town near Cadiz owned by Goodyear), and the United States Soil Conservation Service (which was intent on mapping soils). In both cases the entire county was photographed from an altitude low enough to enable clear glimpses of buildings, let alone forests and fields, and because the flyovers occurred four times (in 1932, 1938, 1950, and 1966), one could quickly and easily discern the timing and extent of strip mining. To discern the societal cost of the destruction, I depended on Puskarich Public

Library records, which indicated the locations of Harrison County schoolhouses that had been destroyed, and a comparative study of plat books published in 1875, 1934, 1980, and 2002. Ads in those same plat books turned out to be particularly useful, for they provided a vivid picture of businesses that were lost.

119. For a quick-and-easy guide to Allegheny Plateau geology and coal formation, see Mark Camp, *Roadside Geology of Ohio* (Missoula: Mountain, 2006), 1–34 (mountain-building events and the appearances of the Findlay Arch near Cincinnati and eastern Ohio's Dunkard Basin), and 149–157 (sedimentary stratification during the Devonian and Carboniferous Periods).

120. For an accurate tutorial on how contour mining actually works, see Harry Caudhill, *Night Comes to the Cumberlands: Biography of a Depressed Area* (Boston: Little Brown, 1963), 309–315.

121. For a description of the way this area looked in 1939, directly after it was largely stripped, see Works Project Administration, *Guide to Ohio*, 461–462. ("Between Bloomfield and Cadiz are a number of large strip mines. Steam shovels following the surface beds of soft coal have thrown up ridges as high as 50 ft. Barren furrows covered sparsely with scrub growth, the heavy odor of burning slack piles, and dismal pools with red water characterize this desolate wasteland. A typical scene is a pony engine dragging a swaying line of coal cars around a sharp bend toward the spindly superstructure of the tipple. The cargo is dumped into a railroad car or truck; then back again through the little canyon go the empties.")

122. For an understanding of how land south of Cadiz looked in 1965, after 38,800 acres there had been stripped, see "Unpeopled," *Cleveland Plain Dealer*, 25 June 1965.

123. Plato would agree. See Book V, *The Republic*, where Plato says guardians are "not to lay waste the land."

124. See "Town Farm Stripped," *Cadiz Republican*, March 7, 1968.

125. Hanna's daughter, Ruth Hanna McCormick Simms, founded the preparatory school I attended in Albuquerque so I have to be careful here. Coal magnate Mark Hanna first made money by building and then running a fleet of lake freighters that shipped iron ore from Duluth to Youngstown, Steubenville, and Pittsburgh, through Cleveland. For more on Hanna's friendship with Warren G. Harding and the "Ohio Gang" in the White House in the early 1920s, see Nick Tosches, *Dino: Living High in the Dirty Business of Dreams* (New York: Doubleday, 1992), 37.

126. This remark apparently surfaced in an 1890 letter from Hanna to Ohio Attorney General David E. Watson, who was in the process of suing Standard Oil. That company was owned by Hanna's high school chum, John D. Rockefeller. See James D. Robenalt, *Linking Rings: William D. Durbin and the Magic and Mystery of America* (Kent OH: Kent State University Press, 2004), 11–12.

127. Jessie Romero, "Money Talks," *Econ Focus*, December 2014, 16.

128. This poster, many others like it, and a complete set of *Coal News* issues dating from 1944 to 1972, are available for viewing at Puskarich Library's Special Collections desk in Cadiz, Ohio.

129. *Coal News*, November 10, 1972.

130. See George Constantz, *Hollows, Peepers and Highlanders: An Appalachian Mountain Ecology* (Missoula: Mountain, 1994), 140, also Caudill, *Night Comes to the*

Cumberlands, 74, 306.

131. Begun in 1802 as a "prayer circle" and disbanded in 1942.

132. Aerial photographs commissioned by The United States Soil Conservation Service indicate that by September 26, 1950 Dickerson Church stood like a lighthouse on a pedestal defined by 90' highwalls on all four sides.

133. For a sobering assessment of the extent to which land has been commodified, see John Medaille, *Toward A Truly Free Market: A Distributist Perspective on the Role of Government, Taxes, Health Care, Deficits, and More* (Wilmington: ISI, 2010), 101–102. ("I have in hand the popular economics textbook, *The Economic Way of Thinking*. Looking at the index, I find no entry for land. . . .")

134. Wendell Berry, "A Native Hill," *Recollected Essays: 1965-1980* (San Francisco: North Point, 1981), 107–108.

135. Though Aldo Leopold is chiefly remembered for *Sand County Almanac*, the 1949 book where he most succinctly states his environmental ethic ("A thing is right when it tends to preserve the integrity, stability, and beauty of the biotic community. . . wrong when it tends otherwise"), his earlier essays on land pathology are no less important. See "The Virgin Southwest," published in 1933, "Land Pathology," published in 1935, and "The Farmer as Conservationist," published in 1939, in Susan L. Flader and J. Baird Callicott, eds, *The River of the Mother of God and Other Essays by Aldo Leopold* (Madison: University of Wisconsin Press, 1991), 173–180, 212–217, 255–265.

136. Bradley Thomas Lepper, *Ohio Archaeology: An Illustrated Chronicle of Ohio's Ancient American Indian Culture* (Wilmington OH: Orange Frazer, 2005), 110.

137. According to archeologist Bradley Lepper, some of the flint "debitage" at Meadowcroft Rock Shelter came from Flint Ridge, in Ohio. See "Ohio—The Heart of It All for Over 15,000 Years," *Journal of Ohio Archaeology Vol. 1*, 4.

138. Camp, *Geology of Ohio*, 15, 164, 209.

139. See Schmidt, *Holy Fairs*, 60. (Schmidt quotes McGready remembering a "Cross Creek" revival upstream from Wheeling in "the spring year of 1787" as a "sweet, solemn, sacramental occasion" and a "time of awakening to many.")

140. For confirmation of this fact, see George Mosul's marvelously written reminiscences of Steubenville, *Under the Buckeye Trees*, printed in 1964, and *Through the Rear-View Mirror*, printed in 1966. Special Collections, Steubenville Public Library, Schiappa Branch.

141. For more on this period in Steubenville's history see Mickey Herskowitz and Steve Perkins, *Jimmy the Greek: By Himself* (Chicago: Playboy, 1975), 15–20, 25–29, 60–63 (downtown Steubenville), 151 (odds-making), 163–165 (political boss Jack Nolan), and 216–217 (Mounds Club); also Nick Tosches, *Dino*, 43–56, 61–67 (cigar stores, numbers rackets, and prostitution), 75–76 (music).

142. Thanks to a 1932 agreement in which Mayfield Road families committed to cooperative control of laundry, casino and speakeasy operations in Cleveland's "Little Hollywood" neighborhood with Moe Dalitz's, Morris Kleinman's, Louis Roth Klopf's and Samuel Tucker's Buckeye Enterprises, the Mayfield Road syndicate protected the Dalitz-directed (and Teamsters-funded) Desert Inn from shakedowns by other Mafia families. See James Neff, *Mobbed Up: Jackie Presser's High Wire Life in the Teamsters, the Mobsters, and the FBI* (New York: Dell, 1989), 25, 218–219.

Endnotes

143. Jimmy Snyder is Steubenville's third most famous citizen, after Dean Martin and Traci Lords, the porn actress whose movies enabled the VCR revolution in the mid-Eighties, and I've never understood why Jimmy (or Traci Lords for that matter, given the class with which she walked *out* of the porn industry) didn't merit a thirty-foot tall city-commissioned mural like Dean Martin did. Some people were appalled by Jimmy's loud cologne and his chunky gold jewelry, not to mention the racist remark that caused him to be fired (appropriately) from his job as a CBS sports commentator (1986), but the fact remains that Snyder almost single-handedly pioneered the art of spread-betting in this country and therefore the world, before holding his own with Brent Musburger on *NFL Today*. Jimmy honed his odds-making skills during the 1940s by studying, on a daily basis, sports sections from small-town newspapers all across the Midwest that had been delivered to him by porters on eastbound trains passing through Steubenville, and by the time of his death in 1996 in Las Vegas he had correctly called 18 out of 21 Super Bowls. His place of rest is Steubenville's Union Cemetery.

144. Tosche estimates that "by the early 1950s some five hundred or so Steubenville families were represented" in Las Vegas, but I think he must have been counting families whose members worked in the service industries, in addition to families whose members managed casinos. See Tosche, *Dino*, 49.

145. See Norman Nygaard, *Twelve Against the Underworld* (New York: Hobson Book, 1947), 109.

146. *Wheeling Intelligencer*, February 7, 1966.

147. Marty died in 2017 in Santa Clara, California about ten years and four months after our last conversation, and I continue to be grateful for the patience he showed me, given the extent of my initial ignorance about Steubenville's importance in the world of illegal gambling. In addition to learning the referee trade at San Quentin Prison and judging 58 World Title Fights, Marty extended his resume somewhat by appearing in Clint Eastwood's *Million Dollar Baby* as "Boxing Referee #5," but I think the job that gladdened Marty the most was his 1957 deployment to Arkansas to protect the "Little Rock Nine." He kept in good touch with those children and delighted in hearing about their subsequent accomplishments.

148. Herskowitz and Perkins, *Jimmy the Greek*, 217.

149. S. B. MacRavan, *A Brief History of Harrison County*, Ohio (Cadiz: Harrison Tribune, 1894), 30.

150. Gerard N. Magliocca, *American Founding Son: John Bingham and the Invention of the Fourteenth Amendment* (New York, New York University Press, 2013), 83–84.

151. Letter to Andrew F. Ross, 10 January 1866, as quoted in Erving E. Beauregard, *Bingham of the Hills: Politician and Diplomat Extraordinary* (New York: Peter Lang, 1989). ("National law . . . must prevent any state from abridging or denying the inborn rights of every person in its jurisdiction, each person being created in the image of the Lord.")

152. Beauregard, *Bingham of the Hills*, 107.

153. *Congressional Record*, 27 April 1866.

154. See Edward Winslow Martin, *Behind the Scenes in Washington* (Kessinger, 1873).

155. *Congressional Record*, 9 April 1869.

156. *Congressional Record*, 16 May 1868.

157. Benjamin F. Kendrick, ed., *The Journal of the Joint Committee of Fifteen on Reconstruction, 39th Congress 1865-67* (New York: Columbia University Press, 1915), 46, 51–52, 61, 83.

158. Senator Roscoe Conkling, while working as a lawyer for Southern Pacific Railroad, flatly asserted in an 1882 argument before the Supreme Court that the Committee of Fifteen had inserted the word "person" into Fourteenth Amendment Section One language because the Committee's members wanted to protect corporations. Conkling, like Bingham, was one of those members, so perhaps the former Senator from New York knew what he was talking about. However, he was also friends with Southern Pacific CEO Samuel Huntington and stood to gain should hearers accept his claim. Hence Conkling's charge was received skeptically and to an important extent still is. Gerald N. Magliocca, for example, doesn't even mention the possibility in the body of his 2013 book (referenced above) about John Bingham and the Fourteenth Amendment; instead, Magliocca dismisses the possibility in a footnote. Other historians, though, have concluded that Conkling might have been right. See Howard Jay Graham, "The Conspiracy Theory of the Fourteenth Amendment: Part Two," *Yale Law Journal*, Volume 48, 171–94.

159. Kendrick, ed., *Journal of the Committee of Fifteen*, 85.

160. *Slaughter House Cases*, 83 US 36 (1873).

161. 94 US 113 (1876).

162. *Santa Clara County v. Railroad Co*, 118 US 344 (1886).

163. 75 US 168 (1869).

164. 125 US 181 (1888).

165. 129 US 26 (1889).

166. Howard Zinn, *A People's History of the United States: 1492-Present* (New York: Harper Collins, 2005), 261.

167. After helping to open casinos in Havana, Monte Carlo, and Las Vegas, Bobby also trained dealers. According to his obituary many late-twentieth-century dealers and casino executives "got their start" at Bobby Ayoub's School of Dealing on Ogden Avenue in Las Vegas. See "Pioneer Casino Exec, Dealers School Owner Ayoud Dies at 77," *Las Vegas Sun*, 27 August 2001.

168. McDougall, *Freedom Just Around the Corner*, 422, 427, 464.

169. See Wilhelm Röpke, *A Humane Economy: The Social Framework of the Free Market*, 3rd ed (Wilmington: ISI, 1998), 229–242.

170. This is a rhetorical question and well it should be, given that our best thinkers and observers have been analyzing the collapse of local economies with great acuity for at least twenty-six years. Christopher Lasch's *Revolt of the Elites and the Betrayal of Democracy* (New York: Norton, 1995) was a prescient read on the abandonment and eventual exploitation (by the wealthy class) of neighborhoods in which they were born, the toll of that abandonment was documented in Charles Murray's *Coming Apart: The State of White America 1960-2010* (New York: Crown Forum, 2012), and that study, in turn, was followed by Patrick Deneen's cogent structural explanation for societal breakdown in *Why Liberalism Failed* (New Haven: Yale University Press, 2019). Yet these works were to an important extent motivated by the need to explain an accelerating class divide that many of us try to ignore through increasingly determined assertions

that America is a "meritocracy." My focus is different. I am concerned, in this chapter, with the ways in which access to First and Fourteenth Amendment rights enabled corporations to accumulate sums of capital that were large enough and concentrated enough to permanently alter and to an important extent control the flight paths of any individual or small business who dares to purchase their products.

171. "The United States," says Turner in his *Frontier Thesis*, "lies like a huge page in the history of society. Line by line as we read this continental page from West to East we find the record of social evolution. It begins with the Indian and the hunter; it goes on to tell of the disintegration of savagery by the introduction of the trader, the pathfinder of civilization. . . ."

172. "We whose names are underwritten . . . covenant and combine ourselves together into a civil body politick . . . and by virtue hereof do enact, constitute, and frame just and equal laws, ordinances, acts, constitutions and officers, from time to time, as shall be thought most meet and convenient for the good of the colony unto which we promise all due submission and obedience." (*Mayflower Compact*, 1620).

173. Excerpted from John Winthrop, "A Model of Christian Charity," 1630.

174. Herman Melville, "The Tryworks," *Moby Dick*.

175. See Ralph Waldo Emerson, "The Young American: A Lecture Read Before the Mercantile Library Association," 7 February 1844. ("In every age of the world there has been a leading nation, one of a more generous sentiment, whose citizens were willing to stand for the interests of general justice and humanity.") Also, see Walt Whitman's poem, "By Blue Ontario's Shore," in which the bard says that "a phantom gigantic superb with stern visage" accosted him. ("Chant me the poem," the phantom said, "that comes from the soul of America, chant me the carol of victory / and strike up the marches of Libertad, marches more powerful yet / . . . A nation announcing itself / . . . We stand self-poised in the middle, branching thence over the world / From Missouri, Nebraska, or Kansas, laughing attacks to scorn.")

176. See Harvey C. Mansfield's and Delba Winthrop's translation of chapter 6 in Alexis de Tocqueville's *Democracy in America, Volume Two, Part Four* (Chicago: University of Chicago Press, 2000), 662–663.

177. Tim Flannery, *The Eternal Frontier: An Ecological History of North America and Its Peoples* (New York: Grove, 2001), 77, 126, 233.

178. Flannery, *Eternal Frontier*, 83–89.

179. Flannery, *Eternal Frontier* 238, 291, 293, 351.

180. Flannery, *Eternal Frontier*, 182.

181. Mark T. Baranoski, et al., *Subsurface Geology of the Serpent Mound Disturbance* (Ohio Department of Natural Resources Report of Investigations No. 146: Columbus, 2003), 2–40.

182. For a while in the late 1990s, archaeologists started to think of Mississippian-themed artwork found in Ohio as an "intrusion" into the culture of the Ft. Ancient and Monongahelan peoples, but according to archaeology curator Bradley Lepper, 2008 research in Ohio's upper Miami Valley "now point[s] toward increasing evidence of direct Mississippian influence." See Lepper, "Ohio—The Heart of it All for Over 15,000 Years," *Journal of Ohio Archaeology Vol 1*, 15.

183. See essays by George E. Lankford and David H. Dye in *Hero, Hawk, and Open*

Hand: American Indian Art of the Ancient Midwest and South, edited by Richard F. Townsend and Robert V. Sharp (New Haven: Yale University Ptess, 2004), 213–214 (where Lankford describes "cosmic dualism" and "diametrically opposed aspects" as on view in late Eastern Woodland depictions of the Mississippian "great serpent"), and 196 (where Dye states that balance was as important as purity, in the Mississippian world, given the "dualistic aspect" to their idea of the cosmos).

184. See Townsend and Sharp, *Hero, Hawk, and Open Hand*, 197, 151 for an effigy pipe image of decapitation (circa 1100–1200 AD) found in Spiro, Oklahoma, on the Arkansas River, and an image of "Birdman" holding a "severed head in his right hand and a mace in his left" on a copper plate (circa 1000–1200 AD) found at the Etowa site in northwest Georgia.

185. Barbara Alice Mann, *Native Americans, Archaeologists, and the Mounds* (Peter Lang, 2003), 226.

186. For an entertaining but respectful description of Johannes Kelpius' New World project, see Bailyn, *The Peopling of British North America*, 124.

187. For a clear, current-day exposition of the difference between premillennialism and postmillennialism see David Walker Howe, *What Hath God Wrought: The Transformation of America 1815–1848* (New York: Oxford University Press, 2007), 285–289. For riskier thinking about millennialism in general and its expression in America, see Harold Bloom, *The American Religion*, 14–15, 293–297. (Bloom thinks of religion as "spilled poetry" and therefore can't be trusted as a theologian; by the same token, though, he sometimes sees things that other people miss, and his perceptions of America's homegrown religions can be insightful.)

188. For more on the difference between low-brow and high-brow varieties of American exceptionalism, see Frederick Merk, *Manifest Destiny and Mission in American History* (New York, Alfred A. Knopf, 1963).

189. Augustine taught that the thousand-year period of peace prophesied in *Revelation* 20 was the sacramental life of the universal (Catholic) church, as instituted by Jesus himself at the Last Supper, and he furthermore argued that, thanks to the Incarnation, eternity is in some fashion "begun" in time. For commonsensical examples of this kind of thinking see Frank Kermode, *The Sense of an Ending: Studies in the Theory of Fiction* (London: Oxford University Press, 1967), 43–64, and especially Josef Pieper, *The End of Time: A Meditation on the Philosophy of History* (New York: Pantheon, 1954), 48–54.

190. See Flader and Callicott, eds, *The River of the Mother of God and Other Essays*, 183, 189–190, 264, 343 (where Leopold employs the logic of subsidiarity to underwrite his proposed land ethic).

191. See Berry, *Unsettling of America*, 114–115.

192. *King Lear* is so thoroughly based in High Middle Ages incarnational logic that it could serve (and, for this reporter, has served) as an almost fool-proof catechetical tool for explaining the entire word-made-flesh conceit, let alone the perils of transcending our human estate.

193. Thoreau, *Walden* (New York: Random House Modern Library College Edition, 1950), 175. ("Why, here is Walden, the same woodland lake that I discovered so many years ago. . ... It is the work of a brave man surely, in whom there was no guile. He rounded this water with his hand, deepened and clarified it in his thought.")

194. Thoreau, *Walden*, 87.

195. Thoreau, *Walden*, 294.

196. See Robert B. Laughlin, *A Different Universe: Re-Inventing Physics from the Bottom Down* (New York: Basic, 2005), 18, 38, 97, 158.

197. For more on Henry Gleason's "correction" of Clements' allegedly too neat constructs, see Michael J. Barbour's marvelously helpful essay, "Ecological Fragmentation in the Fifties," in *Uncommon Ground: Rethinking the Human Place in Nature*, edited by William Cronon (New York: Norton, 1996), 233-243.

198. See Flannery, *An Ecological History of North America*, 192; also Hans Jonas, *The Phenomenon of Life: Toward a Philosophical Biology* (New York: Delta, 1966), 76–89.

199. Barbour, "Ecological Fragmentation in the Fifties," *Uncommon Ground*, 246.

200. When I say "vertically oriented" I am referring simply to Augustine's general bias in favor of faith, rather than the kind of unaided (bias-free) reason Kant aspired (in vain) to employ. That established, it should also be said that Aquinas' more robust confidence in human reason is, in the end, no less faith-based (and therefore out of step with modernity) than Augustine's. For more on the compatibility of Augustinian and Thomistic positions, see Tracey Rowland, *The Culture of the Incarnation: Essays in Catholic Theology* (Steubenville: Emmaus Academic, 2017), 49–68.

201. See Donald A. Hutslar, *Log Construction in the Ohio Country, 1750–1850* (Athens: Ohio University Press, 1992), 44, 58, 69, 126.

Bibliography

Adams, Henry. *The Education of Henry Adams.* Boston: Houghton Mifflin, 1918.
Adams, Truslow. *Atlas of American History.* New York: Scribner's, 1943.
Alexander, Christopher. *A Pattern Language: Towns, Buildings, Construction.* New York: Oxford University Press, 1977.
Ambrose, Stephen E. *Crazy Horse and Custer: The Parallel Lives of Two American Warriors.* Garden City, NJ: Doubleday, 1975.
Athearn, Robert G. *William Tecumseh Sherman and the Settlement of the West.* Norman: University of Oklahoma Press, 1956.
Bailyn, Bernard. *The Ideological Origins of the American Revolution.* Cambridge: Harvard University Press, 1992.
———. *The Peopling of British North America.* New York: Random House, 1986.
Baranoski, Mark T., et al. *Subsurface Geology of the Serpent Mound Disturbance.* Columbus: Ohio Department of Natural Resources: 2003.
Beard, Richard. *Early Ministers of the Cumberland Presbyterian Church.* Nashville: Southern Methodist, 1867.
Beauregard, Erving E. *Bingham of the Hills: Politician and Diplomat Extraordinary.* New York: Peter Lang, 1989.
Berry, Wendell. *The Long-Legged House.* New York: Harcourt Brace World, 1969.
———. *The Unsettling of America: Culture and Agriculture.* Berkeley: North Point, 1977.
Bloom, Harold. *The American Religion.* New York: Chu Hartley, 2006.
Bloch, Marc. *Feudal Society Vols. I&II.* Chicago: University of Chicago Press, 1961.
Bowden, Kenneth, and Meier, Richard. "Should We Design New Badlands?" *Landscape Architecture* 5 (1961), 224–229.
Bouyer, Louis. *The Spirit and Forms of Protestantism.* London: Scepter, 1956.
Bromfield, Louis. *Malabar Farm.* New York: Harper, 1947.
Brownson, Orestes A. *The American Republic: Its Constitution, Tendencies, and Destiny.* New York: P. O'Shea, 1865.
Burke, Edmund. *Reflections on the Revolution in France.* Oxford: Oxford University Press, 1999.
Burns, Daniel J. *Pittsburgh's Rivers.* Charleston: Arcadia, 2006.
Burtt, E.A. *The Metaphysical Foundations of Modern Physical Science.* Garden City NJ: Anchor, 1954.
Camp, Mark. *A Roadside Geology of Ohio.* Missoula: Mountain, 2006.

Caudill, Harry. *Night Comes to the Cumberlands: A Biography of a Depressed Area.* Boston: Little Brown, 1963.
Conkin, Paul K. *Cane Ridge: America's Pentecost.* Madison: University of Wisconsin Press, 1990.
Connell, Evan S. *Son of the Morning Star.* San Francisco: North Point, 1984.
Constantz, George. *Hollows, Peepers and Highlanders: An Appalachian Mountain Ecology.* Missoula: Mountain, 1994.
Copleston, Frederick. *A History of Philosophy Vols. I-III.* Kent: Search, 1946–1953.
Cronon, William. *Changes in the Land: Indians, Colonists and the Ecology of New England.* New York: Hill & Wang, 1983.
———, ed. *Uncommon Ground: Rethinking the Human Place in Nature.* New York: Norton, 1996.
Davidson, Donald, et al. *I'll Take My Stand: The South and the Agrarian Tradition.* New York: Harper, 1930.
Dawson, Christopher. *The Judgment of the Nations.* Washington, DC: Catholic University of America, 2011.
———. *Religion and the Rise of Western Culture.* New York: Image, 1991.
Deneen, Patrick. *Why Liberalism Failed.* New Haven: Yale University Press, 2019.
Durant, Will. *The Age of Faith: A History of Medieval Civilization—Christian, Islamic, and Judaic AD 325-1300.* New York: Simon and Schuster, 1950.
Eyre, S.R. *Vegetation and Soils: A World Picture.* Chicago: Aldine, 1968.
Fenton, Alexander. *A Farming Township: Auchindrain Argyll.* Perth: Countryside Commission for Scotland, 1979.
Fetcher, Robert V., et al. "Serpent Mound: A Ft. Ancient Icon?" *Midcontinental Journal of Archaeology* 21 (1996), 105–143.
Fischer, David Hackett. *Albion's Seed: Four British Folkways in America.* London: Oxford University Press, 1989.
Flader, Susan L. and Callicott, J. Baird, eds. *The River of the Mother of God and Other Essays by Aldo Leopold.* Madison: University of Wisconsin Press, 1991.
Flannery, Tim. *The Eternal Frontier: An Ecological History of North America and its Peoples.* New York: Grove, 2001.
Foggin, G. Thomas. "Coal Mining and Landscape Change: The Case of Harrison County." *Ohio Journal of Science* 77 (1977), 113–118.
Foner, Eric. *The Second Founding: How the Civil War and Reconstruction Remade the Constitution.* New York: Norton, 2019.
Foster, Emily. *The Ohio Frontier: An Anthology of Early Writings.* Lexington: University of Kentucky Press, 2005.
Freeman, Douglas Southall. *Robert E. Lee: A Biography, Vol 4.* New York: Scribner's, 1934.
Freese, Barbara. *Coal: A Human History.* New York: Penguin, 2003.
Genovese, Eugene. *The Southern Tradition: The Achievement and Limitations of an American Conservatism.* Cambridge: Harvard University Press, 1994.
Gilson, Etienne. *The Dream of Descartes.* New York: Philosophical Library, 1944.
Gleick, James. *Isaac Newton.* New York: Random House, 2003.
Gonzalez, Justo L. *The Story of Christianity Vol. I: The Early Church to the Dawn of the Reformation.* New York: Harper Collins, 2010.
Goodwin, Doris Kearns. *Team of Rivals: The Political Genius of Abraham Lincoln.* New York: Simon and Schuster, 2005.

Bibliography

Graham, Howard J. "The Conspiracy Theory of the Fourteenth Amendment, Part 2." *Yale Law Journal* 48 (1938), 171–94.
Guralnick, Peter. *Last Train to Memphis: The Rise of Elvis Presley*. Boston: Back Bay, 1994.
Halliday, E.M. *Understanding Thomas Jefferson*. New York: Harper Collins, 2001.
Hanson, Victor Davis. *The Other Greeks: The Family Farm and the Agrarian Roots of Western Civilization*. Berkeley: University of California Press, 1999.
Hentoff, Nat. *American Music Is*. Cambridge: Da Capo, 2004.
Herskowitz, Mickey, and Perkins, Steve. *Jimmy the Greek: By Himself*. Chicago: Playboy, 1975.
Howe, David Walker. *What Hath God Wrought: The Transformation of America 1815–1848*. New York: Oxford University Press, 2007.
Hutslar, Donald A. *Log Construction in the Ohio Country: 1750–1850*. Athens: Ohio University Press, 1992.
Illich, Ivan. *In the Vineyard of the Text: A Commentary to Hugh's Didascalicon*. Chicago: University of Chicago Press, 1993.
Jefferson, Thomas. *Notes on the State of Virginia*. London: John Stockdale, Bookseller. 1787.
Jonas, Hans. *The Phenomenon of Life: Toward a Philosophical Biology*. New York: Delta, 1966.
Kendrick, Benjamin F. *The Journal of the Joint Committee of Fifteen on Reconstruction, 39th Congress, 1865–1867*. New York: Columbia University Press, 1915.
Kermode, Frank. *The Sense of an Ending: Studies in the Theory of Fiction*. London: Oxford University Press, 1967.
Kerouac, Jack. *Desolation Angels*. New York: Riverhead, 1995.
Knowles, David. *The Evolution of Medieval Thought*. New York: Random House, 1962.
Kohak, Erazim. *The Embers and the Stars: A Philosophical Inquiry into the Moral Sense of Nature*. Chicago: University of Chicago Press, 1984.
Kunstler, James Howard. *The Geography of Nowhere: The Rise and Decline of America's Man-Made Landscape*. New York: Simon & Schuster, 1993.
Lasch, Christopher. *The Revolt of the Elites and the Betrayal of Democracy*. New York: Norton, 1995.
Laughlin, Robert B. *A Different Universe: Reinventing Physics from the Bottom Down*. New York: Basic, 2005.
Lepper, Bradley Thomas. *Ohio Archaeology: An Illustrated Chronicle of Ohio's Ancient American Indian Culture*. Wilmington OH: Orange Frazer, 2005.
———. "Ohio—The Heart of it All for 15,000 Years." *Journal of Ohio Archeology* 1 (2011), 1–21.
Limerick, Patricia Nelson. *The Legacy of Conquest: The Unbroken Past of the American West*. New York: Norton, 1987.
Linklater, Andro. *Measuring America: How the United States Was Shaped by the Greatest Land Sale in History*. New York: Penguin, 2002.
Logsdon, Gene. *The Man Who Created Paradise: A Fable*. Athens: Ohio University Press, 1998.
Lyon, Richard C. *Santayana on America: Essays, Notes, and Letters on American Life, Literature and Philosophy*. New York: Harcourt Brace and World, 1968.
Magliocca, Gerard N. *American Founding Son: John Bingham and the Invention of the Fourteenth Amendment*. New York: New York University Press, 2013.

Mann, Charles C. *1491: New Revelations of the Americas Before Columbus.* New York: Random House, 2005.

Meisel, Anthony C. and Del Mastro, M.L., trs. *The Rule of St. Benedict.* New York: Image, 1975.

Merk, Frederick. *Manifest Destiny and Mission in American History.* New York: Alfred A. Knopf, 1963.

Miller, Perry. *Errand into the Wilderness.* Cambridge: Harvard University Press, 1956.

Mosul, George. *Through the Rear View Mirror.* Amherst MA: Hamilton Newell, 1964.

———. *Under the Buckeye Trees.* Amherst MA: Hamilton Newell, 1962.

MacIntyre, Alisdair. *After Virtue.* Notre Dame: University of Notre Dame Press, 1981.

———. *Three Rival Versions of Moral Inquiry: Encyclopaedia, Genealogy, and Tradition.* Notre Dame: University of Notre Dame Press, 1990.

McCullough, David. *The Pioneers: The Heroic Story of the Settlers Who Brought the American Ideal West.* New York: Simon and Schuster, 2019.

McDermott, John D. *Red Cloud's War: The Bozeman Trail, 1866–1868.* Norman OK: Arthur H. Clark, 2010.

McDougall, Walter. *Freedom Just Around the Corner: A New American History 1585–1828.* New York: Harper Collins, 2004.

———. *Throes of Democracy: The American Civil War Era 1829–1877.* New York: Perennial, 2008.

More, Thomas. *Utopia.* London: Penguin, 2003.

Morison, Samuel Eliot. *The European Discovery of America: The Northern Voyages A.D. 500–1600.* New York: Oxford University Press, 1971.

———. *Oxford History of the American People.* New York: Oxford University Press, 1965.

Neff, James. *Mobbed Up: Jackie Presser's High Wire Life with the Teamsters, the Mobsters, and the FBI.* New York: Dell, 1989.

Niehardt, John G. *Black Elk Speaks: The Complete Edition.* Lincoln: University of Nebraska Press, 2014.

Nisbet, Robert. *The Quest for Community: A Study in the Ethics of Order and Freedom.* New York: Oxford University Press, 1953.

Noll, Mark. "America's Two Foundings." *First Things,* December 2007.

Nygaard, Norman. *Twelve Against the Underworld.* New York: Hobson Book, 1947.

Oller, John. *American Queen: The Rise and Fall of Kate Chase Sprague.* Boston: Da Capo, 2014.

Parker, James. "Pittsburg." *Atlantic Monthly,* January 1868.

Peterson, Merrell D., ed. *Thomas Jefferson: Writings.* New York: Library of America, 1984.

Pieper, Josef. *The End of Time: A Meditation on the Philosophy of History.* New York: Pantheon, 1954.

Pirenne, Henri. *Economic and Social History of Medieval Europe.* New York: Harcourt Brace, 1937.

———. *Medieval Cities: Their Origins and the Revival of Trade.* Princeton NJ: Princeton University Press, 1952.

Polanyi, Karl. *The Great Transformation: The Political and Economic Origins of Our Time.* New York: Farrar and Rinehart, 1944.

Röpke, Wilhelm. *A Humane Economy: The Social Framework of the Free Market.* 3rd ed. Wilmington: ISI, 1998.

Bibliography

Rowland, Tracey. *The Culture of the Incarnation: Essays in Catholic Theology*. Steubenville: Emmaus Academic, 2017.
Santayana, George. *The Genteel Tradition: Nine Essays*. Edited by Douglas Wilson. Cambridge: Harvard University Press, 1967.
Schmidt, Leigh Eric. *Holy Fairs: Scotland and the Making of American Revivalism*. Grand Rapids: Eerdmans, 2001.
Scruton, Roger. *Kant: A Very Short Introduction*. New York: Oxford University Press, 2001.
———. *The Meaning of Conservatism*. South Bend: St. Augustine's, 2002.
Silverberg, Robert. *The Mound Builders*. Athens: Ohio University Press, 1986.
Slaughter, Thomas P. *The Whiskey Rebellion: Frontier Epilogue to the American Revolution*. New York: Oxford University Press, 1986.
Smith, Thomas. *The Mapping of Ohio*. Kent OH: Kent University Press, 1976.
Snyder, Gary. *The Back Country*. New York: New Directions, 1971.
Stauffer, J. and Soskis, B. *The Battle Hymn of the Republic: A Biography of the Song that Marches On*. New York: Oxford University Press, 2013.
Suiter, John. *Poets on the Peaks: Gary Snyder, Philip Whalen and Jack Kerouac in the North Cascades*. New York: Counterpoint, 2002.
Synon, Vinson. *The Holiness-Pentecostal Tradition: Charismatic Movements in the Twentieth Century*. Grand Rapids: Eerdmans, 1997.
Thomas, George C. "Newspapers and the Fourteenth Amendment: What Did the American Public Know About Section 1?" *Journal of Contemporary Legal Issues* 18 (2009), 323–59.
Thoreau, Henry David. *Walden*. Boston: Ticknor and Fields, 1854.
Townsend, Richard F., and Sharp, Robert V., eds, *Hero, Hawk and Open Hand: American Indian Art of the Ancient Midwest and South*. New Haven: Yale University Press, 2004.
Tocqueville, Alexis. *Democracy in America*. Translated by Harvey C. Mansfield and Delba Winthrop. Chicago: University of Chicago Press, 2000.
Tosches, Nick. *Dino: Living High in the Dirty Business of Dreams*. New York: Doubleday, 1992.
Tribe, Laurence. *American Constitutional Law (3rd Edition)*. St. Paul MN: West Academic, 2000.
Turner, Frederick Jackson. *The Significance of the Frontier in American History and Other Essays*. Edited by John Mack Faragher. New Haven: Yale University Press, 1999.
U.S. Army Corps of Engineers. *Ohio River Navigation Charts: Centennial Edition*. Pittsburgh and Huntington Districts, 2003.
Van Rensaeller, Marianna Griswold. *Henry Hobson Richardson and his Works*. Boston: Houghton Mifflin and Company, 1888.
Vogel, W.G. and Berg, W.A. "Grasses and Legumes for Cover on Acid Strip-Mine Soils." *Journal of Soil and Water Conservation* 23 (1968), 89–91.
Wald, Elijah. *Escaping the Delta: Robert Johnson and the Invention of the Blues*. New York: Harper Collins, 2004.
Weaver, Richard M. *Ideas Have Consequences*. Chicago: University of Chicago Press, 1948.
Weigel, George. *The Cube and the Cathedral: Europe, America, and Politics Without God*. Boston: Basic, 2005.

Weisman, Alan. *The World Without Us*. New York: St. Martin's, 2007.
Wiedensaul, Scott. *Living on the Wind: Across the Hemisphere with Migratory Birds*. New York: North Point, 2000.
Witold, Kula. *Measures and Men*. Translated by Richard Szreter. Princeton NJ: Princeton University Press, 1986.
Works Project Administration. *The Ohio Guide*. New York: Oxford University Press, 1962.

Index

abolitionism, 97, 144
Adams, Henry, 98–99
Adams, John Quincy, 192
agriculture, 11–12, 107, 131–33, 190–91
air pollution, 17, 20–21, 200
Akron, Ohio, 136
Alcoa Aluminum, 128
Alexander, Hugo Nunzie, 156
Allegheny County Courthouse and Jail, 98, 104–5
Allegheny Plateau, 15, 25, 217n119
American Electric Power, 142
American Legion Post 482, 202
antithetical intensity, xiii
apparitionist sects, 21
Arabella, the, 178
Asbury, Bishop Francis, 62
As You Like It (Shakespeare), 196
Augustine, Saint, 193, 199, 222n189, 223n200

backpacking, xii, 9, 204–6
Bacon, Sir Francis, 113–14, 116
Bancroft Library, 167
barrelhouse blues, 67
Bartolomé, de las Casas, 214n94
Battle Hymn of the Republic, 96, 120, 158
Bay Tradition architecture, 3
Beard, Charles and Mary, 89, 92, 213n77
Becker, William, 159
Benedict, Saint, 105–6

Benedictine Rule: linkage of ora to labora, 13
  origins, 106
Berkeley, California, 3–9, 203–4
Berry, Wendell, xiii, 145, 196
binaries. *See* false opposites
Big Two-Hearted River (Hemingway), 179
Bingham, Congressman John A., 28, 77, 161–65, 192, 202
bi-polar energy flow, xii, 53, 55–57, 61, 64, 67, 70
Black Elk (Lakota Sioux), 81–82
Black Kettle (Cheyenne), 80
Black Thunder Mine, 85
Bloomingdale, Ohio, 137
Braddock's Field, 38, 127, 128, 130
British Invasion, 69
Brownson, Orestes, 123–24
Brown v. the Board of Education, 160
Brush Run Church, 62
Bucyrus Erie, 27
Butternuts, 97–98

Cabot, John, xi
Cadiz, Ohio: agricultural center, 131–33
  allegiance to Spain, 32
  camp meeting origins, 62, 211n50
  current status, 201
  destruction of, 134–44, 216n118
  similarity to Gillette Wyoming, 84–85
  Whiskey Rebel origins, 33
Cadiz Republican, 133, 134, 202

Index

Calhoun, Senator John C., 86
Calvinism, 56–57, 60
camp meetings, 26, 53–54, 60, 69
Cane Ridge, 26, 56, 61, 69, 70, 210n43
Capital Music Hall, 71
Carnegie Steel, 127, 166
carpentry, 7–9, 13, 130
Carrollton, Ohio, 131
Cellini, Dino, 157
Champlain, Samuel, xi
charismatic experience, 21, 65
Chase, Salmon P., 91, 93, 212n75
civilization v. wilderness, 15, 176
Civil War: as second founding that ended federalism, 93–96
   as polarity-driven storm, 123–24
   as war on tradition-based culture, 97–98, 117–23
   bridge controversy as foreshadowment, 72–73
   Copperhead resistance to war effort, 74
   Emancipation Proclamation as a tactical measure, 88
   industrialization as a cause, 89–93
   Captain John Hunt Morgan's attempt to incite a Copperhead rebellion, 74
   racism in the North, 88
   secession as cause, 93
Cistercian renewal, 5, 106–7
Clements, Frederic, 198
Clinton, President William Jefferson, 172
coal camps, 136
Coal News, 141–42
commons, 32, 37, 119, 140
Conkling, Senator Roscoe, 220n158
Consolidated Coal, 27, 135, 137
Copperheads, 74, 97–98
Council of Nicea, 196, 210n42
Crazy Horse (Lakota Sioux), 76–77, 82, 84
Credit Mobilier scandal, 164, 165
Crook, General George, 77
Cross Creek, 25, 148–50, 218n139
Custer, General George Armstrong:
   attack on the Washita, 80–81

Battle of the Little Bighorn, 75–76, 82–83
   Black Hills expedition, 81–82
   disregard for rules, 79–80
   schooling and youth, 77–78
   role at Gettysburg, 78–79
Custer Hotel, 140
Cutler, Manasseh, 36, 37

Dalitz, Moe, 156
Davis, Bancroft, 166–67, 169–70
Dawson, Christopher, 112–13
Deadwood, South Dakota, 82, 84
decentralized polities, 32, 48–49, 93, 95, 106, 110, 120
Declaration of Independence, 55, 87
de-fealtization, 51, 209n38
Descartes, René, 114–16, 110, 214n96
Desert Inn, 156, 173
Dickerson Church, 143–44
Disciples of Christ, 62
disenfranchisement of the dead and unborn, 119, 215n103
disintermediation, 181
distributism, 113, 203
Divine Right of Kings, 110
Dorsey, Thomas, 67
draglines, 27, 137–40
dualistic tendencies, 188, 222n183
Duquesne University, 65

Edgar Thompson steel plant, 128, 130
Edwards, Jonathan, 57–58, 210n44
Emerson, Ralph Waldo, 55, 182, 196, 221n175
Emancipation Proclamation, 88
Enclosure Acts, 33, 37
Enlightenment, Age of, 26, 47, 119, 196
Environmental Protection Agency, 21
environmental restoration, 12
erosion, 11, 135
end zone, 22, 189, 191–92, 193
Etter, Sister Maria Woodworth, 63–64, 205
Evola, Julius, 112
explosion (postulated): bomb parts, 24, 27

Index   233

concussive impact, 26, 181
detonation proper, 180–81
evidence for, 20, 25–26, 28, 179–80
propulsive characteristics, 183
similarity to Serpent Mound disturbance, 187–88

false opposites: xiii, 11–12, 122–24, 188, 192–93, 194
fee-simple ownership, 50–57
feudalism: as depicted by Moderns, 5, 112, 102–3
    as on view in the historical record, 49–51, 105–6
Field, Justice Stephen Johnson W., 168–70
Fifth Amendment, 163
firestorm. *See* explosion
First Amendment, 172
First American Regiment regulars, 31
First Inaugural Address (Lincoln), 86–87
Flannery, Tim, 185
Ft. Hamar, 31
Ft. Laramie Treaty (1868), 83, 86
Ft. McHenry, 176
Ft. Steuben, 38
Ft. Sumter, 89
Fourteenth Amendment, 28, 94–95, 121, 161–63, 165–69
Fox, Josiah, 17
Franciscan University, 21, 65
Franklin College, 144, 161
freedom, v, 10, 96, 112
French Revolution, xi, 110, 117
Frick, Henry Clay, 128
Frontier Thesis (Frederick Jackson Turner), 23, 176
Frost, Robert, 198, 204

Gable, Clark, 134
Galloway Leveller Revolt, 33
Garryowen, 75, 189, 212n59
Gem of Egypt (dragline), 139
geographer's line, 34, 39, 40, 63, 205
Gettysburg Address, 86–87
Gillette, Wyoming, 84
Gleason, Henry, 198–99

Glorious Revolution, 117
gnosticism, 21, 22, 65
gospel music, 67
Goodyear Corporation, 136
Grant, General Ulysses S., 26, 78, 82, 165
Great Gatsby, The (Fitzgerald), 179
Greek polis era, 13, 49
Greenville Treaty (1794), 38
Guénon, René, 112
Gulf Oil Corporation, 128
Guthrie, Arlo, 69, 173

Hanna Coal Company, 16, 137, 141–43
Hanna, Mark, 141, 217n125
Harney Peak, 81
Harrison County, xii, 17, 54, 137, 140, 143, 149–50, 200–202, 180
Harrison's timepiece, 45
Hendrix, Jimi, 3, 70
Herald-Star, 158
hermitages, 14, 195
hillbilly Augustinianism, 199
hillbillies, 66, 68, 118
Hines, Earl Fatha, 179
H. J. Heinz Corporation, 127
hojoki, 195
Homestead Act (1862), 50, 85, 91
Hopedale, Ohio, 137, 217n121
Huck Finn (Twain), 179
Hutchins, Surveyor General Thomas, 41–43, 205

immediacy, 116, 214n97
incarnational logic: as on view in language, 195
    as on view in Shakespeare, 196
    as on view in sacramentality and Johannine word-made-flesh conceit, 57, 193
    as opposed to dualism, 188
    as opposed to extrinsic logic, 57
    as opposed to disintermediation and immediacy, 115–16, 210n44
Indian Removal Act (1834), 83
Ingram Barge Company, xi, 1–2

Index

Jefferson, Thomas, 33–34, 46–48
Jim Crow statutes, 88
Jimmy the Greek (Dimitrios Georgios Synodinos), 157, 160, 219n143
Jones, Cornelius, 156
Joint Committee of Fifteen on Reconstruction, 161, 165, 220n158

Kansas Nebraska Act (1854), 90
Kefauver Hearings, 156
Kelly, Gene, 179
Kelpius, Johannes, 188–89
Kerouac, Jack, 23, 198, 206
Key, Francis Scott, 176–77
King Lear (Shakespeare), 196, 222n192
Kokushi, Daito, 14
Kopper's Tar and Chemical Company, 128

La Belle Ironworks, 128, 216n111
Lakota Sioux, 27
land: Anglo-Saxon terms for, 49
  as a commons, 32, 37, 119, 140
  as a condition of existential and political freedom, 145
  as a geo-inflected bio-cultural glow, 146–48
  as defined by Moderns and Medievals, 111–12
  as fabric, 17, 140, 144
  as on view in feudal units of measurement, 50
  as falsified in idea of pristine landscape, 11
  as on view in Tennessee Trouble quilts, 147
  as opposed to overburden or upended earth, 18–19
  commodification, 50
Land Act (1785): as an occasion for the advancement of survey methods, 37
  negative effect on homesteaders, 32–33
  similarity to British Enclosure Acts, 32–33, 35, 37
  ways in which it enabled land commodification and eroded committment to place, 32, 49–51, 119
  degree to which it successfully ensured a widespread distribution of land ownership, 37, 46, 48–49
land speculation, 35
Las Vegas, Nevada, 157, 159, 219n144
Lee, General Robert E., 78
leisured contemplation, 12, 121, 193
Leopold, Aldo, 145–46, 194, 218n111
lettered ecosystems, 9–10, 197
Lewis and Clark, 15, 18, 54
Lewis, Jerry Lee, 68
liberal *v.* servile arts, 13–14, 86, 203
Lincoln, Abraham, 86–88, 177
Lisbon, Ohio, 63, 74, 205
Little Bighorn River, 75
Locke, John, 32, 57, 85, 110, 117
lookouts, 14, 23–24, 195–96, 206
Lords, Traci, 219n143
Louisville, Kentucky, 146
Ludlow, Israel, 36, 43–44

McGready, James, 26, 59–60, 149, 218n139
Mansfield, Jared, 44
Marshall, Chief Justice John, 170
Martin, Dean, 157–58, 219n143
Maybeck, Bernard, 5, 7
Mayfield Road crime syndicate, 156, 218n142
McConnell, Harry Burns, 134, 136
Meadowcroft Rock Shelter, 148
Medicine Bow Mountain, 174–75
medieval era: difference between serfs and slaves, 108
  collapse, 116
  genuinely civilized aspects, 108–9
  historical origins, 106–7
  learned aspect, 108
  mindsets, 110–12
  rapid growth of cities as a destabilizing force, 109–10
Mellon, Andrew, 128
Melville, Herman, xii, 181
Mesabi Range, 130

Index

messianic Marxism, 5
Methodism, 58–59, 62, 144
Middle Ages, 5, 51, 102, 103, 105, 112, 116, 121, 196
migratory birds, 15
millenialism, 191–93, 222n187
Miller, Justice Samuel F., 166, 168
mineral rights, 142
Minneapolis and St. Louis Railroad v. Beckwith, 169
Mirandola, Pico della, 102, 116–17, 215n102
Mises, Ludwig von, 171
modernity: as a historical period, 110
  as a project designed to overthrow and replace medieval habits, 113–16
  difference between modern and medieval mindsets, 111–12
  decisive American appearance, 124
Monongahelan culture, 187
Moody, Dwight L., 62
More, Saint Thomas, 12
Morgan's Raiders, 74, 97, 138
Morrill Land Grant Act (1862), 92
Mountaineer (dragline), 138
mountainous terrain, 2, 9, 205
Mt. Rushmore, 85
Munn v. Illinois, 166
Mussio, Bishop John King, 158

National Parks, 5, 85
National Banking Act (1863), 91
National Road, 72–73
nature as defined by post-Christians, 4–5, 11–12
Newton, Isaac, 110
New Western History, 83, 212n71
New World, the, xi
Nisbet, Robert, xii, 98, 120, 171
Nolan, Pinky, 156
nominalism, 115–16, 193, 210n44
Norfolk and Western Railroad, 25, 149
North America (continent), xi, 186
North American Free Trade Agreement, 172

Occam, William of, 115–16
Ocie Clark (line vessel), 1–2, 23–24, 27, 52–53, 85, 100–102, 151–52, 183–84, 203
O'Connor, Flannery, 118
Ohio Central Railroad, 136
Ohio Company, 36–37
Ohio River, xi, 29, 31, 147, 207n4
oscillatory dynamic, 193

Pacific Railway Act (1862), 89, 91, 164
Paul v. the State of Virginia, 168, 169
Pennsylvanian Age (geological), 135
Pentecostalism: anti-sacramental aspects, 61, 210n43
  Assemblies of God, 64
  charismatic renewal, 64–65
  origins in Sister Etter's ministry and holiness churches, 63
  tongues, appearance of, 64–65
  slain in the spirit, 60, 69
Percy, Walker, 118
phenomenology, 194
Pirenne, Henri, 107
Pittsburgh, xii, 16, 72–74, 126–28, 131, 216n110
Play That Funky Music (Wild Cherry), 22
point of beginning, 39
Point Reyes National Seashore, 204
Polanyi, Karl, 160
polarity-driven storms, xiii, 123, 185–86, 188, 195
polarization, xi
potteries, 16, 142
Powder River Basin, 76–77, 84
Powell, General John Wesley, 45
Prairie School horizontality, 3, 7
Presbyterianism, 56
pre-Raphaelite aesthetics, 5–6, 53
Presley, Elvis, 68–69
prosthetic devices. See simulacra
Protestant Reformation, xi, 56, 115
Public Survey System, 39, 44
Puritanism, xiii, 56
Putnam, Rufus, 36, 44

Quattrone, Cosmo, 159, 160

Reese, Lew, 142
Renaissance, the, xii, 100
reversing electrical current, 64, 70
Richardson, Henry Hobson, 103–4
Richardsonian Romanesque, 103–5
rock and roll
  as embodied in Elvis Presley, 68–69, 211n43
  as juxtaposition of alleged opposites steadfastly not fused, 66–68
  as on view at Woodstock, 69
  difference from jazz, 68
  ecstatic experience as an organizing principle, 68, 210n43
  standard definitions, 67
Roebling, John A., 72
Röepke, Wilhelm, 171
romanticism, 4–5, 47, 55, 196–97
Ronsheim, Milt, 137
Roosevelt, Franklin, 171
Roosevelt, Theodore, 171
Rust Belt, xii

sacramentalism. *See* incarnational logic
Sammon, Marty, 159–60, 161, 219n147
Sangre de Cristo Mountains, 9
Santa Clara v. Southern Pacific Railroad, 167, 169
Santayana, George, v, 3, 179, 196
San Quentin Prison, 159
San Patricio battalion, 97
Scarlet Letter, The (Hawthorne), 176
Scio Pottery, 142
Scots Irish: allegiance to Spain, 33, 35
  contrarian disposition, 32, 37, 43
  cultural habits, 54
  holy fair tradition, 210n43
  immigration wave, 31, 207n5
  Presbyterian membership, 56
Scott, Thomas, 164, 166
Second Great Awakening, 56–62
section and range survey method:
  designed to facilitate ward republics, 46, 49–50, 53
  explosion westward, 45
  finetuning, 44
  initial implementation via Hutchins' survey, 41–43
  problematic aspects, 49–51, 53
  rectilinear aspect, 39–43
Serpent Mound, 187–88
sexual licentiousness, xiii, 61, 69, 211n49
Seven Ranges survey, 38–43
shadowgraphs, 193
Sherman, Senator John, 90
Sherman, General William Tecumseh, 84, 200
Sierra Club, 5
Sierras, 9
Significance of the Frontier in American History, The (Turner). *See* Frontier Thesis
Simpson, Bishop Matthew, 62, 144
simulacra, 122, 183, 184, 185, 194, 197
Silver Spade (dragline), 138–39
Sitting Bull, 99
Skagit River, 198
Smith, Adam, 170–71
Snyder, Gary, 3, 15, 23, 195
Sourdough Mountain, 195
Southern Agrarians, 113
spoil banks, 18
Stanton, Edwin McMasters, 26
Star Spangled Banner, 70, 176–77
states' rights, 47
Steubenville, Ohio, 16, 21–22, 38, 54, 62, 152–56, 159–60, 200
Steubenville and Indiana Railroad, 164
Stone, Barton Warren, 60
surface mining: as a practice, 137–39, 217n120
  cultural versions, 19, 154
  problematic aspects to spoil banks, silted streambeds, yellow boy precipitate, and smoldering fires, 137, 140
  reclamation efforts, 137, 141, 143
Swaggart, Jimmy, 68

Tate, Allen, 118
Tharpe, Sister Rosetta, 67

Thoreau, Henry David: 10–11, 12, 13, 14, 195, 198
Tocqueville, Alexis de, 120, 183
topographical maps, 24–25
topography, 140
Torcasio, Tony, 157
tornados, v, 196
total war, 119–20
towboats, 1, 29–30
Treaty of Paris (1783), 31
Turner, Frederick Jackson, 12, 176

Union Pacific Railroad, 91
United States of America, xi, 6, 89, 94, 95, 120, 158, 117, 192
University of California at Berkeley, 6, 92
USS Constitution (frigate), 17, 133
U.S. Geological Survey, 24, 45
U.S. Steel Corporation, 127, 128

Vallandigham, Clement, 74, 97, 161, 205

Waite, Morison, 166, 167
Wagner, Richard, 110, 214n90
Walden project. *See* Thoreau, Henry David
ward republics, xii, 48–49, 133, 199
Washington, George: at Cross Creek, 149
  at Miller's Run, 35–36
  decision to stall western development, 36
  land speculation, 35–36, 208n14
  Watermelon Army generalship, 33
Watermelon Army, 38
Wesley, John, 58, 69
Western Reserve, 146
Westinghouse Corporation, 127
Whalen, Philip, 198
Wheeling, West Virginia, 71–74
Wheeling-Pittsburgh Steel Company, ix, 128, 182
When the Man Comes Around (Johnny Cash), 191
Whiskey Rebels, 33, 38, 41, 88, 149, 180, 186
Whitefield, George, 58, 69
wilderness: current importance of, 197
  as falsely opposed to civilization, 11, 85
wildness as agri-culture, 11–12
Wilkinson, Colonel James, 208n9
Williams, Hank, 67
Winthrop, John, 178, 182
Wister, Owen, 175
word-based knowledge, 118
word-made-flesh conceit. *See* incarnational logic
Woodstock (music festival), 69
World Trade Organization, 172

Yosemite, 9, 126
yellow boy, 19, 140

www.ingramcontent.com/pod-product-compliance
Lightning Source LLC
Chambersburg PA
CBHW022005220426
43663CB00007B/975